AT THE
ALTAR
OF THE
ROAD GODS

AT THE ALTAR OF THE ROAD GODS

STORIES OF MOTORCYCLES AND OTHER DRUGS

BORIS MIHAILOVIC

Every endeavour has been made on the part of the publisher to contact copyright
holders and the publisher will be happy to include a full acknowledgement in any
future edition.

 hachette
AUSTRALIA

First published in Australia and New Zealand in 2014
by Hachette Australia
(an imprint of Hachette Australia Pty Limited)
Level 17, 207 Kent Street, Sydney NSW 2000
www.hachette.com.au

This edition published in 2016

National Library of Australia
Cataloguing-in-Publication data:

Mihailovic, Boris, author.

At the altar of the road gods / Boris Mihailovic.

ISBN 978 0 7336 3567 0 (paperback)

Mihailovic, Boris.
Motorcyclists – New South Wales – Biography.
Motorcycling – Psychological aspects.
Motorcycle gangs – New South Wales.

796.7092

Cover design by Luke Causby
Cover photograph courtesy of Bauer Media Pty Ltd
Text design by Shaun Jury
Typeset in FF Scala by Shaun Jury
Printed and bound in Australia by McPherson's Printing Group

To my late and much beloved aunt, Irene Koudele, who passed away as I was writing this book – but not because I was reading bits of it to her. She was a true outlaw. May the earth where she lies buried rest lightly upon her.

CONTENTS

CONTENTS

INTRODUCTION

A man can travel a fair distance in thirty-six years. Especially if he puts his mind to it. I've certainly done so, and being more pig-headed than a three-headed pig, I have managed to rack up some 2.3 million kilometres, give or take a few thousand.

Much has changed in that time and over that distance. The world is not as it once was, which is to be expected. And neither am I, which is also to be expected. Motorcycles have changed, too. They have gone from being insanely powerful, ill-handling, indifferently braked, semi-reliable projectiles of distilled male rebellion, to even more insanely powerful, great handling, wonderfully braked and very reliable projectiles of distilled male rebellion.

I feel that my personal development has mirrored this most welcome evolutionary process. Consequently, everyone is now better off. Ask my wife. I can now actually tell her with some accuracy when I plan to return from a run. Once upon a time, my return home was contingent upon a host of interlocking variables. Will the bastard motorcycle explode and demand I make efforts to repair it by smashing it with rocks and castigating it with bad language? Will the police finally charge me so that I can get bail, or will they keep me locked in the holding cell until the vomit dries on my clothes and they're bored of laughing at me through the cell's viewing slit? How far will I have to ride back the way I have just come to search for some mate who has failed to materialise at the agreed meeting point, leaving me to scour the valleys into which he might have plunged? How long will my money last? Do I use what I have left for petrol, or do I use it to buy more beer, and hope that I can maybe bludge some petrol from a passing motorist? What pointless lie about my speeding shall I use on the Highway Patrol officer? Is it really Monday? I thought it was still Sunday ...

More importantly, I have finally come to terms with the fact that I am a shit-magnet. I am now at peace knowing I am a sweaty lodestone for a vast array of scandal, horror and quite dire antisocial beastliness. With this knowledge, I have become empowered – and act accordingly. The decisions I make now are not like the decisions I made back when I was ignorant of my particular standing in the cosmos. But I do understand there is nothing I can do about being such a singularity. I just need to stay aware of how things operate in my universe. It is what it is. I am what I am. And what I have always been.

Of course, the riding of bastard motorcycles has only served to exacerbate shit's undeniable attraction to me. Had I decided to spend my life rotting behind a steering wheel, it's certain that shit would have still happened to me, but it would not have been anywhere near as unspeakable as it often turned out to be – or half as much fun. You see, that's the thing. This motorcycling caper really is all about fun – I wouldn't do it otherwise. And when Shit Happening coincides with this fun (as it regularly does when I am involved), the fun factor is not necessarily diminished. In fact, it is sometimes enhanced – a lot. This is not always immediately evident, but that is why the Road Gods invented hindsight, which was very thoughtful of Them.

Normally, the Road Gods are not at all given to thoughtfulness. I should know: I have sat astride Their growling metal altars for more than three decades. I have worshipped upon Their snaking, pitiless temples and I have cursed Them and damned Them as often as I have thanked Them and blessed Them. They have returned the favour. It's how They roll. The shit that comes my way is entirely of Their making, but how I respond to that delivery is entirely *my* responsibility.

It is a working relationship that has flavoured my life like an exotic goulash from the first day I decided to ride motorcycles. Does this mean I have always acted responsibly? Not at all. Does this mean I have done things about which I am not exactly glowing with pride? Absolutely. With the wisdom of hindsight would I have acted the same way and done the same things? Without question.

After all, I am as fallible and conflicted as the next bloke, and hindsight is not something I can access when I'm being fallible and conflicted. I have done stupid things, and I have done *really* stupid things. I still do, on occasion. As a consequence, my life continues to be a rich dish of piquancy, with the occasional rancid cock thrown into the sauce to keep me grounded in reality.

Do I learn from my mistakes? Sure. I also repeat them, but not as often as I once did – there's more to lose these days and the stakes are higher. But I'll still roll those evil dice. Hell, I'm a motorcyclist. I will *always* roll those nasty bones. Viewed through the danger-averse eyes of a peacefully insipid society, my entire existence is one, long, two-wheeled mistake. Viewed through mine, it's the only kind of life worth living.

I hope you'll get a kick out of the stories in this, my second book. Like any writer, I am always hugely flattered when people tell me how much they enjoyed my first book, *My Mother Warned Me About Blokes Like Me*, or indeed any of my work. Because like any writer, I get a kick out of running my home movies inside people's heads and seeing if they smile.

Once again, the tales run in chronological order, beginning from when I started to chew on what I had unwittingly bitten off, all the way through to a recent long-distance ride with my teenage son, Andrew. Once again, I know some of the tales will appal you – they still appal me when I think back on them. Once again, I know some of you will doubt the veracity of the events, and once again I will shrug and ask you if it is at all possible that a man could actually make up any of this shit.

I have changed some of the names of some of the characters in these stories, but only so they can retain a plausible deniability if someone asks them if it's actually them I'm writing about.

Are there more tales I could tell? Oh yes, I certainly hope to. When will they be told? In the fullness of time and when the Road Gods permit. In the meantime, turn the page and enjoy the ride.

LEARNING FAST

I am still at a loss to understand how I managed to survive my first five years of motorcycle riding. It can only be pure dumb luck as there was certainly no skill involved. Sheer craziness seemed to influence every aspect of my life back then. Like everyone I came to know who shared my two-wheeled fetish, I spent many years buying the fastest and most powerful bike I could afford at the time, then get into crippling debt making it faster and more powerful. The thing could never be fast enough, noisy enough, or angry enough. To my simple mind, there was a purity to the concept of a stupidly powerful engine bolted between two wheels, allegedly controlled by a set of handlebars and some squealing rubbish pretending to be brakes. Did that stop me and my friends pinning the throttles on deserted roads or empty (and not so empty) inner-city streets and measuring the girth of our cocks and the heft of our balls, in the hope that girls were watching? Did it fuck.

By the time I was nineteen I was a fully fledged, insane mutant pursuit machine. I would chase any motorcycle that passed me, or go after with a single-minded madness any bike I could see in front of me. Or, if no such challenge presented itself, I would chase my own shadow for the sheer heart-hammering thrill of cheating death and *laughing at the law, which clearly did not apply to me. How could it? I was not dead, nor was I in jail. Sure, I'd come close a couple of times, but I've been told close only counts in horseshoes, hand grenades and thermonuclear weapons. It's got nothing to do with riding motorcycles, right?*

> 'He who would learn to fly one
> day must first learn to stand and
> walk and run and climb and dance;
> one cannot fly into flying.'
>
> **FRIEDRICH NIETZSCHE**

One of the consequences of riding motorcycles is that suddenly you lose all your friends. This is fine, because motorcycles quite effectively fill the hole those feckless, non-riding bastards leave in your life. So you don't really miss them at all. For a while, anyway. Eventually, the driving human need for socialisation with like-minded creatures kicks in and you begin to seek out people who laugh at the same things you do.

I lost my best childhood friend when I took to the handlebars. I didn't think I would, because Alex and I were tight. Hell, I had set him on fire when we were twelve and that kinda thing tends to make or break friendships. Immediately after I had put him out, it made ours. We were becoming increasingly attracted to the motorcycle thing, and as we approached our mid-teens we started making plans to ride around Australia. We even bought a map, seeing ourselves as the wog-kid version of Peter Fonda and

Dennis Hopper in the movie *Easy Rider*; except we were more like Corporal Serbia and Silly than Captain America and Billy. Anyway, upon finishing high school, the plan was to purchase motorcycles and hit the road.

It was a simple plan, but Alex still managed to screw it up by buying a car. He was a few months older than me, so he got his licence first, and two days later there he was at the door of my house with an orange VW Passat sitting on the street behind him.

'Whose is that?' I asked, peering over his shoulder.

'Mine!' he said proudly.

'I thought we were gonna buy bikes ...'

He looked a little uncomfortable, but he had clearly rehearsed an answer. 'Yeah ... umm, look, it's only until you get a bike,' he muttered. 'Then I'll sell it and get one too.' Except when that happened a few months later, he didn't. All of a sudden we didn't have much in common anymore.

By that time, I didn't really care. I had a motorcycle, which I had acquired via parental manipulation, extreme pleading and the telling of vast lies.

I had managed to save half the price of the bike doing part-time work, and then a bit more when I got some brief full-time work as the indentured servant of a crazy Holocaust survivor who ran an army disposal store in the city. In the three months I worked for Mr Aaronovich, and for which he paid me in small notes from the till every afternoon after I had finished sweeping the store entry and the footpath, cleaning the display windows and cases, and straightening the shelves that overflowed with musty-smelling ex-army gear, I vowed I would never again be taken in by classified ads seeking Trainee Assistant Store Managers, when all they really wanted were cleaners.

I was still short a grand, and after many high-level family summits, which began with my father vowing to put an axe through any motorcycle I brought home and eventually ended with my mother in tears on her knees before an icon of the Virgin Mary and my father's guarantor signature on a small bank loan, I was in a bike shop on Parramatta Road and buying the object of my eternal salvation – or damnation, if you believed the muttered prayers of my mum.

That object was a Yamaha XJ650. It had four cylinders, 650ccs and it was red. I was complete. I didn't need friends, I didn't need family. Hell, I even stopped paying attention to the pretty Greek girl who lived in the house behind ours and used to dance to the radio in her underpants most evenings. It was all I could do to keep a job for any longer than a month at a time because working ate into my riding time.

From the day at high school when my mate Gronk first appeared in the car park and let me have a go on his oil-splashed Honda XL250, I'd always had an idea that riding for real, as opposed to sneaking around in the alleyways behind his house, was going to be fun. But I had no idea just how much fun it was going to be.

The first fortnight after the purchase was spent in a haze of euphoric amazement. I even stopped masturbating for a while. My mother grew concerned I had suddenly become a little retarded because I would, in the middle of dinner, stop chewing my food and stare into space with a silly grin on my face. I was, of course, reliving a series of corners, or a particularly fast blast, but to her it looked as if part of my brain had turned into soap. The whole riding experience was so intense it was as if I had to relive it a few times in my head to absorb it and process it.

For the next eighteen months I funned myself stupid by riding everywhere all the time. I had no fear. There was no hesitancy in my riding, I just went at it with single-minded zealotry. I might as well have been retarded.

I didn't have any lessons and no one taught me anything. I lived in Marrickville, an inner-city suburb of Sydney, so there were no wide open spaces and dirt bikes filling my childhood. The only real-world motorcycle-riding experience I'd had followed hard on the heels of my mate Gronk's arrival, astride a disgraceful old Honda XL250, in my high school car park when I was in Year 10 – all of which is documented in my first book, *My Mother Warned Me About Blokes Like Me*.

Gronk's advent was the catalyst for my motorcycle addiction, and I spent many days jigging school and yammering around the lanes and back streets of nearby Camperdown on his bike – and learning whatever I could at the school of Trial, Error, Thrills and Terror. So whatever I had picked up astride Gronk's glorious shit-box, coupled with the fact that I had ridden a pushbike as a kid, seemed to have provided me with a skill-set sufficient to prevent a horrible red death. Which is pretty much how I explained it all to my terrified mother when she questioned me about how I knew how to ride a motorcycle.

'How you learnink raid dis?' she demanded to know one day.

'There's not all that much to learn, Mum,' I grinned. 'It's like riding a pushbike, but heaps easier 'cause you don't have to pedal.'

'Don't be goink too fast,' she pleaded.

My expression was immediately one of shock. 'Never!' I declared and followed that bullshit up with a lie of such epic grandeur it was a miracle the God to whom Mum prayed several times a day didn't strike me dead: 'They don't go that fast anyway.'

But they did. I loved what happened when I made the speedo needle go all the way to the right, but she didn't need to know any of that. In fact, the more ignorant she was of what I was doing, the more blissful I felt she would be. And to this day, I have not changed my mind about that.

So I rode and rode and rode. Day and night. If I couldn't sleep I would go for a ride. If I didn't know what to do on the weekend, I would ride to Brisbane and back. I rode dirt roads, I rode highways, I rode in peak hour, I rode in the rain, I rode with hailstones cracking off my helmet, I rode in state forests and I rode in national parks. I even rode along a beach on the NSW south coast until an incoming tide forced me to ride awkwardly up onto some rocks where I waited endless hours for the tide to recede so I could ride out again. In that year and a half, I clocked up almost 160,000 kilometres.

But I did it all alone. In many ways this was quite fitting, and a bit Zen. After all, we ride alone even when we are riding with a group of other people. If four blokes go for a ride, it's not at all the same as four blokes going for a drive. I got to know myself pretty well on those long rides.

Not every ride is a hell-for-leather death race of pitiless intensity and pulped organs if you screw it up. Once you've mastered the basics, many rides are just you churning out the kilometres, basking in the scenery and bathing in the wind. There's lots of space to think about things. So I did just that. I searched all the rooms of my soul and spent many hours poking about inside my own head-space. I discovered that I liked my own company. I discovered I did not like society all that much. I discovered I would never be a great singer, but I didn't mind the sound of my own bellowing too much and felt I did some of my best work with ancient Serbian battle songs, rather than murdering complex numbers like the Righteous Brothers' 'Unchained Melody'. I discovered I liked to sit by a campfire and stare into the flames and that the darkness held no fear for me. I discovered Australia was full of wonderful, generous, helpful and fascinating people, most of whom did not live in the cities. I discovered I liked speed and danger and risk, and being responsible for my actions. I came to like me and what I was doing with myself and where my life was going – which was nowhere in particular, but as long as it was going there on a motorcycle, I was ever so good with that.

So my life ticked along, until one day I discovered that I needed a new motorcycle. The one I had was simply not terrifying me in sufficient amounts anymore. So I took my XJ650 Yamaha back to the bike shop on Parramatta Road and traded it in for a bigger and vastly more powerful motorcycle. I still had no bike-riding mates, so I was on my own when I did this, and in a bit of a quandary as to what to buy next. I had read all the bike mags I could get my hands on, so I considered myself well informed about what was available. But I also considered myself to be a good rider, so what was one extra delusion in my arsenal of self-beautness?

The bike shop sold Kawasakis, Yamahas and Suzukis, which was fine by me. I had decided a few months back I would never buy or own a Honda because the company's advertising campaigns insisted that I would meet the nicest people on a Honda. Since I was not at all interested in meeting nice people, I was just not gonna buy a Honda. Had the ad campaign stated that I would meet sluts, werewolves, gunslingers, gamblers and drunks, I would have slammed my borrowed money down on the counter in a second, because despite its utterly anodyne ad campaign, Honda enjoyed a great reputation for reliability and performance.

I coveted a Harley, too, but I understood I needed a good deal more evil-ing up before I could carry off that whole hog thing. And besides, the wretched things cost more than twice what a Japanese bike cost.

I didn't have too many options. BMWs were, from what I could see, the province of bearded, Belstaff-wearing stamp collectors, train-spotters and balding middle-aged men who smelled vaguely of urine. Ducatis belonged exclusively to a subset of wild-eyed, long-haired fuckers who seemed to be hewn from obstinacy and delirium, walked with limps, smoked rollies and carried an array of spanners in their pockets. That only left Triumphs (which no one in their right mind wanted to buy in the early '80s as the only things keeping the company afloat were the crazed police departments of Ghana and Nigeria who kept buying them because the jungle drums had told them to do so), and Moto Guzzi, whose owners were several orders of strangeness and oiliness more deranged and oily than the mad swine who owned Ducatis.

My next bike was going to be another Yamaha, or a Suzuki, or a Kawasaki. So while Jerry, the twitchy, lizardy salesman who'd sold me my Yamaha and let me ride it home even though I could not produce a motorcycle licence when I bought it, was looking over the bike and deciding how worthless it was as a trade-in, I wandered up and down the showroom considering my options.

There was a dashing and rather lairy blue-and-white Suzuki GS1000S upon which I spent quite some time rubbing myself. It came stock with a bikini fairing, which caused me not a little anguish. About six months previously I had become overstimulated by press articles about bikini fairings. I immediately went and bought one for the Yamaha, for I very much wanted to be at the cutting edge of motorcycle style. Typically, I was unable to fit the small fairing to my XJ in any way that didn't make it vibrate against the headlight like a jackhammer. Nor could I make it sit squarely, no matter how many times I took it off and put it back on and swore at it. After nine hours of assembly, multiple test rides, fittings, de-fittings, re-fittings and temper tantrums, the cheap crap still buzzed like a Chinese sex toy each time I accelerated. The farce ended, as most of my mechanical farces end, in a sweary fit of Thor-like hammering and destruction of the non-compliant part. And though the Suzuki GS1000S's fairing had been fitted by the factory, I remained suspicious as to its integrity.

Beside it was a decidedly more respectable-looking GS1000G, in a muted two-tone orangey-red colour. But I was unable to take it seriously because it had a shaft-drive and the bike Jerry was devaluing outside also had a shaft-drive. A shaft-drive, I had read in a motorcycle magazine, sapped much-desired horsepower from a motor. I wasn't having any of that. At my age, I needed all the horsepower I could get. It went with my manhood.

Next to that neutered blancmange was a monstrous dark-green and black behemoth that was one-third larger than any other motorcycle on the floor. Or in the world. It was the already legendary six-cylinder Z1300 Kawasaki and it was, to my youthful eyes, intimidation incarnate. I had no business attempting to ride this leviathan. It knew that and I knew that. And it cost two grand more than I had borrowed from the bank, so that settled my inner debate. But I felt like a bit of a girl when I turned my back on it. To this day I still do.

That left three serious contenders.

The Yamaha XS1100 was another shaft-driven monster, but one that allegedly produced enough horsepower to counter-act the shaft-drive's pussification. The bike beside the dirt-red Yamaha was another square-headlighted rocketship that had received a lot of praise in the motorcycle press, the new Suzuki GSX1100EX. It was tarted up in hateful, manly black, with three different blue accents on the tank and a motor that was the performance benchmark of the time.

Beside the EX was *ne plus ultra* of psychopathic Japanese motorcycles, the altogether jaw-dropping Suzuki Katana. It shared the same motor as the EX, but featured styling so far removed from the existing design paradigm of the time as to be almost alien.

I was standing on the threshold of a new age of superbikes, and I just couldn't decide. Should I go with the marque I knew, loved and trusted and buy the Yamaha? Should I sell my soul to the Lucifer-black GSX and its siren call of serious fuck-you power? Or should I take the plunge, bludge another grand off my mum and ride off into the sunset on the wildest, maddest and most outrageous motorcycle ever made and that had been named after the sword samurai warriors used to hack into their own entrails?

I had no idea.

'Okay, Morris,' Jerry declared happily as he wandered back into the showroom and forgot my name again. 'The best I can do on the XJ is a grand. It's got some big miles on it.'

That was about 500 less than I expected, but I was just not equipped to haggle with a man who was wearing a yellow body shirt, tight brown polyester flares and Partridge Family haircut. So I just nodded dumbly.

'So whaddaya reckon you might wanna trade up to?' he grinned.

'I don't know,' I said. And I didn't.

'You like the Katana?'

I nodded again.

'That one's sold, but I can get you another one next month.'

I did not want a bike next month. I wanted a bike now. Jerry, with the scent of my buyer's blood deep in his scaly nostrils, understood that perfectly well. It made him smile with disturbing intensity. I wanted to punch him in the face.

'I can do the black EX for you right now,' he said, showing me his crocodilian teeth. 'And I'll toss in a new helmet.'

I agreed instantly. I couldn't give a shit about the helmet; he was prepared to fuel this thing up and give it to me right now. And part of me wanted a change from the Yamaha and secretly feared its shaft-drive would cause me to sprout a clitoris. An

15

hour later, I was riding my new bike home via Wollongong, a round trip of 250 kilometres.

Its power, after the relatively gentle exhalations of the Yamaha, dried my mouth and turned my eyes into saucers. It was noticeably heavier than my first bike, but it handled much the same, and when I opened the throttle that amazing engine spat me at the horizon with a venom that caused my arse to chew at the seat in delighted alarm.

And so began a love affair that was to last three years and some 260,000 kilometres. I spent money on that bike like a balding middle-aged fool pimping up his Filipina bride. But unlike the bride, the big Suzuki never let me down, always brought me home and ensured that I would now and forever serve as a high priest before the altar of the Road Gods.

But I still didn't have any mates. For a few months, that was still alright. My Suzuki and I were in our honeymoon period, and there was no room in my life for anything but it. Then one afternoon, as I was walking past the Hilton Hotel on George Street in Sydney, and admiring my splendid motorcycling self in the shop windows, I heard a bike gearing savagely down behind me. I turned and saw a nasty, noisy, matte-black Katana lurch to a halt almost beside me. Sartorially the rider was only some fur and a boot-knife removed from Toecutter in *Mad Max*.

'Mmonnis?!' said a muffled voice from inside a black-visored black-and-gold AGV helmet.

I narrowed my eyes and shifted my own helmet down from my wrist and into my hand, fully intending to defend whatever needed defending with my fibreglass bludgeon. The rider flicked up his helmet, and his eyes crinkled in amusement.

'Boris?!' he repeated, a little clearer this time.

'Who are you?' I asked, walking closer and peering at what little I could see of the rider's face.

'Hang on,' he said, put his bike on its stand, undid his helmet and slipped it off his head. 'It's me,' he said.

I still blinked in confusion.

'Frank. From school.'

And the penny dropped. It was indeed Frank from my high school. I vaguely remembered him, but we hadn't been mates – and what I did recall of him was that he was one of those nondescript kids. Neither a genius, nor a jock, nor a monstrous dickhead. And here he was now, looking very cool and very fast and riding what was obviously a horrid home-painted matte-black Katana with a buzzsaw-loud exhaust. And he had a walkie-talkie attached to his hip.

As we shook hands he told me he was a motorcycle courier and asked me what I rode. I proudly replied that I had a GSX1100EX, which you'll recall shared pretty much everything with Frank's Katana except the outlandish styling. So we instantly had something else in common apart from high school.

'I'm finishing work now,' Frank said. 'Wanna come back to my place for a beer? Remember Scott? I live with him. He rides a GPZ.'

I vaguely recalled Scott, Frank's mate at school, and I was inordinately pleased that he rode as well – and he rode a very mighty Kawasaki, which had recently been invented as competition to the GSX I was riding.

'Sure,' I said. It had been a long time since anyone had

invited me anywhere for a beer, and while I didn't want to appear pathetically keen, that's exactly what I was.

'Where's your bike?' Frank asked.

I told him it was parked around the corner.

'Cool. Follow me.' He waited for me opposite Sydney Town Hall, and in a few minutes we were barrelling down George Street to Frank's townhouse in the nearby inner-city suburb of Newtown. It was all I could do just to keep up with him. This had nothing to do with my bike, which was virtually as powerful as his. It was me – and this delusion I had about how fast I was. Or wasn't, as it turned out.

Clearly, Frank was possessed of riding skills, daring and ruthlessness when it came to traffic that had thus far eluded me. He lane-split at speeds that took my breath away, and hammered off the lights as if he was drag-racing for money. As we tore down Broadway, my speedo was nudging 130 kms per hour. His bike sounded glorious, crackling and popping on over-run through its aftermarket exhaust system. I vowed to buy one just like that the next day even if it meant I would once again cheat Mum out of the board I was supposed to pay each month.

And he looked far cooler than me. There was no doubt about that. I was dressed in my normal riding ensemble of blue jeans tucked into black Rossi-brand riding boots, a black leather jacket and some black gloves. My helmet was a silver-and-black AGV with a clear visor. Bar the helmet, which I got when I bought the bike, all of my gear had been bought from Omodeis – a wonderful shop that used to be on Pitt Street, just behind Central Station. I remember so clearly how it smelled of leather, waxed cotton and the ethereal promise of distant horizons astride a motorcycle.

Frank's gear looked a lot edgier and reminded me of the psychotic outlaw riders in what was then my favourite movie, *Mad Max*. Instead of blue jeans, he wore black jeans, and they weren't tucked into prissy black boy-boots. They were jammed into brutish Sidi dirt-bike boots, with cruel buckles on the side and steel reinforcement along the toes. His leather jacket was scuffed and collared with epaulettes (they call them Brando jackets these days), and much thicker than mine. Over the top of this he had a stained, faded sleeveless denim jacket.

I made mental notes as we howled through the busy shopping centre of Newtown, jaywalkers leaping back onto the footpath as Frank's exhaust popped explosions of hate at them.

Note 1. Buy an exhaust system. Do it tomorrow.

Note 2. Buy a Levi's jean jacket and saw the arms off it. Argue with mother about this. Do not lose argument.

Note 3. Buy dirt-bike boots or find someone who is prepared to fight you for his. And fight hard. You must not come second.

Note 4. Stop being a giant sack of trembling, hesitant, slow-riding bitch-poo. Turn the throttle. Do it now. If he can fit that Katana into that traffic gap, so can you. One hundred and forty kilometres per hour is a perfectly acceptable speed down the double yellow lines of a major inner-city thoroughfare. What the fuck did you buy this black monster for? To look at?

I was a somewhat altered Borrie when Frank and I finally pulled up in front of his two-storey townhouse just off the main road.

Scott was out the front washing his Kawasaki GPZ1100, and there was another identical-to-mine black GSX parked next to it, which belonged to a gentle-natured, careful-riding and somewhat skinny bloke called Barry. There was also a fabulous blonde with excellent tits and painted-on jeans sitting on the fence, swinging her legs, smoking and watching Scott wash his bike. She turned out to be Scott's girlfriend, Justine.

Like Frank, Scott was a motorcycle courier. I came to understand that their profession accounted greatly for just how fast these blokes were and how well they rode. As you might understand, a motorcycle courier's life span is mostly measured in weeks. They dance on the knife-edge of metropolitan traffic death for ten to twelve hours a day. They either learn to ride well, or they die. Both Frank and Scott had been couriers for about a year, and they were both very much alive. I was in the presence of minor riding deities.

They all greeted me with good humour, and quite suddenly, it looked like I might have friends again: friends who clearly shared my love of the motorcycle. In short order, I was drinking beer, laughing and passing around a joint as if I'd known these people my whole life. Another bloke called Craig joined us. He lived in the block of flats next to their row of townhouses and rode a big 1100cc Kawasaki shaft-drive. Despite this deficiency, he was as welcoming as the others.

I had to go home for dinner, so we all made some quick plans to go for a ride the coming weekend. We agreed that an excursion to Gosford, via the Old Pacific Highway, was in order. Since I was the new kid, a dash along that famously twisting stretch of bitumen would determine my place in the pecking order. I knew Frank was quicker than me, but I had no idea about the others. I did note that everyone was sporting the latest Pirelli tyres, which were the last word in adhesion back then. By today's standards it would be like riding on ceramic tiles but back then, as your giant, 130-horsepower Japanese bike oscillated and weaved its way around corners, always on the verge of tank-slapping you into the traction braces at the local hospital, you would congratulate yourself on having the stickiest tyres money could buy. And you would ride accordingly.

I will always remember that first ride with Frank and the others from Berowra to Gosford. It started fast and hard and didn't ease off – Frank and Scott engaged it with an intensity I had not seen this side of a racetrack. We must have been doing well over 200 across the Brooklyn Bridge, one of the only straight bits in what is a cornucopia of beautiful corners. They rode closely behind each other, obviously very familiar with themselves and the road, and while I also knew the road, I had never pushed as hard along it as I did that Sunday. We passed everything, and as we began the final, thrilling descent into Gosford, I was shaking my head in disbelief and trembling with adrenalin fizz.

Most Sydney riders are familiar with the Old Pacific Highway. It is a stunning section of bitumen that is rather close to the city. But what was a blessing to riders in the '70s (just after the Newcastle freeway opened for business), '80s and early '90s, has become their curse in the 21st century. The Old Road, as it is now known, was once a free-fire zone for motorcyclists. You went there to learn how to go fast around corners. And some-times, in the process of learning, you would die or end up in a motorised wheelchair oozing faeces into a bag and swallowing laboriously through a tube. For such is the nature of learning how to go fast around corners on motorcycles.

The police now blanket the road every weekend, and the speed limit has been dropped from 100 to 60. But since many motorcyclists have pretty much become unskilled herd animals in today's world, legions of them still insist on riding up there, crashing their vestigial brains out and being booked for everything the Highway Patrol can come up with. I would rather gouge my own eyes out than go there today.

You will recall that the '70s and '80s were simpler and far more Manichaean times. Motorcycling had never been as magnificently Darwinian and more black and white than it was then. If you wanted to ride in those days, there was no room for any doubt or hesitancy. Your desire to ride had better burn with an incandescent fire, and you had to have an innate, almost instinct-driven ability to come to grips with your motorcycle in a short period of time. Failure to do this, and your time kissing the wind and surfing creamy waves of torque would be exactly as Thomas Hobbes observed – 'nasty, brutish and short'.

Do I have to tell you how face-scrunchingly appealing this was to a mildly crazy wog boy with a doting mother, or can you guess? It was the rite of passage into manhood I had always searched for. Sure, it wasn't exactly hunting cave-bears with a fire-hardened stick, but it was certainly a close second in terms of just how much pure screaming terror and manliness could be mainlined into your veins in a nanosecond.

At the time, any sixteen-year-old could buy a machine that could achieve 220 kms per hour in a normal suburban street, sounded like a screaming jet, and made him utterly irresistible to sparkling-eyed teenage girls rebelling against their fathers by taking off their bras and climbing onto the back of such bikes with breathless enthusiasm. There were no nanny-state-mandated, 'Learner-Approved Motorcycles'. You could turn sixteen and nine months and go and buy the most powerful bike in the world, and ride it on your L-plates. There were no cheery instructors full of positive reinforcement slogans and an inane you-can-do-it attitude, even if the unco-ordinated gibbon under their instruction was demonstrably unsuited to riding bikes and was clearly going to die on his way home from the course that afternoon. There were no track days where you could go and hone your skills on a closed racetrack in a relatively safe environment. There were no riding courses and no rider trainers. If you wanted to learn how to ride fast, you learned on public roads, which were thankfully less crowded, but this advantage was offset by comparatively ill-handling bikes with enormous amounts of horsepower. So you did the only thing you could, you learned by following riders who were faster and better than you for as long as you could. You learned by doing and by trying and by judging just how much to push it before it all pushed back. It was a lot like climbing into a fighting cage, putting your hands up and seeing what you could learn from the professional man-beating machine in the opposite corner.

Yes, it did go to horrible bastard shit from time to time. How could it not? What happened then? Well, you gave up riding, and so many did. Or you dealt with it and you grew up a little bit. Fundamentally, you had to learn how to ride all by yourself, or grim-faced men would be scraping you off the bitumen with red-dripping shovels and clucking about the shame and tragedy of it all.

That Sunday, on my first ride with my new mates, I learned a whole lot of new things. I learned that Scott was faster than Frank. Not by much, but by enough to make him heaps faster than me – because Frank was faster than me. Not by all that much, though. And in turn, I learned I was faster than skinny Barry and shaft-drive Craig. I was also faster than another bloke who showed up called Jay. But he was riding an abominable Honda CX500, which was giving away two cylinders and about a million horsepower to the GSXs and the GPZ. The CX had been dubbed the Plastic Maggot by Australian motorcycle riders, who were affronted by its appalling styling and mini-fairing-cum-headlight-nacelle-cum-dribbling-bib, and has remained one of the most hideous motorcycles ever built. Damnably reliable and proficient, like most Hondas, but with zero allure.

What I found most educational was that Frank and Scott rode everywhere fast. The moment they got on their bikes, they were on it. Every set of lights was a drag-race; every set of bends was a late-entry, high-lean-angle speed-fest. Wheelies were popped with amazing skill and regularity, and Scott was certainly the grand-master of lofting the front wheel into the sky. He even performed them between waiting lines of stationary traffic, which made Frank and me helpless with laughter and admiration. I cannot imagine what the drivers must have thought as a giant red motorcycle howled past them on its back wheel, missing their doors by scant centimetres, the exhaust loud enough to cause the children in the cars to cry and yelp in terror. I know this because I saw them screaming as Frank and I followed Scott through the traffic.

I, of course, had no idea how to do wheelies until I hooked up with the two of them. But I certainly taught myself as quickly as possible and in the time-tested tradition of motorcycle hooligans everywhere.

I asked Scott about the mechanics of it. 'Give it about five grand in second as you're rolling along, and dump the clutch. Make sure your foot is covering the back brake in case it starts to flip. Piece of piss.'

I committed this sagacity to memory and found a quiet street. Three hours later I had exploded my fork seals, dinged my steering head bearings, fried my clutch and bounced myself off the side of a caravan and four cars. But I had learned how to wheelie – more or less. I was never proficient enough to essay a 140-kms-per-hour three-gear, lane-splitting minger like Scott, but I did manage the odd two-gear howler when the planets aligned.

Scott also taught me to jump my motorcycle through the air, but the first time I did this it was entirely by accident and scared the furry tripe out of me. Every time after that it was big-time stupid fun. The night-flying caught me unaware the first time: I was belting down Darley Road, an inner-west suburban street at the back of Leichhardt, chasing Scott's taillight. You could attain a fair turn of speed down Darley Road – it arcs in a long right-hander that parallels an old railway line, and Scott and I had certainly attained that fair turn of speed. Suddenly, I saw his taillight veer sharply to the left just where Canal Road runs into Darley Road and a second later it rose at least a metre into the air. But since I had automatically followed Scott when he lurched to the left, I didn't have all that long to marvel at how he'd just levitated a motorcycle travelling at 130 kms per hour, because mine also left the ground, engine screaming, following his into the air. Scott knew about the massive drain that ran across the road right beside the gutter at that point. He'd been jumping it for ages. This was my first time. It was certainly not my last, but it would have been had I not successfully landed the howling Suzuki – and that was more through sheer luck than any skill. Had I panicked and throttled sharply off, the violent shaking of the front-end on landing would have turned into an arm-snapping tank-slapper and Scott would have been feeding me cigarettes as we waited for the paramedics. But it happened all too fast for me to panic. He almost fell off his bike laughing at my appalled facial expression at the next set of lights.

My education as a rider continued apace. Spending every weekend and most weeknights with my new mates laughing a lot, drinking heaps of beer and smoking a bit of dope, we talked about nothing except motorcycles and girls. We rode the Old Road at all hours of the day and night. We conducted land-speed record attempts on the long, straight and mostly deserted factory-lined boulevards in the west of Sydney. We also conducted them on the twisting, hack-surfaced streets of the inner suburbs, which was even more exciting. We rode every winding road we could find around Sydney at every opportunity: Bells Line of Road, the Putty, Tarana, Jenolan Caves, Wollombi via Lemmings Corner, St Albans, Wisemans Ferry, Spencer, Peats Ridge, Bulli Pass, Macquarie Pass, Kangaroo Valley, Royal National Park, Pearl Beach, Patonga, Woy Woy. Some of these roads still had sections of dirt on them, which was just an added challenge. Especially when we'd had a few beers.

We also roamed further afield. Cobar, Dubbo, Tamworth, Mudgee, Wagga Wagga, Griffith, and smaller places such as

Dungog, Gilgandra, Warren, Nyngan, and myriad even smaller places scattered throughout NSW, as well as parts of Victoria and Queensland. Melbourne and Brisbane were frequently visited, as were the fabled roads on the way to them – the Oxley Highway, the Bruxner, the Gwydir, Thunderbolts Way, the Snowy Mountains Highway – they all left their mark on us.

But we did not once leave our mark on them. No, I do not know why. Maybe we were just lucky. I had become a much better rider since I hooked up with Frank that fateful afternoon outside the Hilton – faster, smoother and more confident. My balls were larger and swung lower. My Suzuki had changed as I had added things to make it go faster, shriek louder and handle better. My wardrobe changed, too. I quickly adopted the denim vest over the leather jacket look, and got myself a beaut pair of red-and-black Sidi dirt-bike boots. I even acquired a pair of Balmain Tigers footy socks and wore them folded over the top of the boots, and became the complete incarnation of a motorcycle hooligan.

I began to seek out other riders to measure myself against, and on Friday nights, after maybe doing a quick dash to Watsons Bay – a challenging, twisty, traffic-dodging, inner-city dash from Kings Cross to the southern arm of Sydney Harbour, I would wait on Campbell Parade at Bondi Beach for passing motorcycles. When one went past, I would fire up and tear off after him, the idea being to bitch him in the bumpy, off-camber uphill right-hander that climbed out of Bondi Beach on its way to Bondi Junction. I did this for several weeks, but felt I'd pushed my luck far enough when I passed a bloke astride a Conti-piped Ducati up the inside, probably closer than I might have liked. He panicked, lost the front, slid out and managed to wedge himself under a parked car.

I went back to see if he was alright, and he was. He had a broken leg and his bike was written off, but he didn't seem overly pissed at me. I dragged him out from under the car and we both agreed it was one of those Friday-night things. I sat beside him in the gutter and allowed that maybe I shouldn't have come under his shit as hard as I did. He confessed he should have not lost his shit like a frightened girl and trowelled his bike the way he did. We shared a joint while we waited for the ambulance to come and get him, and parted on good terms.

A type of atavistic madness had enveloped me. I knew it was evident, because my mother spent a lot of time talking to God about me. Clearly, she had some pull as I remained unscathed and unmarked, despite all my high-speed depredations.

I'd only had one accident thus far in my riding career, and that was quite early on in the piece, on the first bike I'd bought. I high-sided myself quite spectacularly as I tried to come to a halt at a Stop sign around the corner from my house. A high-side, if you don't know, is when a motorcycle acts like a stock-whip, catapulting you into the air exactly one nanosecond after it first gets you to squirt hot shit into your pants by sliding its back wheel sideways, then it finds traction, flicks you off and you're on your way to hospital.

The concrete section of road was criss-crossed with 'black-snakes', those insidious, greasy petrified rivers of tar the council likes to pour into joins in the road surface. It was wet and I had no idea what I needed to do when my back wheel lost adhesion, and stupidly hauled on the brakes. The bike vomited me out of the seat, then crashed on top of me, breaking some ribs, a collarbone and tenderising some of my less robust organs. I somehow managed to pick the bike up (it was largely undamaged thanks to my torso cushioning its fall), rode the 150 metres to my house and collapsed in the front yard so the bike's exhaust could sear a nice hole in my calf.

After Mum hauled me out, cleaned me up and drove me to the hospital for bandaging, she made me promise that I would never crash again. So I didn't, for many, many years, until my behaviour became even more erratic and unholy, and all bets were off.

Still, while I managed not to write myself off in all the time I was riding with Frank and Scott, who had also managed not to come to any grief, there were two blokes in our circle who were earning frequent flyer points in almost every major Sydney hospital. The outstanding player was young Dennis, who had come to us astride a ratty red Honda 250 fitted with a full Rickman race fairing in an attempt to hide the shame of his tiny motorcycle. Tall, rangy and determined, Dennis was lit from within by a kind of divine motorcycling madness I have rarely beheld, and beside which even mine sometimes paled. He was constantly dressed from head to foot in brutally scuffed red leathers, so it's not like he met us and then started to crash his brains out. Sliding and tumbling down the street was clearly something he was familiar with.

Sure enough, the evening after I met him at the Illinois Hotel on Parramatta Road in Five Dock – which had become our regular Thursday night meet-up – I saw his bike propped against the front fence of a house in a back street in Ashfield. I recognised it instantly, for there was not another such creation on this earth, and pulled over.

There was a small pool of oil under the bike and it was scuffed and scratched, but I had no way of knowing if that was what it normally looked like, or if the damage was fresh. I couldn't see Dennis anywhere. Jumping off my bike, I went to have a closer look, and saw him lying in the front garden of the house in question. Because he was lying down I hadn't seen him from the road.

'Hey mate,' I called. 'You okay?'

He rolled over, his face a rictus of pain, and looked at me blankly for a few seconds, then obviously remembered me from the night before. 'Hey, mate,' he grinned lamely. 'How you goin'?'

'I'm good,' I nodded. 'You?'

'I think my arm's broken.'

'How'd you do that?'

'A dog ran in front of me. I swerved to miss it and hit the gutter.'

I knocked on the door of the house and asked the frightened lady cowering behind her security screen if we could wheel the bike into her front yard while I took my mate to hospital. Once I explained to her what had happened, she even offered to bring out some water, but I assured her the garden hose was sufficient for our needs. I rehydrated Dennis and doubled him to Canterbury Hospital.

A week later, his arm freshly plastered, he was fanging along Victoria Road – a hellishly busy main arterial road that connects the city to Parramatta – and took the exit that would have led him to Hunters Hill. Except that there was a road crew on the bend laying fresh tar. He lost the front-end and slid into the Armco. I rode out to pick him up and took him to the Royal North Shore Hospital to get his re-broken arm re-set and re-plastered. This became a recurring theme in our relationship.

Over the next year, I either took Dennis to or visited him in St Vincent's Hospital (broken hand and concussion); Royal Prince Alfred (broken ankle, concussion and internal bruising); Concord (concussion and broken collarbone); Sydney (bruising and shock); Balmain (burns caused by his incipient pyromania, not really linked to an actual riding incident); Auburn (cracked ribs and internal bleeding); Westmead (broken leg) … hell, the list is long.

Dennis was one of those unfortunate blokes who just crashed all the time. His accidents were never serious enough to dissuade him from riding or maim him so that he couldn't ride. And so he carried on, his little red Honda becoming more and more battered, and his red leathers transforming into a travesty of protection, though they continued to do their job and kept most of his hide intact. He remained fanatically dedicated to the ride and attended every one we had. He struggled to keep up, but was happy to keep his little bike's throttle pinned wide open in the attempt. And his indefatigable dedication to his bike and the riding of it is what kept us from killing him in frustration. He was a true believer – you don't kill true believers.

Leo was also a true believer, who came to us loaded with a Greek's lust for life and an ex-police Honda Bol d'Or. Suddenly there were four of us contending for a podium at the front of the pack on our rides. Not possessed of any vast riding skill,

Leo made up for it with testicles the size of hams and a total disregard for his personal safety. He was an utter joy to be around – an uncomplicated, super-fit, irredeemably cheerful bloke who burned as brightly as a rescue flare and rode that Honda harder than any cop had ever ridden it.

'It's only a little bike,' he'd laugh whenever I remarked how hard it was to keep up with him when all caution was thrown into the winds of Fuck It All. 'I have to try harder to stay with your big bikes.'

With Leo at the handlebars, there was hardly any difference between his 900cc Honda and his gargantuan gonads, and our 1100cc rocket ships and comparatively smaller man-eggs. Unlike Dennis, Leo was not big on protective gear, and spent most of his relatively short riding career hammering around dressed in jeans, light boots, a singlet and a denim vest. Interestingly, he did have the best Bell helmet money could buy, but since he hardly ever did it up, it all seemed kinda pointless.

About a year into our friendship, he had been at the Illinois Hotel with us on a Thursday night, bubbling with happiness because he'd scraped enough money together to buy a new pipe for his Honda and get it tuned up. We all went dutifully outside to hear him rev it, but then Leo felt we were not fully appreciating his new Kerker pipe and ran inside to get his helmet.

'You gotta hear it through the gears!' he yelled, jumped on, and when the lights went green, he bolted across Parramatta Road and headed down Croydon Road, across the way from the Illinois Hotel. We duly cocked our ears and listened to the Honda screaming its way to red-line in first, then second, then third, then fourth. We all smiled and nodded and declared Leo's

Kerker pipe to be a thing of ferocious aural wonder. We did not hear the bike go up into fifth, but didn't think all that much of it. Leo was taking his time coming back, but that wasn't unusual – he often got carried away and just kept riding. No doubt that was what had happened, and none of us were worried, not even when a car pulled up and asked us if we knew a bloke on a white bike.

'He's gone into the front of a car just up the road,' the driver said. 'Fuck, he was moving, too.'

In seconds we were on our bikes heading down Croydon Road, and arrived at the scene of the accident just as the fire trucks were pulling up. Leo's bike was unrecognisable. It was a charred, smoking ball of metal and plastic lying in the dead middle of the road, directly in front of an HQ Holden that had been turned into the metal equivalent of a forked tongue. The front of the car was resting on the road, its front wheels splayed sideways, and there were vehicle liquids, broken glass and smashed motorcycle crap everywhere. I could see the bike's forks, *sans* the front wheel, lying in the gutter to my right. People in dressing gowns had come out of the surrounding houses and stood with their arms folded surveying the mess. The flashing red lights of the emergency vehicles intermittently painted the whole scene with a stark, flickering grimness.

Leo was dead. He had to be. So I was flabbergasted when he limped up to me, a little bloody and battered, grinning sheepishly. 'That was fucken mad!' he said.

I had no response. I just stared at him.

'I went a bit wide on that kink,' he said, nodding at the slight bend in Croydon Road.

'How fast were you going?' I asked.

Leo shrugged. 'About a hundred and forty.'

'How are you not dead?'

Leo shrugged again. 'One second I was riding, the next thing I remember is flying through the air, skating across the roof of the car and rolling down the road. My helmet came off somewhere.'

'I've got your helmet,' Frank said, walking up. His eyes were like saucers as he handed it to Leo.

Then the police arrived, started writing things down and talking to everyone, including the driver, who was unharmed, and kept walking around his car, shaking his head and muttering unintelligibly.

Leo was charged with negligent driving, paid a fine, and a week later was astride another Bol d'Or, not much the worse for wear. Unfortunately, however, his luck appeared to have been totally used up. A few weeks after his miraculous head-on, a parked car opened its door on him as he was lane-splitting through Marrickville shopping centre. Leo swerved to avoid the door, hit the side of a truck and went under its rear wheels. His skull was cracked like a hard-boiled egg, the fractures running all the way around his cranium, and he spent several weeks in hospital, tied to his bed in some kind of spooky, twitching, spasming coma that unsettled me greatly whenever I went to see him. I spent hours talking to him and holding his clawed hand, but I don't know if he ever heard me.

He eventually came out of the coma, and relocated to Queensland where his parents nursed him slowly back to something approximating health. I ran into him several years later and discovered a Leo who still smiled readily, but spoke haltingly and forgot much of what he had already said. He told me he was not allowed to ride anymore, but he still managed to throw a leg over his brother's trail bike on the odd weekend.

For some reason, other people's misfortunes did nothing to slow me down. If anything, I was just more determined that I would not be one of the ones who ate shit. Resolute about becoming a better rider, I decided that the more I up-skilled myself, the less chance there was of me coming to grief.

I realised early on in my riding career that it was altogether pointless expecting car drivers to see me. I would now and forever remain invisible to them. No matter how many of them I punched in the face, no matter how many side mirrors I smashed off, no matter how many side windows I crashed my gloved fist through, no matter how many bonnets I stood upon and screamed 'Can you fucken see me now, you blind cunt?!' nothing changed. They still pulled out in front of me. They still merged into me. They still drove as if the road was their personal thoroughfare.

Which I understood, because I also treated the road, and still do, as *my* personal thoroughfare. The difference was that I was always like a cat standing on top of a burning shed. I and I alone was responsible for whether I live or died or shitted into a bag for the rest of my life. It was not the responsibility of the car driver. It was not the fault of the road surface. It was *all* my responsibility. Whether I lived or died was almost entirely up to me. I liked that. If I was not able to be responsible for anything else in my life, at least I would be fully responsible for being a good rider. And I had found friends who very much shared this philosophy.

Consequently, our weekends were not full of waiting on the side of the road for ambulances to collect one of us. There was no comforting weeping girlfriends while hospital staff tried to find a co-operative vein to ram a cannula into one of us. We spent very little time on the side of the road dissecting why one of us had ploughed into a tree.

Certainly there was madness and high-speed frenzy, and death leered at us and ran his scythe over our ducked heads every day. But that only made the life-beverage we had each brewed all the more heady and intoxicating. We laughed often and more loudly than other people. We cherished what we had made of our lives, and felt we lived more in a weekend than most people live in a lifetime.

Did we much care that others thought we were batshit-crazy sociopathic death-seekers? Sure we did. It made us all the more determined to be even crazier than they imagined us to be. Shocking people became our way of rubbing their bovine faces into the tepid sludge their lives appeared to be.

The more I managed to appal normal people, the more I felt my lifestyle choices were validated. I knew I wasn't alone. My mates felt much as I did ... and so the madness fed itself. But of course it could not last.

Slaves once stood behind conquering generals as they entered imperial Rome in triumph and whispered, '*Respice post te! Hominem te esse memento! Memento mori!*' ('Look behind you! Remember that you are but a man! Remember that you'll die!'), so that the general would not forget that all glory was fleeting and he was but a mortal and not a god. I did not own any slaves, and the only things that were ever whispered to me as I rode triumphantly about the countryside, was that my female companion was not wearing any panties. But even if I had a slave whispering that shit to me, I wouldn't have listened. I was barely twenty years old. I was deaf to reason and caution and good behaviour. I had a motorcycle that howled like an unfettered demon. Objects in my mirror no longer mattered. What was the point of looking at them? I believed I was far more than an ordinary man and dying was not on my to-do list.

Eventually I drifted irrevocably in a different direction to my friends. Frank had a new girlfriend who was demanding much of his attention. Scott's girlfriend was pregnant, which was affecting a lot of his free time. Craig had likewise set up house with some girl, Barry seemed content to hover on the fringes and keep his bike immaculately stock, Leo had moved away, and that left Dennis, who was now nicknamed Badger, and who seemed as equally unhinged as I was.

He'd stopped crashing his brains out every week, which we both felt was a positive development in our relationship. He had also bought a much larger and more powerful bike, and divested himself of the battered red leathers, so evolution was clearly at work there. For my part, I had been busily getting tattooed with grim reapers and dragons, and had spent many intriguing hours chatting with Tony Cohen, one of Australia's finest and most respected tattooists, about all sorts of stuff. Not the least of which was his long-time membership in the Mobshitters MC, and how much hell-raising fun that all was. A few visits to the club's Hurstville clubhouse certainly bore out much of what Tony and I had talked about.

The seed that had long ago been planted in my fertile brain

was now budding – and being nurtured and fed. I started looking at Triumphs and Harleys with a renewed interest, and while any kind of commitment to a vastly different motorcycling lifestyle was still a few years away, it was certainly inevitable. I had learned a lot about 'fast'. I now wanted to learn all about 'outlaw'.

GOING POSTAL

With the wisdom of hindsight, riding a postie bike around the leafy northern suburbs of Sydney was probably the best job I'd ever had. In terms of being stress-free, simple and fulfilling on some base, bestial level, it was pretty hard to beat. Sure it was repetitious, and because it was, it slowly leached the rich marrow from my soul. And despite the way Australia Post viewed it, I was very pleased I was being paid to ride a motorcycle. The whole telegram and mail delivery thing was, to me, totally incidental to the riding of the motorcycle. Yes, I know it was only a small, buzzy, underpowered motorcycle – but for someone as addicted as me, reclining on a piss-stained mattress and pumping cheap-shit heroin into a collapsing vein was better than not pumping any heroin at all. And it's not like I didn't milk the gig for everything I could.

'We are mothers and fathers. And sons and daughters. Who every day go about our lives with duty, honor and pride. And neither snow, nor rain, nor heat, nor gloom of

        night, nor the winds of change, nor a nation
        challenged, will stay us from the swift
        completion of our appointed rounds. Ever.'

UNITED STATES POSTAL SERVICE

I had to get a new job. The one I had was approaching its use-by date at the same relentless speed a fridge tossed off a building approaches the ground. For two years before starting with Australia Post I had worked for Campbelltown City Council as a surveyor's assistant and draftsman. Not only was it a job I mildly disliked, I was slightly crap at it. That I was doing it at all was entirely due to a woman I had fallen in love with, and who had insisted I 'make something of myself', apparently so she would be at liberty to do whatever she wanted without the hindrance of a boyfriend acting as a brake.

Initially, she felt it would be best for me to become a master plasterer. Then I could take my rightful place among the Gyprock-splashed Italian drunks who made up her relatives, and possibly, if I proved adept at my craft, to conceivably be employed one day by her appalling father – who brewed an appalling type of grape-based brandy in his garage, and fuelled his hatred of me by forcing the frightening concoction upon me and laughing as I lapsed into anaphylactic shock.

But since access to her vagina was like a genetic imperative for me, I essayed this Gyprocking caper for about a month. In that time, I would ride my bike to some benighted building site on the outskirts of Sydney in the darkness before the dawn, and spend the next twelve hours being screamed at in Italian by alcoholics who worked like Mexican mules, and could plaster an entire townhouse (ceilings and walls) in one day.

During that month I smashed many thousands of dollars' worth of plasterboard sheeting with my hammer because I was somehow unable to stand on a ladder, hold a ceiling up with my head and hammer nails into invisible beams on the other side of the plasterboard that was relentlessly compressing my neck into my arse. In between those tragic episodes, I would unload truckloads of plasterboard, fetch food, get water, provide the appalling brandy, go for cigarettes, and search out called-for plastering tools in the trays of shitty, overloaded and mostly unregistered utes. At the end of the day I would ease my throbbing body onto my now-covered-in-crud bike, my hands burning with cramps and my back shrieking in white agony, picture the vagina I may or may not be granted access to as a result of my labours, and idle off home to collapse on my mattress. At the end of the month I had had enough and stopped going, and she stopped granting me splashing privileges to her vagina.

'You need to make something of yourself,' she would explain to my neck as I held her, valiantly and altogether pointlessly attempting to access her toy shop through her firmly crossed legs. 'We can't have a future together if you haven't got a good job.'

To be perfectly honest, I wanted unfettered access to the inside of her panties far more than I wanted any kind of future, but I was young, dumb and easily influenced by hot women who smelled like sexy fruit salads and let me play with their tits.

Right, then! I said to myself. If it's a man with a killer career she wants, it's a man with a killer career she'll get. So after a week

41

of scrubbing myself clean from a month of Gyprocking serfdom and learning how to walk upright again, I decided to do a course in Land, Engineering and Survey Drafting at Sydney Tech. Upon successful completion of which I would promptly score a beaut office job that paid lots of money and then spend the rest of my days smearing myself with my girlfriend's sex juices.

Unfortunately, that girlfriend left me for another man a month into the course.

To make matters worse, I had discovered that most of the course I was doing comprised of insane mathematical sorcery which required calculators that worked in Reverse Polish Notation to solve. Sure, there was some drafting and some surveying in the field with theodolites and levels, but a lot of time was spent inside classrooms trying to comprehend spherical trigonometry and calculating the area of blobs.

I hated maths with a passion. I was shit at it in school and had not got better at it after I left. But I persevered with the course after the no-vagina-for-you girl left me because I needed some form of structure to my life. A year into the course I got a job at Campbelltown City Council, a beaut new thing called a Bankcard (which simultaneously plunged me into stunning debt and acquired me a new motorcycle), and a really long commute to work each day. I lived in Marrickville, and Campbelltown was some fifty-odd kilometres away. My trip to work each day was more than a hundred kilometres (happily against the traffic), and before any bypasses or toll roads had been built in Sydney. The F5 Freeway started at the Crossroads pub at Casula and only went as far as Campbelltown back then, but on a good day, I could get there in about an hour. When I was drunk and racing home late in the evening, I could do the trip in just on half an hour, thanks to the speed-enhancing effects of seven schooners and a tailwind.

I quite enjoyed the commute most of the year, but during winter it was a cold and bitter battle of willpower against hypothermic coma, especially once I hit the freeway. If I was lucky, I could tuck into the dead air behind a truck and pray my aircooled engine didn't overheat and explode as I sheltered from the harsh fangs of the wind. And because I couldn't see anything but the wall of the truck's load rearing two metres in front of me, I would also pray that the truck wouldn't suddenly shudder to a halt and send me spearing under its tray like a bouncing meatmelon. As dangerous as it was, though, at least it was a little warmer than smashing through the Arctic ice-hate unleashed upon me from the end of May until mid-September.

My hands suffered the worst because proper warm gloves for motorcyclists were not invented until the 21st century, and this was still the '70s. I'd bought a pair of sheepskin-lined Rossi boots which did a fair job of keeping my feet from becoming gangrenous lumps of frosted meat. My leather jacket, a woolly jumper and a footy scarf did what they could to keep my heart beating; it was a young and vibrant organ back then, and I foolishly imagined that it would keep on thumping no matter what I would subject it to. But there were times on that wretched freeway when I really did think I was going to die from the cold. And when it rained, everything got exponentially worse and far more fucked and heaps more shit.

I persevered because I didn't really mind the job at first. It paid alright, was relatively varied and allowed me to learn how to do quality circle-work in council cars in various cow paddocks I was meant to be surveying. And about six months into my tenure, when the surveyor and I found six giant dope plants growing on the banks of the Georges River, decided work was over for the day and filled two big hessian sacks with heads the size of deodorant cans, I could see a career for myself there.

Then some bastard invented computers. Yes, they had been invented a while before that, but they were still rare, big-dollar items with as-yet unknown potential. When they finally arrived in the engineering department of Campbelltown Council, I realised my days there were numbered. Not only was I no longer required to hold steady and straight a massive collapsible three-jointed staff atop some hillock, but my (admittedly limited) skills as a draftsman had been supplanted by a machine that could produce a perfectly drawn contour map of an area in a fraction of the time it would take me to do so. And without any errors, bitching, moaning, or cheating on flexi-time.

As the entire drafting staff of Campbelltown Council stood in a circle around the machine that was humming and whirring and producing a plan in five minutes that would have taken the most skilled of us a week, we all knew we were doomed. I had just recently bought a glorious and stupidly expensive set of Rotring drafting pens instead of a set of tyres, so I was hugely pissed off. That night as I hammered home through the traffic, my mind was working overtime, which it normally does when it perceives things are starting to resemble a plate of hot dicks that I was going to eat.

I was three and a bit years into a four-year course at Sydney tech. At the end of this course I would possess a diploma in

Land, Engineering and Survey Drafting with which I could wipe my arse for all the good it would do me. Drafting was to be among the first casualties of the rapidly advancing computer age, and I was hugely peeved at having wasted the last three years studying a dying profession. A week later, I was called into the Chief Engineer's office, handed two weeks' wages and told to leave the building. I went to Mum's that night, clearly in need of nurturing. As she was feeding me up on her marvellous borscht she asked me how my career was going.

'Khow iz job?' she smiled, fussing about her small kitchen. She was very proud of the fact that I was studying 'injuneerink' and that I worked in an office. She'd never coped all that well with my prior job choices, among which was a five-day stint as a door-to-door encyclopaedia salesman; a month as a roo shooter; six weeks as a trainee assistant manager at Coles who did nothing but sweep the storeroom; two months as a shop assistant in an army disposal store run by a deranged Holocaust survivor; a summer's worth as a pre-dawn-to-post-dusk farmhand on a dairy farm; and a roof-tiling slave-thing for some friends of my father's whenever they needed someone to yell at and carry heavy things. The only job she approved of prior to the drafting gig was the year I spent as a Clerical Assistant Grade One for the Department of Technical and Further Education, but that was only because I had to wear a shirt and trousers to work, and therefore, in her eyes, I was like a 'biznizmen'. Why I had to dress like that is a mystery, since all I did was stack course leaflets onto metal shelves and hunt the office cat around the cavernous storeroom using a ruler loaded with heavy-duty rubber bands as a leopard gun.

'Vot you doink now?' Mum asked me after I told her I was no longer an engineer.

'I don't know,' I replied. And I didn't.

She ladled more borscht into my bowl. Feeding me seemed to help my mother think. 'Vy not vorkin in post offis?'

'What as?' I asked her.

'Postmen,' she smiled. 'Iz veri good djob. Iz guvermen djob.'

I put my spoon down with a plop. Epiphany! My mother was a genius. There were only three jobs on this earth that actually paid you to ride motorcycles. The best paying one was as a professional motorcycle racer. But I was fifty kilograms too heavy and 1000 kms per hour too slow. The next option was as an enforcer of the law and revenue-raiser for the state government. But I was philosophically indisposed to ever being a policeman, no matter how much I wanted to have a revolver strapped to my jodhpur-clad hip and a sexy leather hat jammed onto my head. That left Australia Post. Sure, there'd be no high-powered motorcycles, gun battles, bribes or Champagne-splashed podiums and hot racetrack babes with bags full of cocaine waiting for me in my motorhome. But getting paid to ride anything was, as far as I was concerned, light years better than being paid for not riding.

For the next month I scoured the newspapers waiting for Australia Post to advertise its quarterly entry exams, rode around NSW and lived off my Bankcard. One sunny day in March, I turned up at the then Institute of Technology on Broadway, and sat for the entry exam to become a postman. I initially thought they had to be taking the piss and that I had stumbled into some kind of sheltered workshop where mentally damaged people were given things to do on bits of paper to keep them from scaring citizens on the street. Halfway through the test I was starting to wonder if the questions were actually trick questions, and the answers not as obvious as I first thought. Here were three triangles and a circle, and I was to pick the shape that was not the same as the other shapes. Surely it could not have been the circle. I scrutinised the three triangles closely. Perhaps one of them was not as the other two. Was there an invisible fifth shape? What did 'not the same as' actually mean?

'If you have a pencil, a pen, a marker and a pillow, which is the one you cannot use to draw things with?' Another impossibly deep and entirely Machiavellian conundrum. I could certainly draw things with a pillow if I dipped it in paint or dragged it through the sand. What if the pen was empty? What if I could not get the lid off the marker? We were allotted an hour and a half for the exam, and since I had finished in about twenty minutes, I spent the remaining time going over each and every multiple choice question in case I had somehow misread it or misunderstood it.

I walked out of the exam extremely concerned. If the questions really were as easy as I found them to be, then it was obvious Australia Post was not seeking rocket scientists to deliver its mail. And rightly so. But the questions appeared to be so ridiculously simplistic, it was as if Australia Post just wanted someone who had mastered breathing and blinking.

And, as it turned out, that someone was me. A fortnight later I received a letter saying I had scored highly in the exam, and was to report for work at the post office I had actually requested. The post office was Chatswood, and since it served what is known as the lower north shore of Sydney, I figured it would be a right pleasant place to work at. My figuring proved to be quite correct, but I did not get a job as a postman.

It seemed that my exam results fated me for an even more auspicious career: I was to be employed as telegram dispatch rider, or 'telegram boy', as we were known by the post office staff. I initially thought this whole 'boy' thing a bit demeaning given I had long ago ceased being anyone's 'boy' but my mum's. But on further consideration (which was subsequently borne out by the job itself), it proved to be the best job in the world for a bloke with the attention span of a prawn, a boredom threshold a centipede couldn't trip over, and who was rather averse to the 4.45 am starts demanded of postmen. And, unlike that bullshit drafting gig I had, telegrams were obviously the way of the future. It was humanity's fastest way of communicating in writing. Your written message would streak across the world, literally hours from the time you lodged it at your post office, and then a few scant hours later, someone like me would deliver it to the recipient. What could possibly be more efficient than that?

My career thus secured, I set off for my first day at work, more than stupidly pleased with myself. When I rode my big, black, noisy and deeply antisocial Suzuki into the laneway adjacent to the post office, I was pleased to behold three other motorcycles parked on the narrow footpath beside the entry to the loading dock. Two were dirty, well-used trail bikes, and the third was a very slick-looking, red 1983 Moto Guzzi Le Mans III. I lurched my growling monster onto the footpath beside the trail bikes and looked closely at the rear tyre of the Guzzi. This is the motorcycling equivalent of dogs sniffing each other's bums to determine alpha maleness. If I beheld chicken strips (unused portions of rubber on the edges of the back tyre), then I would deem the rider to be a mincing pretender with shrivelled bitch-testicles and little skill. If, on the other hand, I witnessed a tyre scrubbed savagely to its walls, and the rubber balled with hard-cornering venom, I would consider the rider a manly man, with goodly amounts of skill, courage and aplomb.

My examination revealed the middle ground. There was some cowardice evident; the chicken strip was there, but it was not a big one. This could mean that the rider was competent but not insane, or that he just commuted a lot and had not yet had the chance to lash out in a meaningful way. I decided to stay my judgment for the moment, and went to knock on the big doors that opened onto the loading dock.

The post office building straddled the loading dock, and opposite the doors I could see a garage that housed three red Honda CT110s – the ubiquitous Aussie postie bike, and to this day the highest-selling bike in Australia. They are beloved of farmers, learners and commuters, are capable, willing and behave much like a proper motorcycle rather than a small-wheeled scooter. With their centrifugal clutch, changing gears requires nothing more than banging it into the desired cog with your left foot. I did initially turn up my 1100cc-riding nose at the insectile-looking jigger, but I grew to admire and love it over the next two years. It was very much a 'go anywhere' motorcycle, as I was to discover to my delight, time and again.

I knocked and was admitted into the mailroom of the post office by a small, middle-aged Italian bloke called Joe, who took me in to see Col, the postmaster. 'You'd be the new telegram boy,' Col said, shaking my hand and indicating I should sit down. 'Here's your uniform, and I want you to know this is a Grade One post office.'

Clearly, the look on my face informed Col – a beaut Koori bloke and former boxer – that I was either retarded or ignorant. 'A Grade One post office means that we are very busy, and that means you will be delivering a lot of telegrams,' he explained slowly. I nodded. I did not sign up to bludge and lots of telegrams meant lots of riding, as far as I was concerned.

He then showed me the toilets, waited outside while I changed into my new uniform, briefly introduced me to some of the staff who weren't serving at the counter, then left me to the tender mercies of the two existing telegram boys, Simmo and Davo, to be trained up.

Simmo and Davo were lounging by the telegram machine, exuding ineffable coolness, smoking Dunhill Reds (it was the '80s, so everyone smoked everywhere all the time) and giving me the once-over. And who could blame them? I was certainly a sight to be onced over. My uniform was brand new (unlike their magnificent stained-jeans-and-postie-shirt ensembles), and consisted of a scratchy shirt that made me sweat like a moose, a pair of magical dark-blue polyester pants that would melt into your screaming leg-flesh each time you brushed against a hot part of the delivery bike, and a set of clog-like steel-capped boots that would (and did) fly off your feet when you went to kick the attack dogs that beset you as you went about your duties.

Davo stubbed out his durrie, his eyes made narrow by the sting of the smoke, pulled himself to his feet, and stuck out his hand. 'G'day,' he said. 'I'm Davo. I do Chatswood. This is

Simmo. He does Artarmon. Simmo's leaving at the end of the week, so you'll be doing Artarmon when he goes.'

I shook their hands and waited eagerly to see what 'doing Artarmon' entailed. They sat back down beside the telegram machine and I sat down with them. They both lit up and Davo picked up a small stack of envelopes marked 'TELEGRAM'. 'We'll go out in a sec,' he said. 'I'm just waiting to see if there's any more before ten.'

The telegram machine we were looking at was a beige-coloured chattering box that resembled a fat typewriter. It would stutter into life at various intervals and produce brief and often cryptic messages on a long yellow roll of paper. The senior postal clerk would then tear off the telegram, fold it into an envelope and await further developments. Those developments were us delivering the telegrams. But we didn't just rush out each time a new telegram appeared. We would wait until several had built up in the box and then do them all in one hit. Of course, just how many telegrams it took before critical mass was reached and a delivery took place varied all the time and depended on many factors. All of which Davo and Simmo made sure I knew about.

For example, if several telegrams came just before knock-off time at 5.30 pm and they were not on the way home for the telegram boy, they could certainly wait until the following morning. And to avoid uncomfortable questions from senior staff about why Monday's telegrams were still sitting in the box on Tuesday, Davo made me understand that Monday's telegrams could also happily await Tuesday delivery in their leather pouch on the bike in the garage where no one except us ever went.

Similarly, it was highly unlikely that any telegrams were

51

going to be delivered in the half hour before lunch commenced, in the hour after lunch when digestion was taking place, or in the first hour of the working day when our crucial nicotine and caffeine levels were being adjusted. Of course, since we read every telegram before it was placed in its sealed envelope, we made exceptions to these rules. If the telegram dealt with the death of a relative, we almost always delivered it immediately. Likewise if the telegram contained details for picking up children at airports. But if you were just wishing some bastard a happy birthday, or bludging money off your parents because you've been gambling and losing in Macau, we were certainly not about to bend the rules for that.

As we waited for both 10 am and more telegrams, the motorcyclist conversation began the way every motorcyclist conversation has begun since motorcyclists had decided some time in the distant past that this would be the initial way we would measure the size of our cocks.

'What do you ride?' Davo asked between puffs of Dunhill.

I told him. He nodded noncommittally and Simmo nodded along with him. My GSX was a serious machine, and by default, that might have meant that I was a serious rider. Or it might have meant that I was a massive wanker on a stupidly over-powered motorcycle. Either way I knew they'd be out later to examine my chicken strips.

'We do a bit of dirt-riding,' Simmo explained when I asked about the trail bikes outside. He was a touch defensive, I thought, but I held my fire because I was still the new boy, it was my first day, and for all I knew the fucker had six national Enduro titles to his name.

'So who owns the Guzzi?' I asked, finding neutral ground. Whoever owned it was clearly some kind of deeply weird and disturbed bastard because that was the only type of person who owned Moto Guzzis in the '80s.

'That's Terry's,' Davo said. 'He's a postie. He's got the riding beat.'

Chatswood had twenty-five posties, each of whom had a beat (delivery route), but only one of those was a riding beat. Judging by Davo's tone, this riding beat was much coveted, both by the other posties and the telegram boys (who were, I found out, sort of like posties-in-training), but Terry's ownership of it was apparently ironclad. Of his incipient Guzzi weirdness there was no mention. Clearly, the bastard would bear watching. But at that point I didn't need to concern myself with this: my job was to deliver telegrams.

Except it wasn't my job just yet – it would only become my job when Simmo left. For the moment, I had to be content with smoking cigarettes, watching Simmo and Davo watching the telegram machine, and generally soaking in the busy ambience of a Grade One post office. And it truly was busy: there were four people relentlessly chucking parcels into a twelve-mailbag centrepiece that was the 'mailroom' just to the left of where I was sitting. These parcels were delivered to the back door by Australia Post trucks from some mail centre, opened and redistributed into mailbags in the centre of the room by Joe, the Italian bloke who ran the mailroom, and his three female offsiders.

To my right was a door leading to the public area of the post office and a big counter behind which stood the postal clerks, and my immediate boss, Jeff, the senior postal clerk. He did the money orders, wrangled the telegram boys and sported the greatest mullet any head had ever seen. Its centre-parted, haughty grandeur is seared into my mind like a blistered brain tumour to this day. Immediately behind me was the postmaster's office, where Col sat and worried about the drug fiends, knucklemen, tramps and thieves who were his cadre of night-sorters and postmen, and who worked upstairs.

'Right,' Davo said, standing up and interrupting my observations. 'Let's go.'

It was ten o'clock and the three of us trooped out the back door where one shiny new Honda CT110 and two ratty Honda CT110s were parked and waiting, like three red promises of urban adventure.

'You know how to ride one of these?' Davo asked.

'Of course I fucken do,' I lied. I had never ridden a Honda CT110 and had always viewed them as something a clown might ride in a circus rather than as a serious motorcycle. But there was no way I was ever going to admit that to my new work colleagues.

'I forgot the fucken telegrams,' Simmo grinned and went back into the post office while Davo and I geared up.

When he returned, he stuck a handful of white envelopes marked 'Telegram' into a small brown leather pouch that swung on the handlebars in front of me and told me to follow them. Which is how I learned to shit into the laughing mouth of the Grim Reaper on a bike that didn't have the power to pull the crust off a bowl of custard.

I was astounded when Davo and Simmo took off on their postie bikes like grease-smeared demons. I had always imagined

I had a respectable amount of kung fu when it came to slicing through traffic on my Suzuki, but I was not the fragrant steam off Davo and Simmo's bracing piss. These blokes were an order of magnitude crazier and more skilful than I was at this stage of my riding career. Nowhere was a no-go zone for their postie bikes – footpaths, walking tracks, service-station forecourts and shopping plazas were treated in the same contemptuous fashion as normal suburban traffic. If it was in front of you, it was meant to be overtaken. No gap was too small, no traffic light was too red, no pedestrian too angry, and no Give Way sign was any kind of impediment to the swift delivery of Her Majesty's telegrams. Which, I had to keep reminding myself, was what we were doing.

My heart was jackhammering in my chest when we pulled up at the first delivery point – a handsome sandstone mansion not far from Chatswood shopping centre. I would eventually learn where every street in Chatswood and Artarmon was in relation to every other street, and my brain functioned much as a GPS does today, without the annoying recorded voice. But on that first day it was all I could do just to keep Davo and Simmo in sight as they leaped off gutters, used driveways as launching pads for wheelies, and utilised footpaths as salt lakes where speed records were set.

'Do you know what the life expectancy of a telegram boy is?' Simmo asked me when I returned from handing over the telegram to a nice lady with blue hair who answered my knock.

'An hour?' I offered.

'About three weeks,' Simmo grinned.

'How come you two are still alive?' I asked.

Simmo's grin got wider. 'We're fucken good.'

The implication was obvious. They were good and I was crap and I should probably stop by at a funeral home after work and choose a casket.

'Don't worry,' Davo patted my shoulder. 'You just need some practice.'

About ten minutes later, I was getting lots of practice crashing through the scrub of the nearby Lane Cove National Park, where the two blokes went to hone their skills on a daily basis. When they stopped for a smoke on some fire trail, I pulled up in the hope that they would take pity on me at least until my eyes had stopped bouncing around in my skull. I was sweating like a mule in my wondrous polyester uniform with my postie bike decorated with branches and leaves from every bush I had managed to plough through.

'Are we allowed to be here?' I puffed, more than slightly concerned that where I was with my undelivered telegrams bore no relation to where I should be with my undelivered telegrams.

'Postie bikes are allowed to be fucken everywhere,' Simmo advised me. This, as I discovered, was an absolute truth.

Where postie bikes could go was only limited by the bravery of the rider and the applicable laws of physics. The *Motor Traffic Act* apparently did not dare apply to the men who carried Her Majesty's telegrams about Her Majesty's kingdom. And rightly so, I came to believe.

The only difficulty was the nebulous concept of what was *actually* allowed and what we *assumed* our postie uniform allowed us to do. As far as Australia Post was concerned, we were to abide by the *Motor Traffic Act* at all times, except on those rare occasions when we had to mount a footpath to access a mailbox. The reality of telegram delivery was an entirely different thing, however. And besides, people are conditioned to respect a uniform and automatically assume that whatever that uniform is doing is totally legitimate. I'm pretty sure the staff at the Lane Cove National Park did, on occasion, wonder why I was smashing my way through their lovely park's foliage and over their lovely park's lizards on my postie bike. But when one of them eventually stopped me and asked me, I informed him I was delivering a telegram to a man whose mother had just been killed in a car accident and his silly questions were standing in the way of familial grief and mourning, and I was left alone. Likewise I was never stopped by a police officer for careening down a footpath at 80 kms per hour, or questioned about why it was necessary to use driveways as ramps for wobbly wheelies or why slipstreaming bare centimetres off a car's bumper bar was all necessary for the proficient delivery of telegrams.

That evening, as I recounted my day's adventures to my then girlfriend, Rachel, I felt I had found my life's work and the best job a motorcycle nut could ever dream of. I was still of this view when I tore a medium-sized divot of meat out of my calf three days later. It was all my fault. I should not have been trying to drag Simmo off down the footpath while dragging my feet. Had I not been dragging my feet, or more specifically, my left foot, it would not have got itself caught between a brick fence and the L-shaped steel bracket that supported the red Australia Post saddlebags each bike was fitted with, as Simmo nudged me off line. I got him back a week later by distracting him long enough for him to ride into the back of a parked car, so it was all good.

I also covered myself in glory by not claiming workers' compensation for the injury and forcing Col to fill out endless paperwork, and look for a replacement while I healed. I always did my best to make my boss's life hassle-free and it always paid dividends.

At the end of my first week when Simmo left for greener pastures, Davo and I settled in to rule the streets of Chatswood and Artarmon. We didn't work too hard, had lots of fun, and delivered lots and lots of telegrams pretty much on time and to the right people.

Our telegram delivering sessions were interspersed with helping Joe in the mailroom, sorting parcels into the right sacks and going out in the afternoons with postie van drivers to collect the cash tins from the twenty-odd public phone booths scattered around Chatswood. I initially wondered why a van driver could not do this on his own, then after I had met a few of them, I understood just how militant, unionised and fundamentally bone-arse lazy they were. Sure, not all of them. But certainly lots of them were grossly obese bludgers who just drove from phone booth to phone booth, while the telegram boy did all the work replacing the coin boxes.

Some six months into my new career, it was deemed by people higher up the pay scale than Col that the Chatswood–Artarmon area only needed one telegram delivery boy, and Davo was given the chop. Col was clearly traumatised by this occurrence and, concerned that I might be similarly traumatised, asked me if I required counselling.

'Counselling for what?' I asked him. I was genuinely nonplussed by his anxious question.

'Well, you understand you'll be required to deliver to two suburbs now and I'm worried the extra work might prove stressful. On top of that your work colleague has been made redundant and that can make the work environment stressful.'

I blinked at him in amazement. Stressful? Riding around the pretty, leafy suburbs of northern Sydney like a mad bastard on a government-issued motorcycle for a few hours a day was not, under any of my terms of reference, something that could ever stress me out. All this really meant was that I would spend more time on the bike.

'I'm good, Col,' I grinned at him. 'I can handle Artarmon and Chatswood, no problem.'

'That's great,' he nodded. 'But anytime it gets too much for you, you let me know and I'll look after you.'

'Thanks, mate,' I said. And I *was* grateful. Col was, up to that time, the best boss I had ever had; unlike the assortment of slavers, despots, tyrants and psychopathic shoguns I had previously worked for.

So then I ruled alone, but not without challenge. In between the stunt-riding, top-speed runs down Delhi Road and enough skill-honing Enduro-style madness through Lane Cove National Park to rival the Dakar, there was a constant beastly threat of which I always had to be aware. And I do literally mean beastly. One of the earliest lessons I learned was that telegram delivery boys were several rungs down the food chain from dogs. And Chatswood certainly had its fair share of dogs.

First there were three of us telegram boys. Then there were two. Now there was only me – and what seemed like 50,000 dogs. Happily, 49,995 of them were small, amusingly decorative, mop-like beasties who yapped at me from behind locked screen doors and low fences. Sometimes they managed to sink their tiny fangs into a polyester trouser leg – a futile act of trivial canine savagery that barely caused you to break stride. However, there were five other dogs in Chatswood which I came to view with a little more seriousness.

Four of them roamed in a pack on the outskirts of the suburb and I only ever encountered them if I was running telegrams down to the big condiment factory on Smith Street. I think they lived rough and free in Willis Park, a big green area on the other side of Eastern Valley Way, the road that delineated the border of Chatswood. I'd always wanted to explore Willis Park on my postie bike, but the opportunity never arose.

These dogs were obviously strays, and consisted of one medium-sized cattle dog plainly bristling with mange and hatred, one smaller bitzer who was covered in sores and ran weirdly on three legs (but at the speed of a galloping ostrich), and two giant mongrels which looked to be the motley bastard offspring of rabid leopards and carnivorous antelopes. They were relentless in their loathing of the postie bike and would course after it for miles – once chasing me all the way into the shopping centre and causing the good matrons of Chatswood to shriek in horror as this smelly suburban wolf-pack pursued me through their midst.

I tried everything to shrug them off, including spraying them with water (that only cooled them down and allowed them extra speed) and lashing madly at them with a whippy car antenna I found in a gutter. But I found I could not ride and lash the slavering fuckers at the same time and I was concerned that if I crashed they would be onto me like hyenas on an injured wildebeest.

Each time I went down to their end of Chatswood I was on a higher alert than North Korea. They came so close to getting me one day, the bottom of one pants-leg was crusty with their diseased saliva. I went home that night, called my mates and told them to bring their guns and had every intention of conducting a shooting safari through suburban Sydney. I was brought to my senses by a series of bongs and beers Rachel kept serving.

I finally solved the problem by riding slowly enough for them to be hugely tempted by my extended leg, and as they closed in to lock their jaws on my calf, I gunned it through a red light. They came slavering blindly after me and were promptly murdered by a series of cars that missed me by centimetres. I did not look back, but I could hear the combined sound of screeching tyres and yelping dogs through my helmet and over the sound of my revving bike. I felt this was a good result. Their days of slavering canine terrorism were at an end. These days, the local council would doubtlessly deploy a task force of trained dog-catchers at the first complaint, but back then my grievances were met with stoic indifference and the attitude that this all came with the telegram-delivery turf. To be perfectly fair, I only ever whinged about it once, Col did call the council, and I have no idea what efforts had been made to rid the suburb of the dog pack. But the fact that they continued to hunt me with impunity meant that I was forced to take matters into my own extreme hands. *C'est la guerre.*

The fifth dog was an entirely different beast who lived in one of the cul-de-sacs near Lane Cove National Park. Terry, the postie who rode the Guzzi, warned me about him because the monster was on his beat. The mad glint of genuine fear in his bloodshot eyes convinced me he was graveyard serious. I didn't get to deliver a lot of telegrams down that end of Chatswood, but the very next time I did, I was confronted by the beast. It was almost as if he somehow knew Terry and I had spoken of him, on the 'speak of the devil and he shall appear' principle.

This gigantic and heavily scarred bull terrier would stand in the middle of his street like a gunslinger awaiting a showdown at High Noon. He (it could not have been a bitch) had absolutely no fear of me, or the bike, or anything, it seemed, that lived, breathed or moved upon the face of this good earth. Even local cars would drive carefully around him. Thankfully for the residents of the cul-de-sac he wasn't there every day, because if he was the mail in that street would never, ever, ever fucking ever, have been delivered.

He was there the day I had to deliver a death telegram, which was one of those telegrams that could not wait for another occasion. It just so happened that I owned a bull terrier at the time, so I had a pretty good idea about the breed's unique characteristics. I knew for sure that if this was the kind of bull terrier I thought it might be, then I did not want to tangle with it.

There are two kinds of bull terrier and one is thankfully far and away more prevalent than the other. There is the kind that hates all life, but specifically human, and enjoys the taste of hot blood rushing down its powerful throat as its impossibly potent jaws pulp the bones of a foolish telegram boy. But such creatures are very rare. The vast majority of bullies quite adore humans, are good natured, gentle, and only now and again disposed to murdering other dogs. As a result, this type makes a great companion but a pretty crap watchdog.

I was hoping this scarred and pitted fiend was the latter kind of bull terrier and normally busied himself slaughtering French poodles, Dobermans, German shepherds and labradors. From where he stood waiting for me in the middle of the street, it was impossible to tell. His ears were up, his stance was aggressive and his slitted battle-narrow eyes glinted with intelligence and meaning. I tried not to stare at him, since I knew dogs interpret direct eye contact as a challenge, and turned my head while keeping my eyes on him. The idle of the bike might have been angering him as well, but I didn't dare turn it off. Bull terriers are not greyhounds, but nor was I. There was not a turn of speed I could achieve with two legs that would enable me to outrun a bully bent on bringing me down like a blue-uniformed zebra. That postie bike was my lifeline.

There was also no question about the telegram not being delivered. A man's mother had died, and he would certainly want to know that. And probably as soon as possible. But there was also no question about me fighting some primeval mammalian monster with my bare hands in order to facilitate this delivery.

There was only one hope and it lay back up the road a ways. I turned my bike around and rode back up Delhi Road to the small grocery store. I made a quick purchase, tossed it into my saddlebag and rode back down the hill to where Cerberus awaited.

The thing hadn't moved. Propped in the street like a fanged barricade, it was like he'd been carved from stone. I pulled the can of Spam from my saddlebag, opened it, dumped the pink meat on the ground and back-pedalled the bike five metres.

'Come on, boy,' I purred, my voice like gentle, welcoming honey. 'Come and eat some yummy piggy goodness. Come on, puppy.'

I knew that bull terriers loved food in much the same way that sharks felt about blood. Mine would sell his soul to dog-Satan for a piece of pizza and all the others I had met had been similarly disposed. It was a fair bet Cerberus was likewise inclined.

'Come on, puppy,' I cajoled. And puppy came. He wagged his spike-like tail a little, then proceeded to consume the Spam with great relish and more tail-wagging. While he was licking the bitumen, I idled gently around him and rode up the street to deliver the telegram. As I rode back, the bull terrier watched me go and wagged his tail again. From that day, there was always a can of Spam in my saddlebag and Cerberus actually started to look forward to my occasional visits, when I provided the odd snack, and he refrained from eating me. We never got into a patting relationship, but that was probably for the best.

As the months went on, I settled into a comfortable routine at Chatswood Post Office. My boss liked me, my fellow workers didn't actively despise me and I did my job efficiently and with good humour. Col even let me have a crack at being a postman for a while, but the early starts and banal sameness of the one beat soon had me begging him to give me my telegram gig back.

'You know they'll be phasing telegrams out eventually,' he told me after I had finished pleading my case.

'When?'

'I don't know for sure, but telegram traffic is declining. Computers and electronic mail are the future.' It was starting to sound a lot like Campbelltown Council again. He put me back on the telegrams.

Several things started happening in my life in the preceding months. I had bought a Harley and was edging my way into an outlaw motorcycle club, and my weekends and nights were filling with the associated atavistic madness. My relationship with Rachel was inexorably edging towards its use-by date, for all sorts of reasons, but mostly to do with my changing persona. And the fact that I had met another girl.

I had also taken to writing letters to *Ozbike* magazine, a publication dedicated to the celebration of customised Harley-Davidsons and outlaw motorcycle clubs. My letters were invariably opinionated, angry and outrageously badly written. But they were published and I was very chuffed.

I was also starting to grow bored with delivering ever fewer telegrams and spending more of my time slouching about in the mailroom with Joe and the neurotic, slow-moving staff working for him. When he retired and the ruling baton looked to be passed to one of the many despotic, chinless psychopaths angling for the gig, a few more lights went out in my state of Georgia.

Then one day I came up with a great idea and went to see Col. 'Col,' I said. 'I reckon I should ride a postie bike to Melbourne and raise some money for charity.'

Ever since I had started to transmogrify into an outlaw, Col had taken to staring at me in concern a few times each day. Tattoos had appeared where none had been before, nasty-looking rings had taken up residence on my hands, barbaric earrings dangled from my ears, my beard was becoming rather formidable and aggressive, and my only concession to the postal uniform was a very worn blue shirt with the Australia Post logo half picked off, so that it read 'LIA POST'. He had even asked me not to rev my Harley so loudly when I came to work in the morning because it set off car alarms (which is why I did it).

He stared at me with extra concern when I told him what I had in mind. 'What charity?' he finally asked.

I shrugged. 'I don't give a shit. Pick one.'

'Leave it with me,' he said.

My timing was pretty good. A week or so before my proposal, Australia Post had sent around one of its interminable staff announcements, declaring that each post office and its staff should consider doing something for the community. I was at a stage in my life where I could not have given less of a shit about my community, and had on the previous weekend hammered several nails into the coffin of bikie respectability by throwing a member of the community through a plate-glass window outside the Stoned Crow wine bar in Crows Nest when I found him sitting on my bike. But I did see this announcement as a way I could have some fun – riding a postie bike to Melbourne appealed to my joy-glands in all sorts of ways.

When I left Col's office, I actually sat down and scribbled out a formal proposal, had it typed up and placed it on his desk the next day. A week later he called me into his office. 'Management likes your idea,' he said with a wry grin. 'They reckon it's a great PR exercise.'

'Cool!' I squeaked. 'What happens now?'

'You need to pick a charity, and we'll organise everything else.'

I decided that spinal research was something I could

give a vague shit about, given so many motorcyclists ended up smashing theirs into jelly, and contacted the office of the renowned spinal surgeon Doctor John Yeo. He proved to be receptive, gave my proposed odyssey his imprimatur and a month later I was on my way to Melbourne astride a postie bike.

Interestingly, it was not a Honda CT110. The powers that be deemed the little jigger unsuitable for such a journey, and not wanting my blood on their hands, gave me a Honda 125 trail bike which was used by Australia Post in rural areas. For my money, I got a proper-sized motorcycle, albeit generating more or less the same kind of power as the smaller CT110 due to its greater weight. In real terms, the CT110 would have been more comfortable; its seat was thicker and wider and less of a dirt-oriented spanking paddle. Dirt-riders spend a lot of time standing up on the pegs in their efforts not to die among the undergrowth, so seat comfort is not large on their list of priorities.

As I whirred past Campbelltown at my top speed of 87 kms per hour, I had several concerns. The first was that this was actually the stupidest idea I had ever come up with and in all likelihood it would see me either dead when a faster-moving truck ran over me, maimed in some ditch if the truck missed me but the fury of the wind-vortex that followed it sucked me off the road, or drooling insanity claimed me from all the near-death experiences I was doubtlessly going to have.

The second concern was that they had given me a brand-new bike with 1.2 kilometres on the clock, and I was now revving the red-line bastard fuck out of it on the freeway. It was entirely possible the white-hot piston would eventually exit through the top of the motor, sear through the tank and smash me in the face.

My third concern was the bright-red Australia Post van dogging my heels. Behind the wheel was my personal mechanic, Jim, and beside him was an Australia Post PR girl, Diane, and her ever-present clipboard. We were to spend three days getting to Melbourne, stopping off at various post offices along the way to receive donations, and I was a little anxious about how they would deal with me when I went insane, or needed emergency medical attention when a semi fucked up all my shit. At that moment, all that was keeping me alive was Jim keeping the van as close as he could to my back wheel, and his van was easier to see and harder to run over the top of than my tiny trail bike.

We got as far as the outskirts of Mittagong when the bike's engine seized, slammed my nuts into the tank before I could get the clutch in, and almost caused Jim to run straight over the top of me. I heard his tyres squealing through the pain-noise my newly mashed testicles were making in my head, and silently screamed at the Road Gods to give me a swift and only briefly excruciating death.

'What happened?' Jim asked after I'd painfully waddled the bike to the side of the road. Diane remained in the van with her clipboard, making notes and looking completely lost. It was obviously her first such expedition, too. And at least we had that in common, because when I first met her at the start line at Chatswood Post Office that morning, it was clear to both of us we were not going to be friends. I was everything she clearly despised in a man, and she was not at all my idea of a hot chick. So after she worked out how to pronounce my surname, making copious notes on the matter, she pretended I had ceased to exist.

I liked Jim a lot better, and he didn't seem to mind me. A straitlaced Australia Post mechanic, he smiled a lot and seemed very pleased to have been selected to go on this grand adventure.

'I think the engine's seized,' I grimaced, leaning forward with my hands on my knees, which is the standard male-with-busted-balls-seeking-relief position.

Jim quickly confirmed that was indeed the case.

'Guess that's it, huh?' I said, secretly pleased that this madness was over through no fault of my own, and I would be home that evening telling my mates what a stupid arsehole I was to have ever come up with such a plan.

'I'll get the spare bike,' Jim said.

'What spare bike?' I asked.

'There's a spare bike in the back of the van,' he smiled, and went to get it. It was obvious that Australia Post had taken my proposal quite seriously.

In ten short minutes I was back on the road. But at a much reduced speed and with strict instructions from Jim not to keep the throttle pinned at the red-line.

'Try and run it in for the next two hundred kays,' he said. 'Work through the gears, ride at different speeds, take it ...'

'I know how to fucken run a bike in,' I snapped as I rode off. And immediately started to follow his instructions.

Several interminable hours later we all rolled into Gundagai and took up residence at a motel that had been pre-booked for us. Dinner at the motel restaurant that evening was a strange affair. Diane sipped mineral water, scrawled things on her clipboard and avoided looking at me. Each time I tried to crack a joke she would look pained, but each time Jim, who had managed to nurse a single beer all the way through entrée, main and dessert, made a funny remark she would come to life and giggle like a partially blocked drain.

I drank four beers and two bottles of red wine in an attempt to dull the horror of the ride so far. It was going to be a long, frightening journey for me. The next day was going to be a particularly lengthy one because Diane had decided we were to detour via Wagga Wagga and visit the post office there, where there was apparently going to be a big reception and media.

'Will you be okay to ride?' she clucked as I drained the second bottle of cheap red and considered having another one.

'Yeah, I could manage a lap or two of town right now, if you're interested,' I grinned.

Diane looked appalled. 'No, no,' she spluttered. 'I meant tomorrow.'

'Sure I will,' I said. 'Why wouldn't I be?'

She looked a little confused and turned to Jim for support. Jim stared intently into his schooner glass.

'Well, I just thought that with all the wine and beer ...' she finally said.

I forced a laugh. 'Don't worry, sweetheart,' I winked at her. 'I'll just have a few lines in the morning and Jim will have his work cut out keeping up with me.'

She looked totally confused. 'Lines?'

I nodded. 'Speed. Great for hangovers.'

'Are you talking about drugs?' she puffed, her eyes wide with horror.

'Yes, I am,' I winked at her. 'You want some?'

She looked like she was about to throw up and left the table in a big hurry.

Jim's shoulders were shaking. He was laughing so hard his eyes were clenched shut. 'You horrible bastard,' he panted.

'What?' I blinked and smiled at him.

'Do you have any drugs?'

'Fuck off,' I said, shaking my head. 'Like I'd bring drugs on this trip.'

'I didn't think so. But she's fucken spinning out.'

I nodded. 'Yes, she is. Great, isn't it?'

Jim shook his head, and then stifled a yawn. 'I'm going to bed, mate. Big day tomorrow.'

I bade him goodnight, ordered another beer, drank, went back to my room, rolled a fat joint and walked down the deserted street to smoke it.

The next morning we turned off the Hume Highway and made our way via Henty, Culcairn and The Rock. We stopped a few times so Diane could take promotional photographs, and each time she would peer at me closely and ask me if I was feeling okay.

The third time she asked, I told her I was a little off-colour. 'Do you think you could get me some smack?' I whispered loudly.

'Smack?' she blinked.

'Yeah, smack. Heroin. I need some heroin.'

She recoiled in horror.

I was unrelenting. 'Look,' I said through gritted teeth. 'The speed I took is really fucking strong. The heroin will take the edge off. Do you think you could get me some in Wagga?'

She fled to the van and no more photos were taken that day.

As soon as we stopped at Wagga Wagga post office, Diane was out of the van and inside the big old settler-era building. I half-wondered if she was trying to score some smack for me. Of course I hadn't taken any drugs apart from the joint I smoked the night before, but that was not going to stop me riding Diane around like a Shetland pony at a country fair.

Jim and I waited outside for half an hour but Diane didn't return. Nor was there any reception committee or media.

'I'll go see where she is,' Jim said.

'I'll wait here,' I said, rather obviously.

My mood was not pleasant. I was mildly hungover, I had been riding this stupid dirt-bike for what seemed like forever and over a billion horrible and very slow kilometres, I had been forced to pose for impossibly naff photographs, my hands had gone numb from the vibrations, my arse felt as if a railway sleeper had been forced between my cheeks, and I was still two days from Melbourne – a trip I normally did in around eight hours.

Jim returned. He looked worried. 'Diane is very upset and cannot continue,' he said.

'What's wrong with her?' I asked.

'She's scared of you. She thinks you've gone mad on drugs.'

'So what's she going to do?'

'She's going to hire a car and go back to Sydney.'

'What are we going to do?'

Jim grinned at me. 'I guess we'll keep going to Melbourne.'

I nodded. I was more than halfway now. It was longer to go back than it was to go forward. And so we went forward, or rather, southward.

Our next overnighter was in Albury and since we did not have to stop for photos and I could now ring the 125's neck without blowing it up, we made fairly good time. Trucks would still blast past me at 120 kms per hour, which was 40 kms per hour more than I could do, and their bow-waves would invariably force me onto the shoulder of the road. The tyres would scrabble for traction on the off-cambered dirt and the handlebars would judder in my hands as I fought to keep the bike from sliding totally out of control, and then somehow I'd manage to force it back onto the bitumen. It was hard work and when we finally rolled into Albury, I was fucked.

Dinner that night was a very beery and laugh-out-loud affair. Without Diane around, Jim let himself go and had about nine schooners with his steak. I matched him and had a joint before bed.

The next day we stopped at Seymour Post Office because Diane had told Jim there was to be a reception and media waiting for us there. No one at Seymour Post Office had any idea about anything to do with my riding to Melbourne. The postmaster said that the nearby mail centre might be the place, so Jim and I went there but after making us wait at the back door for forty minutes while they asked around inside the building about a reception, we were finally told that no one there knew anything either.

I droned on to Melbourne, Jim following closely behind. The final 250-kilometre stretch was appalling, all divided road, but in the decades before the Victorians had sown its entire length with speed cameras and Highway Patrol officers without fathers, it served as a divine high-speed proving ground. My friend Frank and I once raced a brown turbocharged Porsche 911

140 kilometres from Wangaratta to Seymour on that highway. The Porsche was driven by a smarmy young prick in a white skivvy whose pretty blonde girlfriend had smiled at me and Frank in a Wangaratta petrol station. We left the servo and proceeded down the highway at our normal touring pace of about 140 kms per hour, when the Porsche shot past us as if we were standing still. The guy must have been doing over 200 kms per hour – which suited Frank and me just fine. Frank was on his matte-black Suzuki Katana, which had had a bit of work done to it, and I was on my faithful and stupidly fast Suzuki GSX1100, which had also had a bit of work done. We were probably good for about 230 before shit got weird and possibly exploded. So we set off after the Porsche, overhauled him with a bit of effort, to which he responded with a little more effort and passed us again. He was as tapped out as we were, but he wasn't about to back off and neither were we. So we sat behind him all the way into Seymour, when we had to stop for petrol again (230 kms per hour tends to turn a simple four-cylinder 1100cc motorcycle into an insatiable fuel-raping monster), while the smarmy skivvy-clad prick sailed on to Melbourne, doubtlessly to gloat about how he beat those two wankers on their stupid motorcycles.

I replayed this duel in my head as I droned along the road at 78 kms per hour, half-hoping one of the many trucks that roared past me would move two metres to the left and end my suffering under its dusty black tyres. But that was denied me. Jim had my back.

Eventually I spied the giant grassy hill on my left that marks the imminent appearance of Melbourne, and a relatively short time later I was idling down Sydney Road. I was to make my way to Melbourne's GPO, where once again there was meant to be a reception and media. As the massive GPO building loomed up beside me, I was gobsmacked to see people waving at me from the footpath and a police officer directly ahead of me, indicating to me to mount the footpath. As I did that, a corridor of applauding people appeared on either side of me. Ahead of me was a large banner that read 'Congratulations, Boris! Well done!' There were several cameras clicking at me and a table set with drinks, sandwiches and cakes. I stopped and a tall man in a suit shook my hand and more cameras flashed. I think he told me he was the postmaster of the Melbourne GPO.

'Good on you, mate!' he said to me. 'What a great effort. We're all very proud of you.'

'Thanks,' I smiled lamely. It was all suddenly quite embarrassing, and after the previous non-events in Wagga and Seymour, quite unexpected.

I got stiffly off the bike, and someone handed me an orange juice. I gulped it down and a sandwich was thrust into my hand. I ate that. I was being bombarded with questions by people who might have been media, or just curious passers-by.

'How was it?'

Fucked.

'Did you enjoy the ride?'

Go fuck yourself.

'How much money have you raised?'

Fuck knows.

Of course I didn't say any of that.

'Boris has raised more than $5000!' the big bloke who was shaking my hand when I arrived said from somewhere to my left.

More people applauded. And as I looked around, rather sheepishly, actually (this was more public attention than I had ever received), I spotted my good mate Terry in the crowd. He had promised to meet me at the GPO and take me to his place, then double me to the airport the following day.

He was smiling, but shaking his head, as if to say: 'You wanker. Good on you, but you're still a wanker.'

I certainly felt like one. None of this accorded with my view of myself: this public accolade was as galling to me as toothpaste rubbed into a weeping wound.

Riding a 125 trail bike from Sydney to Melbourne was not a feat deserving such applause. It was certainly no great achieve-ment. Lots of people had done it before me and lots more would do it after me. I had a support vehicle and all my expenses had been paid for. Hell, I didn't even do this for any altruistic rea-sons – I did it to get out of work. And now, with all these people clapping and feeding me chicken-and-lettuce sandwiches and orange juice, I felt like a giant fraud as well as a wanker. I even felt bad for messing with Diane's head, but that quickly passed when I recalled her sneery, holier-than-thou attitude when we first met.

I swallowed my sandwich, found Jim in the crowd, thanked him for riding shotgun on my slow-moving arse, and left as unobtrusively as I could with Terry.

'How was it?' he asked me as I climbed onto the back of his bike.

'Fucked,' I replied.

I flew back to Sydney the next day. It was Saturday. On Sunday my girlfriend moved out. On Monday I was in Col's office explaining to him that I wasn't really a crazy drug addict, and that Diane was over-reacting to some harmless shit-stirring.

'Asking Australia Post's senior press liaison officer to buy you heroin is not harmless shit-stirring!' Col insisted.

'Sure it is,' I shrugged. 'It's not like she was going to actually do it.'

'But she was!' Colin railed. 'She says you were so insistent and threatening she felt like she had no choice.'

I had possibly overplayed it a little, but this was not the time to back down. 'Maybe you should speak to Jim,' I said. 'He was there. He heard how it went down.'

'I have spoken to Jim. It's thanks to him you haven't been summarily dismissed.'

Good old Jim. He still had my back.

'So what now, mate?' I asked. 'Are you and I good?'

Col looked at me for a long time before answering. 'Yeah, we're good,' he finally said.

But we weren't. Not really. And it wasn't just Col. Nothing felt right anymore.

There were barely any telegrams to deliver. The moll in the mailroom spent all her time whining through her nose at me for one reason or another; the last mate I had at the post office resigned; my girlfriend had left me; my new girlfriend was still unsure if she adored me adequately enough; my landlord no longer wanted me living in his house with my horrible mates, half of whom were still unsure about the whole outlaw motorcycle club thing, while the other half felt that stabbing the first half with knives would assist them in making up their minds; and to top it all off the primary case on my Harley was leaking oil.

Then one day, not long after my conversation with Col, the editor of *Ozbike* called me. 'I really enjoy your letters,' he growled into the phone. 'We have a position here for a cadet journalist you might be suitable for.'

'Whassit pay?' I asked.

'What do you get paid now?'

I told him.

'It doesn't pay that,' he said.

'So what does it pay?'

'Well, if you quit your job and go on the dole, I'll give you $20 on top of that.'

It was an offer I could hardly refuse. So I didn't.

THE LAST SUMMIT

The Easter motorcycle races at Bathurst were an integral and organic part of my life as a motorcyclist. Each Easter I would make my way to the Holy Mountain and wallow in its lunatic embrace. It was as raw and pure an experience as any motorcycle rider could ever find: for a few brief days we were as one atop that hill, bound together by the bike and the ride and by experiences shared and dangers faced. We were also bound by our mutual hatred of the police who went out of their way to harass and abuse us. And we responded exactly as they expected, and indeed goaded, us to respond. This relationship's critical mass was reached in 1985, and very much like a messy divorce between a fundamentally linked couple, there were lots of tears and broken furniture. And a clear loser. That loser was the motorcyclist. What the Australian motorcyclist lost on that crazy, hyper-violent night in his battle with the NSW police was Bathurst – the annual focal point for the brotherhood and passion that once united us all. But human nature is always thus. It is precisely as Oscar Wilde observed it to be. Each man does indeed kill the thing he loves. And we killed Bathurst because we loved it so.

> `'Madness is rare in individuals —`
> `but in groups, parties, nations`
> `and ages it is the rule.'`

FRIEDRICH NIETZSCHE

It was a very different Borrie who snaked his way up the dirt road to the top of Mount Panorama to the Borrie who'd first stuttered his way up that self-same road an age before. Almost everything about me was different. I looked different. I rode differently. I dressed differently. I walked differently. I thought differently. And unlike my first attendance, there was not a single excited drop of piss in my pants as I confidently made my way to the top of the Holy Mountain and what would turn out to be the very last traditional Easter motorcycle racing weekend I, or anyone else for that matter, ever attended at Bathurst.

Eight years had passed since I first wended my way up this road, eyes wide with wonder, to baptise myself in the beery, smoky and impossibly outrageous font of motorcycling. Then again, it could have been seven years. Or even six.

I had ceased counting after the first three Bathursts, and then they all kinda blurred into a whole bunch of sequential Bathursts. But it doesn't really matter.

In that time, I had ridden almost 700,000 kilometres on various motorcycles, seen lots of Australia, drank vast vats of booze, worked my way through a bunch of girls and made some quite outlandish and improper friends. It was 1985 and I was at a crossroads in my life. I could feel it. My world was changing and I was changing right along with it. This feeling kept me awake at night and made me fractious and moody and quite often violent – it was a dangerous time for me and everyone around me. I was feeling immortal and strong and righteous and I was taking greater risks with my riding. Hell, I was taking greater risks with everything I was doing; it was as if I somehow assumed nothing bad would happen to me – but of course bad stuff did happen to me, but not the kind of stuff that would put me off or slow me down. And no matter what happened, I would just chalk it up to a life experience and move on to the next brilliantly stupid thing I wanted to try.

The motorcycle I was riding up the Mountain was very much a manifestation of my mindset. I'd scored a job at Australia Post, bought a brand new Suzuki GSX1100EX and promptly began mutating it into an immensely powerful, indifferently handling and savagely loud monster that terrified me as much as it thrilled me. I had poured countless dollars into it, over-capitalising my purchase like some primitive Balkan peasant who builds a pig-sty out of Italian marble.

From memory, the bike cost me about $5000, and I had quite easily spent another $15,000 on it, buying Akront wire rims; Yoshimura exhausts and cams; various carburettor assemblies; dago-orange Marzocchi shock absorbers (which I mounted upside down so that the remote reservoir hung at the top because that was head-noddingly cooler than mounting them the traditional way); fork braces; Laverda handlebars; braided cables; a heavy-duty clutch; sexy candy-apple red paint … the list went on and on, I kept spending and spending, and I could not have given less of a shit.

It's not like I needed to save up for a house deposit or had a serious drug habit to pay for. I actually didn't have any other interests. I had no hobbies. I had no diversions. All I had was motorcycles. And all I did was ride these motorcycles from place to place and have adventures and shit.

For quite a long time, I could not imagine a more complete sense of sublime and all-encompassing contentment. I was sharing a small house with my mate, Mark. My rent was reasonable, my job paid alright, my girlfriends were not high maintenance and my needs were simple and modest. I owned nothing that needed ironing, slept in the nude and lived in two pairs of jeans and maybe six T-shirts. I had one jumper, one leather jacket, a shitty pair of vaguely water-resistant wet-weather pants, one pair of gloves and one helmet. My clothes could all fit into one garbage bag and I had no furniture to speak of. Mark at least owned a bed. I slept on a mattress I had bought in a secondhand shop, but only because my girlfriend Rachel said she felt like a homeless whore whenever we fucked on the floor atop my old sleeping bag. And I only put the sleeping bag there because the carpet was suspiciously sticky from some former tenant's atrocities. But Rachel was a good sport, and promised to buy me sheets if I bought a mattress. After holding out for a few weeks I finally relented and my sex life was incrementally improved as a result, so I never regretted the purchase.

As time passed, I was being inexorably drawn towards the fierce truths I felt were to be found in outlaw motorcycle clubs.

They were there waiting for me, I was convinced of it. Of course, I had no idea if the truths I sought were real or just a projection of my naïve desires. All I knew was that I had to find out.

This seed had been planted while I was still a non-riding teenager. My best friend, Alex, and I were in town and coming home from seeing *Blazing Saddles* – the funniest movie we two fourteen-year-olds had ever seen. We were standing on Elizabeth Street where Bathurst Street runs into it, right next to where the Hyde Park obelisk, Sydney's miniaturised version of the Washington Monument, pokes itself into the sky at the edge of Hyde Park. Except our version is a sewer vent, rather than some kind of democratic icon. Anyway, Alex and I were burbling at each other about the film and waiting for the lights to change, when the sound of mechanical thunder stopped us mid-sentence.

Two brutal-looking and impossibly noisy motorcycles idled up and stopped at the lights where we were waiting to cross. I'd been reading *Easyriders* magazine for a while and I knew the bikes had ape-hangers, sissy bars and shotgun pipes. And I could see they were being ridden by two of the heaviest, nastiest, beastliest and coolest motherfuckers I had ever seen. The two of them were wearing road-hammered sleeveless denim vests adorned with badges I could not make out. Their muscle-knotted and barbarically tattooed arms were bare and raised to face-height by the handlebars; their jeans were grease-sinks; their boots cruel and heavy; and their hair an unkempt wilderness. They were magnificent ... and clearly not of this earth.

It was a Saturday afternoon and people just stared at these two men sitting on their explosion-emitting motorcycles, their chins high, looking for all the world like 'Go And Get Utterly Fucked' personified. As it happened, they had pulled up next to a pub where a large crowd of mods was drinking. Mods were scooter-riding, flash-dressing pseudo-hooligans, and quite a big sub-culture in England which had, in a somewhat diluted form, made its way to Australia.

Now I did not hear what was said, but I saw both the outlaws' heads turn to the crowd of scooter-toughs on the footpath, whose scooters stood like a wall between the two parties. Alex and I were across the road and way out of earshot. Maybe nothing was said, but I do think something was.

I then saw one of the bikers turn off his bike, kick his side-stand out, lean his bike onto it, get off, and I saw the colours on his back – a leering, earring-ed skull on an inverted black triangle, with the words 'Gypsy Jokers' arced across the top of his battered denim vest. He then unwound a metre of steel chain from his sissy bar and stalked meaningfully into the large crowd of mods. As if a leopard had suddenly dropped into a herd of squawking pelicans, panic ensued in an instant. Scooters were knocked over, people were trampled, and I saw a body come crashing out of the pub's corner window. I then watched the Gypsy Joker walk casually back out of the now much less crowded pub, wind his chain back onto the sissy bar, say something to his mate who had sat there like a tattooed sphinx the whole time, kick his bike into life, get on and ride off in a fading litany of barking thunder.

I was dumbfounded. Never in my life had I seen such a display of massive steel balls and iron-spined daring. A lone man walks into a vast crowd of enemies, throws one of them through a window, then leaves as casually as if he just bought a take-away beer. His back watched the whole time by his brother, with whom he's neither discussed his actions nor formulated any plan. No talk. No bullshit. No hesitation. Just immediate and irrevocable commitment and action.

At fourteen, it was the greatest thing I had ever seen. I was already stupidly enamoured with motorcycles, and now I was convinced that I had beheld the absolute apotheosis of the motor-cycle rider. To me, those two outlaws were coolness incarnate and toughness personified. I knew nothing about outlaw clubs other than what I had read in a few magazines, and I had never actually seen any outlaw motorcyclists in real life. Australia in the mid-'70s certainly had outlaw motorcycle clubs, but they weren't obvious or in the media, no one ever talked about them and the authorities would have laughed themselves stupid had anyone suggested that these greasy, tattered, hairy and decidedly scary-looking motherfuckers were 'organised crime'. To most people they were just 'mad bikies'.

To my fertile teenage mind, there was nothing mad about them at all. Just the opposite, in fact. By my thinking, they were sanity incarnate and their clubs appeared to be the sim-ple answer to a world that was becoming increasingly more complex the older I got. I understood them as iron-clad brother-hoods governed by honour and respect. Membership demanded unquestioning loyalty and rewarded you with the same. I was good with all of that.

They were islands of non-conformity in an increasingly con-formist world. That certainly appealed to me because I always found trying to conform difficult. Mind you, the vast irony of conforming to the rules and regulations of an outlaw club as a response to not conforming to society was entirely lost on me as a teenager. Teenagers have no time for irony. What they do have time for is insanely loud motorcycles, adventures, girls, parties and good times – and this is precisely what I imagined awaited me if I ever became a member of one of these brilliant organisations.

They were clearly anti-authoritarian, which also appealed to me a great deal. I was very much that way inclined myself – I actually could not understand how anyone could be 'pro' authority. And I still don't.

Anyway, that afternoon, a seed was planted which eventually poked its grim and crazy stalk through the fertile soil in which it had lain dormant for many years. In the fateful year of 1985, as my bike growled its way to the top of Mount Panorama and my girlfriend pressed her soft bits into my back and made all sorts of happy noises, it was ready to grow a few more centimetres.

Behind me rode ten other motorcycles and behind them came two utes loaded to the gunwales with everything twenty-odd people might need to assist them in becoming batshit crazy for the next four days. I was very excited – I had never done the Easter races in this fashion. Once again, something old and familiar had been made new and exciting to me.

The preceding year had been seminal in my life – and extremely fast-paced. So much had happened in a short period of time: I had grown apart from many of the friends with whom I had been riding for years, and had forged new and different friendships with other riders who shared my world view. We had not formed a club, per se, but there was certainly a lot of discussion on the subject. It was obvious to us all there were quite a few obstacles to be overcome before we could call ourselves an outlaw club or seek to join an existing one, and a good deal more water would need to flow under that particular bridge, but many of the basics were in place. And we were about to see how all of that worked on top of the Mountain.

It was most certainly a completely different paradigm to the one I had previously been operating under. Every year, since I had started riding motorcycles, I would load up my bike with camping gear and ride to Bathurst. Once there, I would put up my small tent and immerse myself in the Mountain's unique atmosphere. As the years went by and my circle of riding friends grew from zero to a few, I would go up there with them and we would all camp together. Once settled, we would proceed to howl at the moon, pass out in our own filth, crash our bikes on the dirt tracks, throw shit at the cops, lament our disabling hangovers each morning while drinking stoically through them, meet new people, remember people we'd met before, fall into a variety of campfires, eat the most appalling dietary horrors imaginable, and ultimately return home damaged, debauched and disgusting.

This year, it was all very different. For starters, I had brought my girlfriend. How she was going to cope with what went on up there was anyone's guess. Then with the new mindset my friends and I had adopted, we figured we'd set up a big marquee in addition to our normal smaller tents for sleeping in, and form a type of compound, complete with a gas-operated barbecue, Eskies full of ice and booze, a stack of fold-out chairs and a brace of tables, a pair of utes to do the heavy lifting with the firewood and booze-runs into town, and a host of creature comforts that would reflect our new view of ourselves. Since a few of us brought our girlfriends along, we thought there'd be far less bitching and moaning if the girls didn't have to sit in the dirt or on lumps of wood.

As we erected our tents and the marquee, set up the chairs, started the fire, lit the barbecue and cracked open the first beers, we beheld what we had wrought and we deemed it to be good. It was late afternoon on the Wednesday before the Easter long weekend began properly on Good Friday. The three camping sites atop Mount Panorama – Reid Park, Sulman Park and McPhillamy Park – were still only sparsely populated, but would fill rapidly on the Thursday and be chock-a-block by Friday morning. We made the call to arrive the day before and get a good spot – which was more or less the same spot I had been camping at since I started going to Bathurst.

That first year I had put up my tent equidistantly between the caretaker's cottage and the McPhillamy Park gates and had returned to much the same spot every year after that, just like a man will continue going to the same tattooist because there is comfort in familiarity. And when you've gone completely insane on drugs and alcohol and you're cloaked in madness like a medieval beggar who thinks he's a swamp-bear, familiarity is important. No one wants you waking up in someone else's tent. There are even fewer people who want you climbing into their tent and settling in beside them for the remainder of the night. So when the time comes to hibernate, you need to be able to find your campfire and your people and your tent.

This I had learned the first year I went when I was chased from a strange campsite by half-a-dozen disgruntled alcoholics after mistakenly passing out in one of their tents thinking it was mine. There was no chance of that happening this year. Our gigantic orange forty-nine-square-metre marquee could be seen from space. It was at least two metres taller than any other temporary structure on that mountain at that time so I was confident that no matter how smashed I was, I would be able to find my way back to it.

Such inane confidence only serves to demonstrate that I really had no idea how smashed I could possibly get. But I was sure gonna find out, though I did not know this on that gorgeous Wednesday afternoon.

I opened my third beer and levered myself up beside Mudguard, who was sitting on the lowered tailgate of his borrowed-from-work ute, sipping beer and rolling a joint. To this day, Mudguard remains the Michelangelo of joint rolling. He is fast, efficient and produced numbers that were consistently perfect in terms of density and awe-inspiring in terms of shape. Everything I know about rolling joints, I learned from him, but my best efforts are mere regional radio masts compared to his Eiffel Towers of smoking excellence.

'We done good,' Muddy said, lighting his smoothly elegant masterpiece, puffing it into crackling life and passing it to me.

'Yes, we did,' I agreed, smiling benignly to our left at the sunset bathing the top of the Mountain in a lambent golden light which was reacting very favourably with the drugs and booze in my system. I felt decidedly lambent and golden myself.

'I brought some acid,' Muddy advised me as we sat there,

sipping, toking and enjoying the sunset. 'I've also got some amyl nitrate, a block of hash, some shakers, a bit of crank and a bunch of pills.'

I absorbed this information along with a big lungful of dope-smoke. 'Is that amyl shit what the poofs use when they're bum-fucking?' I asked.

Mudguard nodded.

I grinned. 'We gonna be doing some bum-fucking?'

He punched me in the shoulder. 'Fuck off!' he laughed. 'It's a mad rush. You gotta try it.'

I nodded. I had every intention of trying it.

'What's crank?' I asked. I knew what shakers were. They were pills truck drivers took to stay awake. I had never taken any, but I knew from friends that they made your skin crawl, your head itch and if you took a lot of them, they gave you the shakes, hence their name. But I had no idea what crank was.

'It's speed mixed with coke,' Muddy explained, looking around to see if we were being overheard. 'I don't have much, but enough for you and me.'

'Speed?' I blinked. I had heard of this drug, which had only recently surfaced in Australia, and everything I had heard about it indicated this was precisely the kind of drug psychopathic motorcycle hooligans needed to be taking by the shovel-load.

Mudguard grinned like a fiend. 'Yeah, mixed with coke.'

'Cocaine?'

Mudguard nodded. I had never had cocaine, either. Clearly, this was going to be a weekend of discovery and enlightenment.

'Want some acid?'

Just like amyl, shakers, cocaine and speed, I'd never taken

acid before. I have to admit the thought of hallucinating atop the Mountain was a little off-putting. Acid had been around for a long time, and because I am a control-freak, I was never drawn to it. The thought of seeing things that weren't there did not appeal to me.

'Maybe later,' I said, dragging deeply on the joint. I was nicely stoned at the moment and enjoying a familiar and pleasant buzz from the beer-and-dope combo.

'Sure,' Muddy grinned. 'We got all weekend.'

So we sat and smoked and sipped and stared at the sunset and then Rachel came over, looking a little alarmed. 'What's wrong?' I asked, offering her the joint.

She shook her head, and her eyes darted from me to Mudguard and back again.

'What's wrong?' I repeated. Clearly something was not right. It was not like Rachel to knock back a smoke.

'Knob's here.'

A cold spike of hate poked its way into my guts. 'Where?' I said through gritted teeth, and hopped off the tailgate. 'In our camp?'

'No, no,' Rachel shook her head. 'He's just over the track from us with some guys.'

'You cool?' Muddy asked, stubbing out the joint.

'I'm fine, mate,' I said evenly. 'I just need to sort this out once and for all. Make sure no one interferes.' And then I went to see Knob.

Knob was Rachel's old boyfriend, the one she was with before we got together. And we had been together for two years. In that time, I had been forced to beat the bleating bitch-shit out of

Knob twice, primarily because he refused to accept he was no longer a contender for her affections, but also because he just kept appearing where I was and putting his hands up to me. What was I supposed to do?

This all began when Rachel and I had hooked up very shortly after she left him. It was all a bit weird, because I had once actually double-dated with him and her and one of her girlfriends. Knob rode a Honda and was part of a group of mates I was riding with for a few years, and he wasn't a bad bloke, but we were never going to be close.

Pretty much from the first time I met Rachel there was a mutual attraction between us. Neither of us acted on it; she was an honourable girl and faithful to her boyfriend, and I was never one for cutting someone else's grass. But as time went by, the attraction only increased and she subsequently left Knob in a welter of angst. I waited a decent period of time – I think it must have been about three days – then I rode over to her house at twice the speed of sound and we pantingly consummated what turned out to be a relatively long and mostly happy relationship.

Except that Knob just couldn't let it go. I don't actually blame him – Rachel was quite the catch. I was batting way out of my league, but I was certainly batting, and I was nothing if not medievally possessive about my women.

The first time he and I came to blows was on the terraces at the old Amaroo Park racetrack, northwest of Sydney, during the legendary Castrol Six Hour race. It was not all that long after I had taken up with Rachel, who was looking particularly shit-hot that day, as a bunch of us drank beer and watched the motorcycle madmen dice for glory in the natural amphitheatre of

Amaroo – one of the most brutal and therefore most visually entertaining race venues in Australia. So Knob's love wounds were still fresh. And when you factor in a fair amount of beer-drinking in the warm sun, and seeing your red-hot ex-girlfriend in skin-tight jeans and a little off-the-shoulder crop-top cosying up to the bloke she left you for, shit just has to happen.

Knob bellied up to me and declared that I was all sorts of arsehole in a loud and beery voice. I told him to fuck off and punched him in the face. He fell down, so I helped him up and punched him a few more times. I could hear people cheering and clapping, but when I turned to look, all I saw was Rachel looking horrified. And quite scared. So I stopped punching him while the crowd booed and urged me to 'Smash the cunt!' some more.

Knob stumbled off, wiping the blood from his face, and from that day he stopped hanging around with us. I didn't waste any more time thinking about him, and Rachel was upset for maybe another hour or so, then things settled down and we carried on with our lives.

A year or so later, I was starting to hear from mutual acquaintances that Knob was gunning for me and my comeuppance was imminent. I wondered why it had taken him such a long time to come looking for a re-match, briefly lamented not flogging him more effectively at Amaroo Park, then forgot all about it. The following weekend I was at the Illinois Hotel on Parramatta Road at Five Dock. The Bandidos MC were having a bike show and being a great lover of outlaw motorcycle club bike shows, I was there when the doors opened. Around lunch-time, I was standing at the bar, talking to Big Adam, one of the members, and feeling pretty bloody beaut about myself, the universe and everything in it.

'Why is that bloke giving you the fucken eye?' Adam asked, nodding over my head at the back of the bar, quite an easy thing for Adam, who towered over my six feet like a tower looms over an igloo.

I turned around and there was Knob at the back of the public bar, gurning, grimacing, rolling his not-very-big shoulders and glaring venomous hatred at me. He was there with a few mates, all of whom were patting him on the back and clearly offering him all kinds of encouragement. Because of my proximity to Big Adam, however, they were obviously unsure of the lay of the land. Attacking someone at an outlaw bike show can be fraught with peril, especially if you don't know who that bloke is with.

But I wasn't with anyone. I was there on my own and had no affiliation with the Bandidos. I just vaguely knew Adam, and we both just happened to be at the bar and struck up a brief conversation. But Knob and his mates didn't know that.

'I think he wants to go you,' Adam said around his glass.

'I think that would be great,' I said to Adam. I sure wasn't about to start something at his club's bike show, but I also wasn't about to turn into a bitch.

When Adam nodded, offering tacit permission, I pushed myself off the bar, took a few steps to my left, put my hands up and wiggled my fingers at Knob in that universal 'Come get some' gesture.

Knob came off that back wall like a Melbourne Cup starter out of the clanging Flemington gates. Cheered on by his mates he flew across the room, dodging around patrons and tables, and steamed straight at where I was waiting for him in front of the bar. When he was an arm's length away, I stepped sideways, grabbed his hair with my left hand and his jacket with my right hand and drove him face-first into the bar. I was just about to start stomping his spine into jelly when the publican called a halt to proceedings.

I moved off to another part of the bar, while Big Adam and a few of his brothers watched Knob's mates help him out of the pub. His face was a mask of blood, which was understandable given how hard the tiles that made up the main bar of the Illinois Hotel are when compared to Knob's soft and quite stupid skull.

Once again, I got on with my life. I never told Rachel about the incident. I knew she wished Knob no harm, but she also knew that if I ever got my hands on him and she wasn't around to supervise, what she wished and what was going to happen were polar opposites. And here he was at Bathurst.

I could see him standing on the edge of the dirt track, one of the many criss-crossing the camping areas atop the Mountain, separating our campsite from where he and his three mates had pulled up and started unpacking their bikes. Except Knob wasn't unpacking. He was standing there, arms akimbo, glaring at me as I made my way towards him.

'I wanna talk to you,' he said, pointing his finger at me as I drew closer.

Which was all well and good, but I didn't want to talk to him. I wanted to beat the shitting red bastard fuck out of him, and it looked like I was gonna get my chance.

Rachel was not going to interfere. Mudguard would see to that. Knob's friends would not intervene. My friends would see to that, and were indeed already coming around behind Knob's mates. It was going to be me and him, on top of the Holy Mountain, as the sun set. All it needed was a soundtrack.

The only sounds anyone heard were my fists splatting meatily into Knob and the constant subterranean cussing that accompanied each blow. I punched him and punched him and punched him. He fell down several times, and each time I hauled him up by the hair and punched him some more. I was absolutely determined to dissuade this vampire-like motherfucker from coming at me ever again.

In return, I think he punched me once. On the shoulder. Or it could just have been one of his arms flailing wildly. Eventually I stopped punching him. He was lying in the middle of the dirt track, writhing a little, and I was panting like a dog. I had punched myself breathless. So I took a few deep breaths as Knob slowly struggled to his hands and knees.

Not one of his friends had moved to help him thanks to my mates having come among them advising against such foolishness. There was no crowd around us. There was no yelling. There was no crying. There was just me breathing deeply, a low swirling of dust, and Knob leaking a substantial amount of blood into the grey dirt.

Then I started kicking him, but only a few times. He was done and I was tired; nonetheless I felt an instructive kicking was a must. I kicked him so he would understand that Rachel was off-limits to him at least until the ice caps had all melted and the saints had descended from Heaven. I kicked him so he would understand that all those other times I *didn't* kick him, I could have, but chose not to. I kicked him so he would understand I was truly grim, dire and horrible and would not hesitate to demonstrate my utter dastardliness to my girlfriend's stupid ex-boyfriends. And finally, I kicked him just because I wanted to. And then I limped back to my compound because my right leg hurt a little.

Rachel had not seen what had happened – Mudguard had kept her inside the marquee – but she was not dumb. Seeing me grab one of our water drums and start washing the blood off my face, hands and arms kinda gave shit away.

'Is Knob alright?' she asked.

'No,' I said quietly.

'You didn't kill him, did you?'

'No,' I shook my head. 'Probably not.'

As it turned out, Knob lay there for about ten minutes. His friends were too spooked by whatever my mates had told them to go anywhere near him until they were sure I was finished. Finally they must have figured I was done, went and picked him up, and about an hour later we saw them all ride away. Knob was being pillioned by someone and his bike was being ridden by one of the blokes who must have been a pillion. I opened a beer and spent a lot of time that evening staring into the flames of the campfire.

The following morning was crisp and clean and full of wood smoke and revving motorcycle engines. The Mountain was filling up – by lunch-time camping space was at a premium. I went for a walk and, as always, I was drawn to the lodestone of the police compound, and observed it wasn't only me who had changed in the past year. Large berms had been raised to the right of the compound as you faced the track, the fence surrounding it looked higher and there was new fencing to its right and left. Tall towers crowned with massive floodlights loomed over the squat brick police building, and as people clutching beer cans ambled past, a few burly policemen stood in a cluster behind the fence and watched us all watching them. The vibe was not pleasant.

In prior years the whole 'rioting at the police compound on Saturday night' situation was kinda weird. Some years, despite our best efforts and veritable meteor showers of flaming toilet rolls raining down on them, the cops simply refused to be drawn past the gates of their fortress. So we would get bored and go back to our campsites. Other years, they would come charging out of the gate like bison in rut before the sun had even gone down and while we were still looking for rocks to chuck at them.

It was interesting to note how the police had evolved over the years. The first time I witnessed a police compound 'riot', the cops were pretty much dressed in their normal uniforms, dispensing justice with their standard-issue batons, fists and feet. As the years went by, they acquired helmets, coveralls, Perspex shields and much longer batons, and used the Bathurst Easter bike races as a proving ground for their Tactical Response Group because no one really cared too much about them semi-annually beating the sass out of motorcycle-riding drunks.

From the motorcycle-riding drunks' perspective, it was all fun and games until they actually caught you and dragged your baton-tenderised body through 200 metres of dirt, rocks, glass, cans and swearing, only to fling you into a cell inside the compound building to await transportation to cells at the foot of the Mountain for 'processing and charging'. Then it was not so much fun. Though there are apocryphal tales of some high old times inside the cells until the alcohol wore off and the disciplinary beatings commenced.

Still, some years were better than others. The year the police deemed it clever to direct their baton-charges with whistle blasts worked a treat until a bunch of motorcyclists found some whistles and started whistling signals at them. Confusion reigned as the cops responded to our whistle-blowing rather than their own, milling around and making false starts as various commanders waved them back into their defensive lines and all sorts of burning and brick-like things rained down upon them, along with our derision.

The following year they beat us like braying mules, and emerged the next year sporting T-shirts declaring themselves to be the winners of the year before. That year's riot was a Mexican stand-off.

And so we came to 1985 and the higher fencing, lights and berms – though what purpose these dirt embankments were meant to serve was lost upon me that morning. What wasn't lost on me as I wandered around the top of the Mountain was the somewhat tense atmosphere. I couldn't put my finger on it exactly, but the whole place felt edgy. Gone was the easygoing bonhomie I had experienced every year throughout the campsites. People seemed a little keyed up, for reasons I could not readily identify. Few seemed keen to share a beer and swap 'Where ya from?' tales, and the half a dozen campsites I did saunter into offered scant hospitality.

This kind of atmosphere is quite infectious. When I returned to my own camp, I felt the same tension and noted we weren't being particularly hospitable to roving blokes either.

I also noticed the police driving around the area with annoying frequency: stopping and getting out of their vans, adorned in their riot gear and walking through campsites all around us. I believe they viewed it as 'proactive policing' and imagined these displays of 'strength' would somehow intimidate us all into placid subservience. Which actually only shows how little the stupid bastards understood about how beer, drugs and a crowd's mentality responds to this kind of intimidation.

By the time the sun set that Thursday afternoon, the whole Mountain was wound tighter than an archbishop's scrotum. I even saw the first mass fight I had ever seen on Mount Panorama. A bunch of blokes not too far from where we were camped commenced rocking and rolling with another bunch of blokes. They knocked over tents, kicked apart campfires and stomped each other with resounding vigour. As the brawl engulfed several other campsites, we made preparations to repel boarders if they drifted into ours, but fortunately that didn't happen. It only ended when one of the combatants jumped onto the top of a car and killed its roof with an axe. This seemed to calm everyone down, as such overt displays of violent insanity often do. It's like putting out fires with explosions – they remove all the air a blaze needs to burn.

Interestingly, the police watched all of this from a van parked only fifty metres away and did nothing. Given that they'd just spent the whole day wandering around the camping areas mob-handed, peering into people's tents, breaking up the traditional bull-rings and drag-races, and generally being rude, officious and intimidatory – all with the supposed intention of clamping down on 'disorder' – we kinda figured their hypocrisy was outstanding.

Here was their big chance to stop a serious outbreak of mass violence, involving tent poles, axes and lumps of wood wielded by many hooting, battle-scarred warriors, and they chose to sit in their van and observe instead.

Disgusted, Muddy and I retired immediately to the tailgate of his ute and began going through his drug stash. 'We need to go get some more firewood,' I said to him as he painstakingly sorted through the chemicals.

'And we will,' he grinned, his eyes on the task at hand. 'But we shall not go unprepared.'

So we prepared. And I was never the same again.

In the next twenty minutes, he and I ingested the crank, backed up with a few sniffs of amyl nitrate (which made my vision tremble and head pound as if a massive steel-capped boot was trying to kick my eyes out from within), spotted an obscene amount of hash, swallowed six shakers each (three times the recommended dose), washed them down with a beer, another two sniffs of amyl nitrate (the pounding was off the scale and I saw dancing explosions at the edge of my sightline), guzzled another beer and a bit of neat bourbon, swallowed two each of Muddy's unidentifiable pills, and followed up with a seven-paper joint the size of a cat's front leg. I did refuse the acid he offered me, feeling that there was no mileage in overdoing this.

Then we got into the front of his ute and drove off to get firewood. It was late afternoon on Thursday when we left. I wandered back alone into my compound at dawn on Friday, greeted by a horrified and extremely worried Rachel and lots of pissed-off mates who had spent much of the night searching for me and Mudguard. I was wearing someone else's T-shirt. My jeans had been tattered around the legs and flapped evocatively as I stumbled along. All the belt loops had been ripped off as well. The soles of my boots were melted. There was blood all over me, most of which wasn't mine. I was sporting several deep bites on my arms (human) and a few on my calves (animal – probably a dog), and a large clump of hair was gone from the back of my skull. Several of my teeth were loose, my ears rang and I had pissed myself at some stage. But it was almost dry, so it had been a few hours back. My ribs ached and I was very thirsty, but not at all hungry, and surprisingly, in a fairly even-tempered state of mind.

'What happened to you?' Rachel demanded.

I was wondering this myself, but no matter how hard I tried to recall, the night was mostly a massive blank, broken up with vivid bursts of chaos. I do remember every drug I had taken kicking in at once and Muddy driving like a deranged, screaming demon straight over a giant woodpile. I remember falling out of the ute, laughing hysterically, and throwing the scattered firewood into the back of the still-idling ute with great vigour. Unfortunately the firewood was already spoken for and we had not just run over the pile, we had also managed to level a six-man tent and a large fire with a hotplate full of snags on it. The owners of all this stuff were not amused, as you can imagine, and I had flashes of appalling violence being visited upon me. I remember a dog barking. I had flashes of stumbling wildly, laughing and weeping, through campfires and over tents, some with people in them. At some stage I knew I was on the race-track, but only because I recall Muddy telling me I had to get up or I was going to get run over. I have a clear vision of sitting in a very comfortable chair and eating a very large steak. I remember being incredibly tall, as if I was sitting on someone's shoulders. And I remember being under a car, but whether I was hiding, being hidden, looking for Narnia or had been run over is entirely unclear. There are many long hours missing from that night, hours that are utterly blank and lost to me for all time. Which is probably a good thing.

After Rachel had cleaned me up a little I must have fainted because the next thing I knew I was trying to get out of my sleeping bag and it was afternoon again. Saturday afternoon. Fuck. I had lost an entire day being a twitching, comatose drug-fiend. Rachel was no doubt impressed with just how hardcore this whole Easter weekend was turning out to be. I knew I sure was.

Nonetheless, it was now Saturday, which meant I was due at the police compound for the traditional annual gathering of deeply disaffected and peeved motorcycle riders, catastrophically pissed non-bike-riding locals who came up each year to get it on with the cops, a few concerned ambulance drivers and some television media people, who had been driving around the campgrounds all day.

Mudguard had returned while I was out cold, and was now out cold himself. I saw no sense in waking him up after being told he was in far worse shape than I'd been in – unable to speak and with no idea where his ute was. I begged Rachel to stay put, stay safe and not leave the camp, and left five of the blokes to guard her, the other two girls, the snoring Mudguard and our campsite. Then with twelve good and true men, I made my way to the police compound just as the sun was offering up yet another glorious golden farewell.

A sizeable crowd had already gathered around the compound, which had its front gate open and a few police admirals and field-marshals standing and observing the crowd with imperial disdain. A mass of people congregated on top of the nearby toilet block and in short order a lit petrol-soaked toilet roll arced its comet-like way into the nearby crowd from the assembly on the roof. It was duly picked up and thrown back to accompanying shrieks of laughter and so it went back and forth a few times while the police field-marshals looked on. They then disappeared inside their compound, replaced by some lower-ranked myrmidons and a few armoured Tactical Response Group brutes in their blood-repelling overalls.

None of this was lost on us. We watched the cops as closely as they watched us. A 'Pigs suck!' chant started up, and we all eagerly boomed it out at the top of our lungs, all the time edging closer and closer to the compound. The people on top of the toilet block were lighting another toilet roll and throwing it among themselves and the police had inched back so that they were standing across their still-open compound gate.

Then a bloke with a female pillion rode his bike straight through the crowd, across the front of the police compound and the girl lifted up her T-shirt to flash her tits at the cops. The crowd roared happily. The bloke on the bike did a U-turn and as he headed back the way he had come, the TRG cops simply coat-hangered him and the girl off the bike, and dragged them both inside the building within the fenced-off compound.

The crowd lost its mind. A hail of mostly empty beer cans came raining down on the cops. Most fell short, but enough of them came close enough for the cops to retreat inside the

compound to the thunder of 'Pigs suck! Pigs suck! Pigs suck!'
The sun had gone down and the floodlights went on. Squinting
through the glare we could see clumps of heavily armoured riot
police assembling inside the compound. They were clearly not
planning to sit this year out.

A few cans and rocks were thrown at the floodlights, but they
were too high, as was the cyclone wire fence behind which an
inordinate amount of state violence was being prepared for us.
So it was kinda pointless trying to toss shit over it. And no one
was game enough to get too close to the fence.

The crowd was large and growing larger as people increasingly came over to see what was going on. Which is what
people do when there's lots of noise somewhere near them
– they go to investigate. Of course, everybody knew all the
action was at the police compound. That's where the action
was every year. It was tradition. But when you take into account
the excessive amount of angst, tension and naked anger on
the Mountain that year, there was no doubt in anyone's beer-
befuddled mind that it was gonna kick off in a very large and
messy way.

You also have to factor in the whole drug aspect – which is
the one thing none of the university studies after the riot even
mentioned. Nor did the cops or the media. No doubt the reason
for this is that none of those people were in the crowd, or if they
were, they were certainly not being offered small foil-wrapped
dabs of methamphetamine for five dollars from an assortment
of dodgy-looking villains.

Speed was a relatively new drug in Australia then, and it
made a big public debut at Mount Panorama that weekend.

That is why people were edgy. That is why people were fighting. That is why there was so much aggression. Snort crazy bathtub chemicals for several days, drink your bodyweight in beer, be subjected to overt and patently hostile policing that prevents you from letting off any steam via the customary bull-rings and drag-races, and what did anyone think was going to happen on Saturday night at the police compound? Exactly what happened. And what happened is that we ran completely and utterly amok, caveman-style. Neanderthals celebrating after a mammoth hunt could have taken lessons.

We rioted for nine hours. Nine hours. Who the bastard-fuck riots for nine hours *without* being evilled-up on drugs? We'd certainly never rioted for nine hours before. Without that shit-mean methamphetamine poison roaring through our bloodstreams, we would've simply run out of puff after three hours and had to have a lie down.

In the very early stages, the largest proportion of people in front of the police enclosure were just looking – only a few were actually throwing stuff. But the crowd was big and the vibe was aggro, and more and more people joined in the throwing. It was all gaining a quite irresistible momentum. Which is precisely what the Channel Seven news crew understood when they drove their rented white Ford station wagon out the front of the baying, beer-can-chucking crowd and parked it. The blokes then got out of the car, removed all their gear, moved fifty metres away, set up their camera and tripod, and yelled at the crowd to burn their car. So the crowd promptly did, all the while being filmed doing it, and on the next news broadcast all of Australia was treated to edited footage of the manifestly insane bikie menace that threatened to engulf the country, and was starting with the news vehicles of their beloved media outlets.

My mum was watching the news the night they screened it. She knew I was at 'Budherst', as she called it, so she immediately began a series of prayer meetings with God. She later told me she went to church on Sunday and lit a candle for my safe return. Of course, she never imagined I would come to harm at the hands of the police. She was very worried the motorcycle hoodlums she could see incinerating the Channel Seven car would somehow hurt me. It never occurred to her that I could have been one of those motorcycle hoodlums.

I was actually right beside the car when it was being unloaded. I heard the producer and cameraman talking about how great this footage was going to be, even as they removed their gear. I remember thinking at the time what a champion bunch of blokes they were letting us torch their car for the cause, then promptly bought $20 worth of speed from the nearest sniffling ferret, slammed it up my nose and went in search of more rocks.

Out in front of the police compound the TRG was forming in lines. One faced out, one faced to the left and one faced to the right. The crowd just kept getting bigger and the rain of missiles was unending. There were now Molotov cocktails in the air, along with bricks sourced from a crowd-demolished beer-kiosk near the track. When a few police officers were hit they did the fire-dance to howls of approval from the mob.

The police compound almost backed onto the track just down from where it arcs in a fast left-hander out of Sulman Park and begins its twisting, nightmarish descent from Skyline. In all the previous years, no one had ever thought of actually surrounding the compound by massing on the track. Our past riots had been rather disorganised, ad hoc affairs consisting of frontal assaults on the police gates, all of which were easily repelled and the compound was thus also easily reinforced via buses full of angry, keyed-up reinforcements trucked up from Bathurst.

As any student of siege warfare will understand, if you can surround the fortress, the defenders will struggle to re-supply themselves with extra warriors. So after first setting fire to the track then heaving a burning forty-four-gallon drum through the windscreen of a speeding police van coming up from Conrod straight, it actually appeared that the crowd was gaining the upper hand.

Attracted by the flames, I went down behind the compound and was mildly shocked that we would actually try to burn the bloody track, and even more surprised that we managed to set fire to it at all. For the first time I saw cops with riot shields running awkwardly behind their enclosure, swinging their long batons and tripping over their feet. It was dark back there. They had not thought to light up that area, and it provided many attackers with good cover. I saw one bloke ducking down behind the Armco railing as three cops raced by, then rising up and nailing the last one in the back of the head with an empty Jack Daniel's bottle.

Then I beheld Conan standing atop the embankment. His name probably wasn't Conan, but it should have been. As I moved closer I beheld his puissance with awe. He stood alone and shirtless, clutching a steel Stop-sign pole, minus the Stop sign, but still with the big lump of concrete at one end. A line of TRG police had formed at the bottom of the mound.

'Carnyacuuuuuuuuuunnnnnttttssss!' he screamed at them, the pole swaying from side to side, his shoulder muscles twitching with the effort, his face contorted with battle fury. And of course the cops 'carned'. Waddling straight up the side of the steep mound, they were met with a mighty swing of Conan's concrete-crowned steel pole and came crashing and tumbling down the embankment in a chaos of riot shields, flying helmets and despair. The crowd behind Conan and the mobs on the track and in front of the compound bayed and howled in thunderous ecstasy. Twice more the TRG formed their line and essayed the mound and twice more Conan batted them back down. The fourth charge was successful and the police finally stood atop the embankment, puffing behind their Perspex, while Conan was savagely beaten and dragged off to their dungeons to the cheers and catcalls of the mob.

It was now well past midnight and the crowd showed few signs of settling. The missiles still rained down, the TRG mounted more baton charges and culled the slow ones from the herd. The Mountain literally throbbed and thundered with mob-hate. I was physically exhausted, but I couldn't bring myself to leave. What if I missed something? What if the mad bastards actually succeeded in storming the bloody compound? Would they mount the heads of the cops on star pickets and immolate everything in sight? Would they smear themselves in the gore of the enemy and dance among the flames? Would the news crew be filming this or would their cur-entrails be roped about the necks of the mightiest warriors? And where were my mates and where the fuck were the drug dealers?

Of course it was unlikely the police would cede their fortress without serious bloodshed. Thus far, no one had been shot by the cops, nor had anyone shot at the cops (despite them reporting that they had been fired upon). But that all might very well change if the crowd did look like seizing the compound.

Around 2 am, busloads of cops started arriving. The track didn't burn for very long, and the TRG had managed to clear it for a few hundred metres in both directions behind their compound. The reinforcements were duly deployed and the crowd simply deflated itself like a giant flannel-and-leather clad inner tube.

I limped and swayed my way back to my campsite, which was watchful, but quite peaceful. I was the last to arrive back, my mates having returned an hour before me. Rachel hugged and kissed me, told me I smelled like a dead animal, and a resurgent Mudguard handed me a beer. I shook my head, asking for water instead. My throat had seized up and felt like a wound scraped raw with some demon's broken talons. My chest ached. My feet throbbed. My back was an expanse of distilled suffering. Mentally I was numb. I had seen and done things I would not soon forget, and when I tried to make sense of what had happened, I failed. I now had a clear picture of what mob-mentality is, how powerful it can be, and how utterly hopeless and ultimately worthless that brief orgiastic might is.

The cops won. They were always going to win. All we had done was usher in a whole new raft of restrictions and regulations that would kill the Easter races at Bathurst forever. Certainly, we had scared the shit out of them, and to be perfectly honest, out of ourselves as well. There was no way anything like that would ever be permitted again, anywhere.

And so it came to pass.

The following morning I went back to the compound to see what it all looked like in the harsh light of day. It was incredible. The demolished beer kiosk could be seen scattered, brick by brick, across a vast expanse around the large cleared area in front of the enclosure. There were billions of beer cans strewn among the masonry. You had to watch where you stepped or you could have turned an ankle. The burned-out shell of the news car was still smoking and a few hardy beasts bounced on its roof and bonnet. There were a few police, in normal uniforms, chatting with some motorcyclists in front of the compound gates, which were wide open. The atmosphere was subdued and everyone looked a little ashamed, amazed and affronted by what had happened the night before. The tension that had been building up for the last few days had dissipated and we were all a bit numbed by the evening's insane excesses.

I actually watched a few races that Sunday, astounded as always by the skill and bravery of the racers who tested themselves against one of the most unforgiving racetracks on earth. I didn't touch any more alcohol or drugs for the rest of the weekend. My brain was sludge. I would forget what I was saying halfway through a sentence, or lose my balance while standing near the campfire and stagger a little as gravity threatened to overwhelm me. I dozed off at some stage and fell off the camp chair I slouched in. All the food I ate tasted like ashes and the inside of my mouth was a mass of stinging ulcers and chewed tongue. I had never before damaged myself as profoundly as I had that weekend. I was a physical and emotional wasteland. My body had served me up with several months of serotonin in the space of three days. I had battled fiercely with an old enemy, I had fought madly with unknown animals, riders and demons, and I had warred heroically with a collective nemesis and I had not emerged unscarred.

No one who participated in the Great Riot of 1985 had. And all of society is still paying the price for our Easter madness.

HAY, HELL AND BLOODY MILDURA

It is hard to have fun with your mates when the cops treat you like the Nazi Brownshirts were treating the Jews in pre-war Berlin. They smash or seize your personal shit, harass you on the streets, demand laws to outlaw you (does anyone else see the irony and pointlessness of outlawing outlaws, or is it just me?), remove your legal right to silence, shut down your business, feel up your girlfriend, hover over your wedding in a helicopter, dress up in full battle armour as if they were some kind of military phalanx, and generally pretend they are saving society from the scourge of the Jew ... oops, outlaw motorcyclist.

It is, of course, a farce played out for the media. And yes, it inconveniences and annoys the outlaw motorcyclist, which is really why it all goes on. Arrests are made, charges are laid, and the media is notified of the efficacy of the state in its duty to protect everyone from everyone else, but few convictions are ever made. And no one cares about that bit, because no one really knows about that bit.

Ironically, if the Brownshirt shit-storm didn't happen, then the outlaw motorcyclist would be concerned that he had somehow failed in his outlawry. So it is all weirdly self-serving and self-perpetuating.

Society needs its bogey-men. Ask Adolf. He'll tell you. And bogey-men need society in order to be bogey-men. It's how this shit works. In all honesty, though, the outlaw motorcyclist has as much interest in destroying or even interacting with society as an ape has in doing complex algebra. A criminal is by literal definition an outlaw, but an outlaw motorcyclist is not necessarily a criminal. There are certainly criminals in the ranks, just as there are criminals within the ranks of the police, the priesthood and the business community. Criminals are everywhere in our society. And because our society is rich and varied, and proudly waves its pluralism about the place, outlaw motorcycle clubs are also a part of it, in a holistic sense, at least.

By his very nature, an outlaw motorcyclist seeks to live outside normal society as much as he can. Total isolation is not possible, especially if he holds down a job and has a family, but no one can argue that an outlaw motorcycle club member is not an inward-looking person, because he certainly is. He doesn't like society and it doesn't like him … except it sometimes might admire him a little bit. And write songs about him. And ape his uniform. And wish it had his haughty attitude. He is a little bit scary and a little bit threatening – not actually to anyone personally or directly, unless you get up in his shit, but to the social order.

And we just can't have that, can we? Or must we have just a little of that? You know, to make us all feel a bit better about ourselves? Maybe to add a little frisson of outrage to our mundane lives? I don't know. I'm not that deep a thinker. But I do know that an outlaw motorcyclist just wants to be left alone.

Once, not all that long ago, he pretty much was. Which was great, because that meant he could have some fun with his mates.

'These are the times that
try men's souls.'

THOMAS PAINE

The decision to go to Mildura was taken, as all momentous decisions are taken, under the influence of strong liquor. There were probably drugs involved too, but drugs were involved in pretty much everything my mates and I did in those days.

The fact that we had worn out our welcome in many of the picturesque coastal towns during our club runs also had a bearing on our plan to ride to Mildura. For a change of scenery, as it were. Then there was the fact that as towns go, Mildura was a big town. And a big town has certain bonuses that a small town does not have: primarily a larger population of young women who would, in all likelihood, not be averse (initially, at least) to the company of smelly, bearded, tattooed men with hunting knives strapped to their hips and offensively loud motorcycles wedged between their legs. Our reasoning in this regard, as you might appreciate, was flawless, and borne out by experience. We had been to lots of towns, and invariably, after a polite pause while we ensconced ourselves in the pub, the local girls would arrive having made themselves as pretty as possible. Then they would stand around acting all shy and coy while belting back rum-and-cokes like holidaying shearers, whereupon the festivities would commence.

Naturally, the male relatives and friends of the girls would also come along and belt back rum-and-cokes like holidaying shearers, which is what many of them were – big, rangy, brutally strong country lads who were not easily intimidated by big, rangy, brutally strong, well-armed outlaw motorcyclists. Both camps also understood that if push came to shove, things would get messy. Most times things did not get messy and a kind of watchful and wary cohabitation of the pub ensued. Of course, sometimes shit did get messy and smashy and bloody, because alcohol, especially rum (often the locals' drink of choice west of the Divide), tends to brave up all the boys on both sides a treat. As a lady called Clara Brown, a contemporary of Doc Holliday and Wyatt Earp, wisely observed back in around 1880, 'When saloons are thronged all night with excited and armed men, bloodshed must needs ensue occasionally.' Nothing has changed in that time.

As you will understand, the first ten drinks makes everyone chatty and friendly, and few people actually go to pubs looking to start shit. We certainly didn't. We were simply passing through, and while it was quite impossible for us to back down from a confrontation, conflict was not something we actively sought. But it was the next ten rums that always flavoured the evening's social goulash.

Familiarity does indeed breed contempt. And after hours of communal drinking with simple villagers who were not at all familiar with the dynamics and triggers of outlaw motorcycle clubs, the simple villagers sometimes overstepped invisible boundaries and chaos instantly broke out. These boundaries may have been something as simple as one of them climbing onto one of our bikes parked outside the pub. The simple villager, now twelve rums into his Saturday night, and reassured by our general bonhomie inside the pub, sometimes felt he would like to try one of the bikes out for size. Or something. He would lurch his drunken way outside, drop his moleskin-clad arse onto someone's seat and lever the bars from side to side. This would happen quite quickly, and usually before one of the watching prospects (probationary members who were delegated to do all the stuff none of the members ever wanted to do, which was part of their quite lengthy initiation into the club's membership) could actually stop him. So the prospect would then help the simple villager from the bike by smashing him repeatedly in the head with a ring-bedecked fist. Further unpleasantries would follow.

These were just the things that happened on runs, even short Sunday ones, and none of us ever spent any time thinking of what might be. We were very much like dogs in that regard. We lived in the moment. The future was something that would reveal itself to us in the fullness of time, but in no way would that future dictate how we lived in the present.

So we decided to go to Mildura, a searing 1000-plus kilometres from Sydney, and began preparing ourselves for the journey. We figured six days for the trip: two days to get there, two days to experience the glory of one of Australia's most iconic inland towns, and two days to limp back home stinking of righteousness.

Mildura is almost directly due west of Sydney, situated on the other side of a geographical feature known as the Long Plain (and while it is indeed long and very plain, it really should have been called the Massive Empty Area Of Bloody Fuck-All Nothing), in the middle of which sits the town of Hay. This town was immortalised in Banjo Paterson's poem *Hay and Hell and*

Booligal, which first appeared in 1896 and enumerated the many dubious ecstasies to be found in the isolated Riverina town of Booligal, which, according to Banjo and verified by myself, is certainly less enticing than Hay.

Hay is a sizeable town by comparison with Booligal, but it's still an oasis in the middle of a vast emptiness – an 'I can see the curvature of the earth!' kinda emptiness. It's an emptiness and a vastness that really defies description. It has to be seen. It's a hollow, almost soundlessly booming expanse that has to be ridden through on a motorcycle to be properly appreciated.

Driving a car through the Long Plain to Hay and out the other side to Balranald on your way to Mildura on the banks of the Murray is a doddle. You turn on the stereo and the air-conditioning and try not to fall asleep as you sing along with the music. Riding it on a motorcycle is altogether different. You're not insulated by glass and steel and chilled air. You're *in* that vastness. It's rushing at you and past you and waiting for you and following you all at once. You can taste it if you open your mouth. It sucks your eyes dry in summer and snap-freezes your insides in winter. It is pitiless, indifferent and eternal.

The road is not smooth and you will be speeding to get it over and done with as quickly as possible, so your internal organs will kiss your bones from time to time, and not in a happy way. But you will not back off, because backing off means you'll spend longer riding the straight, flat, featureless insanity for longer. And you so don't wanna do that. Part of you even kinda hopes you'll get pulled over by the cops for speeding to grab a break from the lurching, wind-blasted monotony of the ride.

The lunatic emptiness begins just outside West Wyalong, stops briefly at Hay then redoubles itself all the way to Balranald. Or if you're really seeking more endless sky and infinite plain, the small town of Ivanhoe by way of Booligal is worth a visit. As we fuelled our bikes in West Wyalong this time and contemplated the road ahead, none of us were considering any crazy detours to even more isolated places.

'How far's Hay?' Evil wanted to know. Evil always wanted to know how far the next town was. He always asked and I always knew and told him. Our obsessive-compulsive disorders were thus compatible.

'It's about 250 kays,' I said, cinching down my old, battered and much-hated helmet as tightly as I could, knowing full well that after the first bump, it would ride up on my head, whereupon the wind-blast would turn it into a parachute that would relentlessly strangle me with the strap I was now tightening.

The other five riders gathered around and Terry, who had ridden up from Melbourne a week before on his newly purchased black FLH Shovel, produced a hip flask. He had a belt, passed it to Mark who sniffed it suspiciously, had a sip, handed it to Badger who just passed it on to Dead Bob and Ankles to finish off.

It was a cloudless day in early spring, so the temperature was pleasant. The sky was a perfect, depthless blue and there was even a slight breeze. If we were girls we'd have been wearing pretty summer dresses. Instead, we were caparisoned in leather, denim, steel, hair and tattoo ink, and weren't at all uncomfortable. We'd timed it pretty right in seasonal terms. It can hover well into the forties in summer in the middle of NSW, and the last time I had come through here it was early February and it felt like I'd been seared with a blowtorch. I had resolved not to do that again in a hurry.

Seven of us had set off from Sydney at dawn and seven of us had made it to West Wyalong by early afternoon. This in itself was a minor miracle. Certainly, there had been a few small mechanical issues – broken clutch cables, a lost number plate, a flat tyre, some kind of weird intermittent electrical gremlin plaguing Terry's new bike, and some of Evil's luggage had fallen off somewhere the other side of Bathurst, but since he could not remember what it was or if it was important, we just carried on.

Somehow we had managed to avoid the usual catastrophic mechanical failure which would see at least one of us waiting on the side of the road for a ute to be organised. Runs where every single member who set out on his bike and subsequently returned home on his bike were just non-existent. Something *always* went to shit. That nothing had yet gone to shit was worrying me, but marijuana, alcohol and methamphetamines always managed to distract me enough to carry on with an elegant, albeit sometimes fragmented, stoicism.

'Is there petrol between here and Hay?' Evil asked as we stood in a group, smoking, stomping the aches out of our bones and shit-stirring each other.

'Is there anything between here and Hay?' Dead Bob asked.

'There are five small towns,' I said, unfolding my map, squatting down and spreading it on the ground. 'North Yalgogrin, Weethalle, Rankins Springs, Goolgowie and Gunbar.'

'They have petrol?' Dead Bob wanted to know. It was a fair question. One of them had better have petrol – none of us had the range necessary to get to Hay.

'Of course they have petrol,' Mark avowed. 'Where the fuck do you think you are? Ethiopia? This is the main road between Sydney and Adelaide, you fucken spastic.'

Dead Bob looked out onto the main street of West Wyalong. It was empty of traffic. 'Must not be peak hour,' he observed flatly.

Our plan was to arrive in Hay that evening, immerse ourselves in the local pub culture, then suitably befouled, essay the Hay Plain the following day and spend our Saturday night fevering up in Mildura. We finished zipping up our jackets, gave the bikes a quick once-over to see if anything more had vibrated loose, pushed our lids harder onto our heads and turned west for Hay.

There was no petrol at North Yalgogrin. There was petrol in Weethalle, but it was deep underground inside the tanks of the closed petrol station. We stopped to consider our options. This was around the point of no return for two of the bikes, so if we went on and there was no petrol at Rankins Springs, that's where those two bikes would stay. If the rest of us then carried on to Goolgowie and there was no petrol there, then that's where we'd stay.

Weethalle appeared deserted, so there was no one we could ask. Knocking on someone's door when you looked like us was quite counterproductive, and forget trying to pull a car over. Cars do not stop for outlaws on motorcycles. Unless you make them by heaving a big rock through their windscreen, but we weren't at that stage yet.

So we sat there for a while looking at each other, wondering what to do. Then I just rode off in the direction of Rankin Springs and the others followed. Sometimes an executive decision has to be made and what will be, will always and forever just fucken be. As it turned out there was fuel at Rankin Springs, but Terry's bike had clearly not enjoyed that last fifty kays and refused to start. Evil, being the resident and only prospect with us at that time, pushed him up and down the road until the bike finally kicked into life, then, with the sun setting directly in our eyes, we made for Hay.

I could see kangaroos off to the side, and the number of relatively fresh carcasses littering the highway told me they weren't scared of measuring themselves against vehicles. They were sizeable brutes, too. There's an old bushie view that you can happily run over kangaroos in your car provided they aren't any bigger than the white posts on the side of the road. This does not apply to a motorcycle. I have seen blokes run over a small cat then spend three months in hospital while their pancreas learned its business again.

Our seven Harleys made a lot of noise. We had always considered muffled exhausts to be the province of the shy, retiring and law-abiding. None of us could honestly tick any of those boxes, so our bikes hacked thunder through unmuffled pipes in a way that would make calving icebergs sound muted. I hoped that the noise would keep the kangaroos at a distance, and I had also fitted a moose whistle a mate had sent me from Canada as an added precaution. It was a piece of cone-shaped plastic some four centimetres long and a centimetre in diameter. I understood it to work by emitting a high-frequency sound humans couldn't hear (but moose apparently could), when air was forced through the wide end of the cone as you rode. I had thus far not hit a single moose and was vaguely confident that kangaroos would also flee in terror at the noise that was said to work so well on moose.

We saw the lights of Hay just as the sun dipped below the horizon and the pack bunched up to make a grand and glorious entrance into the town. If only Terry's bike had not begun to miss and fart and stutter and shoot flames out of its exhaust pipes, this entrance would indeed have been something to behold. As it was, he limped to the front of the pub on a bike that sounded like a washing machine full of rocks tumbling down a hill.

'That's not good,' Mark said, watching Terry paddle his now-stalled bike backwards against the footpath with the rest of the bikes.

'Nope,' I agreed, safe in the knowledge that while it was indeed not good, it was also not going to be my problem, since I was the least mechanically inclined of all the blokes. At times of mechanical bastardry, I was certainly happy to offer advice and make pointed observations, and even to pass the requested tools. Since I had no business making any attempts to diagnose, let alone repair any problems, I normally just stood in the background rolling joints and quietly wishing outlaws would have chosen more reliable motorcycles to get their evil on with.

Dead Bob and Badger joined Terry beside his bike and the rest of us went inside to drink some beer. As usual, the publican was mildly apprehensive, but when he saw there were only a few of us, he relaxed, smiled and even shouted us the next round.

'Your mate having a few problems?' he asked.

Ankles shook his head. 'The thing's been carrying on since Bathurst. I'm amazed it got here.'

I took a few beers out to Terry and the others, who had begun disassembling the battery cover after failing to find anything untoward with the points and the ignition.

'It's got to be electrical,' Terry declared. There are only two possible causes of motorcycle bastardry – electrical or mechanical. Mechanical bastardry normally manifests itself with the accompaniment of horrid noises, sometimes with smoke and geysers of heated oil from places from which no such oil is meant to spout. Electrical bastardry is usually silent, but every bit as dire and often quite incomprehensible unless one is well versed in such voodoo sorcery.

None of us were so versed, and as I sipped my beer on that gentle outback evening, I was reminded of this as Terry jammed a screwdriver against some electrical component and was rewarded with a sharp, sparking crack.

'It's got power,' he observed, flinging the screwdriver onto the road and shaking his hand.

'And the pub,' I said, putting my hand on his shoulder, 'has vast amounts of beer. And a pool table. And a jukebox. And pies!'

Terry looked up at me from the gutter. 'You are the wisest motherfucker I have ever met,' he grinned, picked up his screwdriver, wiped his hands on his jeans and followed me back into the pub.

An hour or so later we were having a ball. The jukebox was slamming out Johnny Cash songs, the locals were buying us the odd beer and we were returning the shout, so it seemed that the Road Gods were in their heaven and all was right with the world. Whatever was wrong with Terry's bike might repair itself overnight. Don't laugh. This has been known to happen with Shovelheads. And while there weren't any girls in the pub just yet, we understood there might be some imminently. We also understood there was another pub in town if this one got boring, and we were advised that the local police, both of them, were young, lived locally and were altogether reasonable human beings.

Then Mercedes walked in the door. I'm pretty sure her name wasn't Mercedes. In fact, I really have no idea what her name was, but she had a Mercedes-Benz hood ornament hanging around her neck that flashed and bobbed between a pair of quite entrancing bra-less boobs jiggling joyously beneath a black turtle-necked sweater. Skin-tight jeans and boots dealt with her somewhat pudgy nethers and her head was crowned with a veritable mane of tousled auburn hair.

Evil instantly fell deeply in love with her. And since she was the only game in town right then, one cannot blame him. He was beside her at the bar before she even had a chance to check out the rest of the man-talent arrayed around the place.

'You look fucken fantastic!' he brayed. 'Wanna drink?'

'Rum and coke, thanks,' she replied coolly, not really looking at Evil. She didn't appear to be looking at anything in particular. From where I was on the other side of the pool table playing air guitar with one of the cues as Johnny began the second verse of 'Ring of Fire', her eyes seemed unfocused and not a little bit crazy. For our purposes at the time, this was not a bad thing at all.

Evil immediately ordered six double rum-and-cokes, which is always the best way to commence these pub romances. It saves you having to go back and order another round, which then leaves your intended unattended and open to approaches from other men. Being a prospect, Evil also understood that his needs and desires were always less important than the needs and desires of the members. So his six-drink game plan was sound.

Mercedes turned out to be not much of a conversationalist, and I was starting to think she was a little dim, or full of Valium, or maybe both. But she had an outstanding pair of tits and seemed completely enthralled with Evil, who was already at the hands-on stage of their evening. He was admiring her Mercedes-Benz medallion by resting his hand on her chest and turning it over and over in his fingers. She didn't seem to mind this at all and kept pushing her boobs against his paw and smiling and nodding.

Ankles was also watching them, and being one of the nicest and most good-hearted men I have ever met, went and bought another six rum-and-cokes for the happy couple. Then he came over and helped me sing the last verse of 'Folsom Prison Blues' with Johnny.

'Members buying prospects drinks?' I grinned. 'You're gonna ruin them.'

'I felt sorry for the poor bastard,' Ankles shrugged. 'You know the second he goes to the bar Badger or Dead Bob will be onto her like flies on shit. Then Evil's gonna sulk and you know what happens when Evil sulks.'

I nodded. I was highly aware of what happens when Evil sulks. The last time he sulked was in a Sydney pub that he, Ankles and I were drinking in one sunny Sunday afternoon. It had a wonderful beer garden and big tables and there were lots of girls sunning their legs while lubricating themselves with white wine.

That particular afternoon, Evil was making adjustments to the soles of his shitty boots with a large hunting knife. He made quite an amusing sight, seated astride one of the benches at our table in his tattered socks, muttering and sawing at one battered boot-sole, while the other waited its turn among the myriad beer glasses on the table. Management soon decided the whole flashing hunting-knife thing was a bit much for their Sunday-afternoon guests and sent a barmaid over to ask Evil to put the knife away. Smart pub management would always send a girl to ask us to tone it down, understanding that it was entirely unlikely we would take offence at a girl making such a request.

'Yeah, but look,' Evil said to her, holding up a boot with a flapping sole. 'I was just cutting this crap so I don't trip over the fucken thing.'

The barmaid smiled in fake sympathy. 'People have complained about the big knife,' she shrugged.

'Yeah, fair enough,' Evil nodded, a little perplexed by what people had the temerity to complain about. 'But I wasn't gonna stab anyone. I was just fixing my boot.'

The barmaid nodded. 'I know. But you know what people are like.'

Evil knew perfectly well what people were like, which is why he didn't like many of them at all. He put the knife away as asked, then proceeded to sulk, presumably over the way of the world. He sulked for about ten minutes, refusing to speak to anyone, clearly dismayed at the thought of honourably continuing his Sunday afternoon after being chastened by a girl about crucial boot repair.

Next thing he accidently knocked over his drink, which made a big puddle on the ground, which he then stood in – and because he had not yet put his boots back on, his afternoon just got exponentially worse. The three young, trendy couples at a nearby table burst into laughter. I do not know to this day if they were laughing at Evil, or it was just poor timing on their part, and it really doesn't matter. They had been surreptitiously watching Evil's antics since he had taken off his boots and set about repairing them with his knife, and while he was oblivious to their snide glances and snickering, I wasn't. And quite suddenly, Evil wasn't oblivious to them anymore either.

'What the fuck are you laughing at?' he spat and started for their table. Clearly, it was a rhetorical question. He wasn't interested in an answer. And none was possible.

Their laughter died instantly, then Evil was among them like a ball of hairy, tattooed fury. He flipped the table (no mean feat given it was made out of lengths of railway sleeper and he was wearing wet socks) and began grabbing, punching, kneeing and kicking everyone at hand. Male or female, Evil did not discriminate – he beat them all with equal abandon. But he did spend longer beating the three blokes. The women he mainly slapped. He told me later he wished he'd remembered to put his boots on because he'd hurt his feet kicking the blokes.

It was over pretty quickly, as these things tend to go, and we left the pub, though with a great deal more dignity than the three couples who had just learned an object lesson about laughing at, or being thought to laugh at, sulking outlaws.

That evening in Hay, there didn't appear to be any danger of Evil lapsing into a sulk. Mercedes was now onto her sixth rum and was drinking it while sitting on Evil's lap. The bloke could not have been happier: he was on the road with his mates, his bike was running fine, a member had just bought him a round of drinks, and he had the only girl in the pub on his lap. He lacked for nothing. From my perspective, it made me happy to see my mate so happy. Happy Evil was always a better deal than Sulky Evil.

The pub was filling up slowly, mostly with blokes and a few older women, and I could see some of the other blokes eyeing up Mercedes, who had now been persuaded to dance for Evil's viewing pleasure. It was clear they were wondering if she might be persuaded into spreading her love around. Now before you start sticking psychotic rapist labels on people, it'd probably be a good idea if I was to explain how most of us related to sex at that time and in our rather unique paradigm. Always remember there was an insane amount of drugs and alcohol involved in most of the things we did. Now, while marijuana and beer aren't known as aphrodisiacs, methamphetamine is a different story. Get properly whacked on speed, and talking shit and not sleeping will be the least of your issues. Having honkingly filthy fiend-sex until your genitals look like they've been scrubbed with sandpaper, on the other hand, will *not* be the least of your issues. It will, in fact, be the paramount and dominant issue. For many, many hours. So there's that to consider.

You might also want to contemplate that, as Waylon Jennings sang, ladies love outlaws like babies love stray dogs. Not all ladies, of course, but a goodly amount of women were drawn to outlaws like lemmings are drawn to cliffs. We were never, ever, hard up for female companionship. Then there's the fact that some girls actively seek out the company of more than one bloke at one time. Just as there are blokes who fantasise about having sex with entire female volleyball teams, there are women who fantasise about having sex with a whole male football team. And, as I discovered, if a football team is not available, then an outlaw motorcycle club is most certainly a worthy substitute. We even had a name for such girls. They were called 'onions', presumably because they were multi-layered (get it?). They weren't all that common, but they certainly weren't all that rare, either.

So, combine crazy sex drugs with promiscuous women, and you'll have a clearer picture of what we were dealing with at the time. Of course, if it became evident that a girl was keen for more than one bloke to party with, it didn't necessarily follow that twenty blokes lined up for a go. Some blokes aren't into that kind of thing. Some blokes will watch, and some will wander off because they couldn't care less. I normally found myself in the latter category. I have always been ruthlessly fussy about the kind of girls I wanted to swap spit with: for me spit-swapping is a private affair. So while some of my mates were not in the least bit discriminatory about who they fucked, where they fucked them and who might also have been there at the time, the rest of us were rather better adjusted.

I actually remember one horrible beast of a woman who cohabited with a member's girlfriend for a time. This great, lumpy 120-kilogram female cheesebag was simply appalling in her sexual appetites and disgraceful proclivities. Whenever we were over, she would pig out on the drugs we brought, hose a litre of cask wine into her vast belly, then let us know in no uncertain terms that she was nude, rude and ready to ride in the bedroom adjoining the living room.

The first time it happened we were all backslapping, hooting and braying like donkeys. It was novel and mental and sordid in exactly the right amounts. But when it began to happen every time we went there, it started to creep us right out. It got to the stage where we would draw cards to see who lost and got to skulk into the bedroom and service the moaning she-brute. I cheated every time. There weren't enough drugs on earth to make me want to climb aboard that particular train.

While I was certainly not about to board the lewdly gyrating Mercedes choo-choo, it was patently obvious Evil had bought a first-class ticket, but Dead Bob and Badger were also at the ticket booth. They were happy to concede first place to Evil – he had, after all, invested the most money in terms of rum-and-coke purchases and was giving her generous pinches of speed to keep her focused – but they were in dispute about who should go next.

'Get fucked,' Badger said to Dead Bob as they propped up the bar and watched Mercedes's arse shimmying away in front of a grinning Evil. 'He's my prospect. I'm sponsoring him. I'm going after him.'

'Fuck off,' Dead Bob said, waving dismissively at Badger's claim. 'You take fucken ages. You always take fucken ages. I'm done in twenty seconds. You won't even know I've been there. Don't be a bastard.'

'Am I on a fucken clock here?' Badger asked. 'I take as long as I take.'

Dead Bob grinned like a fiend. 'You're always taking your fucken time,' he sneered. 'You fucken ride like you fuck, too.'

Over by the pool table, Mark, Terry, Ankles and I were in hysterics listening to them chew on each other.

'Outside, cunt!' Badger barked. They both stalked outside like gunfighters, and we followed honking like clowns. Evil and Mercedes followed too, their arms around each other. Badger got on his Sportster, fired it into barking life and as it warmed up, he told Dead Bob what the deal was. 'Get on your shit-heap,' he said, pointing at Dead Bob's ageing, rust-pitted FX Shovelhead, which had just undergone a top-end rebuild and boasted some go-fast internals courtesy of the wizards at Carillo and S&S. 'And line the fuck up over there.'

He was pointing across the street. 'The first one to the end of the shops wins.'

Dead Bob fired up his bike, just as some of the locals joined us on the footpath.

'Two outta three!' Dead Bob yelled over the staccato thunder of two Harleys being eagerly revved.

Badger gave him the thumbs-up and beckoned me over. 'Can you start us?' he asked, his eyes glittering with determination and maybe a dozen rum-and-cokes.

'Sure,' I grinned, clapping him on the shoulder. 'Out in the middle of the street?'

'No!' Badger barked. 'On the footpath. I'm too fucken drunk to race on the street.'

I was pretty drunk too, so his statement seemed perfectly reasonable, and Dead Bob was already staging on the opposite footpath, the front of his FX propped against a shopfront and his back tyre whooshing and vomiting fast-tumbling clouds of grey smoke into the air. Some of the locals were clapping, others were staring in shock.

Badger promptly took hold of his Sportster, which had also had some mild engine work done and due to its slightly lesser weight had been known to offer a decent turn of speed – despite it having a smaller-capacity motor than the bigger Shovelheads the rest of us were riding – and wheeled it against a closed newsagency beside the pub to begin his warm-up burn-out. The cheering locals cheered louder. The shocked locals looked even more shocked.

Evil and Mercedes had taken this opportunity to grope each other against the front of the pub, and from where I was standing in the middle of the street as official starter, the whole scene looked decidedly surreal. It was getting on to ten o'clock, the only noise in Hay was the noise we were making, and the smell of burnt rubber, alcohol and dazzling fresh outback air made for a heady mix as I raised my arms up to start the drag-race.

'One!' I bellowed, thrusting both arms in the air. I was answered by a thunderous rev from both sides of the street and some hooting from the small crowd outside the pub.

'Two!' The revs got louder and part of me wondered why none of us were concerned about how far these two blokes still had to ride, and just how ridiculously fragile their bikes that still had to cover a considerable distance actually were.

'Three!' I shrieked and dropped my arms by my sides as Dead Bob and Badger roared off the start and up the opposing footpaths to a chorus of cheers and yelling.

Badger won by half a bike-length. They rode back down the middle of the street side by side, yelling at each other and laughing like madmen. The spectators outside the pub applauded them and I noticed that having hoiked up her black turtle-neck top, Mercedes was now swinging her sizeable pale boobs from side to side. They looked like two plastic bags of suet, but that may just have been the unflattering lighting.

'Again, you cheating fuck!' Dead Bob shrieked, gunning his bike back to its start position on the footpath. Badger likewise gunned his Sporty onto the opposite footpath and I took up my position in the middle of the road. Which is where the police paddywagon found me a few seconds later. It flashed its blue lights, two young officers exited and walked over to where I was standing and sipping at a half-empty beer can.

'Shoot him!' I heard Terry yell at them from the footpath.

I saw one of the cops grin slightly as they approached. 'Good evening, mate,' he said. 'You in charge?' As those words left his mouth Badger and Dead Bob, obviously tired of waiting for me to start the race, started themselves and thundered off up the footpaths, which prevented the police officer from hearing my answer.

'Sorry,' he said when the noise receded up the street. 'What did you say?'

'I asked what I was meant to be in charge of,' I grinned.

'All of this,' the police officer indicated with his hand.

'No, officer. I'm just the starter.'

'So who's in charge of the club?'

'No one, really,' I lied. 'We just kinda make it up as we go along.'

'So what's your President badge all about?'

He sort of had me there. 'I'm on leave,' I bullshitted then burst into laughter.

They smiled but didn't join in. 'How long are you in town for?'

'Just overnight,' I said, around a mouthful of beer.

'Gone tomorrow?'

I nodded.

'Where you off to?'

I shrugged. He nodded. He knew I wasn't going to tell him, but he had to ask.

'Can you do me a favour?' he asked.

I just looked noncommittally at him.

'Can you please ask your blokes to not race on the footpath? The bloody locals will think it's okay, start doing it, and that will cause us all sorts of problems.'

It sounded like a reasonable request. And I was, right at that moment, in a most reasonable frame of mind.

'No worries,' I nodded. 'So we can drag-race on the road then?'

The police officers exchanged looks, then the talkative one fixed me with a meaningful stare. 'Not while we're fucken here,' he said evenly.

I nodded.

'We good?' he asked.

'We're good,' I smiled.

They got into their van and drove slowly off. I walked back to my mates on the footpath. The locals had all gone back inside the pub the moment the police had appeared.

'They didn't fucken shoot you,' Terry said, his voice edged with disappointment.

'You bastards can't race on the footpaths anymore,' I explained. 'The cops reckon it'll make the locals crazy.'

'But we're in the middle of a championship!' Badger spat. 'It's the best of three. I'm winning!'

'He said you can race on the street but not when they're here,' I advised them.

'Bullshit,' Terry blinked, and all of them looked rather nonplussed.

Almost all of our many experiences with the police had been less than positive, especially when we were engaged in anti-social buggery like drag-racing on the footpath. So we were all a bit unsettled by what the constable had told me.

'You sure he said that?' Mark asked.

'I asked him if we could drag race on the road and he said, "Not while we're here."'

'I love this fucken town! Come on, arsehole. You've got another race to lose,' Badger declared to Dead Bob and went back to start his bike.

Dead Bob won the next race, and Badger won the third and deciding one. Cashing in on the excitement, Evil had managed to get his hand into Mercedes's jeans and was busily rubbing her up. It reminded me of a man planing a timber beam. So things were all pretty festive and happy and beery. None of the locals seemed to be getting ornery, none of us seemed to be getting prickly, and the publican was still smiling whenever any of us went to the bar to order another round.

It was while I was ordering one of these rounds that another girl of interest arrived at the pub. She was of interest because she was dressed in ultra-tight white jeans, a singlet top a size too small, and was crowned with staggeringly bleached bone-white hair. She also had a lot of make-up on and a pocket full of coins which she immediately started feeding into the jukebox. She slammed a few of them down on the pool table where Terry and Ankles were playing doubles with two of the locals, thus claiming her turn to play the winners of the current game.

The winners were always going to be Terry and Ankles. The winners were always whoever had Terry on their team because Terry played pool like Paul Newman played pool in *The Hustler*. But Terry didn't hustle, never crowed when he won, and he only ever played for drinks, which is probably why he remained un-stabbed.

After dispatching the locals, Mark immediately offered himself up as a partner for the new girl. Her name was Jodie, she had been born and bred in Hay, as had her parents and her parents' parents. She was a super-local, knew everyone in the pub and played pool passably well. But she had no idea who Mercedes was.

'Who the fuck is that slut?' she demanded to know the minute Evil walked in with a slightly dishevelled Mercedes under his arm.

'Who the fuck are *you*, ya moll?' Mercedes hissed back, detaching herself from Evil and making for Jodie, who hit her in the head with her pool cue.

'Get fucked, ya fucken slut, that's who I am!' she said, brandishing the pool cue at Mercedes, who had retreated a step and was holding her face with one hand. Jodie had used the thin end of the cue, so the blow did nothing more than shock Mercedes, who recovered quickly and went at Jodie like a runaway bus.

The two of them collided beside the pool table and fell to the floor in a welter of cursing, spitting, yowling and bitch-venom. A sack with two cats in it would have been less hostile. It all happened so quickly and with such atavistic savagery that no one made any attempt to break it up. It was engaging as hell to watch. So we did. We observed as Mercedes and Jodie tore at each other like a pair of cheaply perfumed chainsaws, knocking over tables, spilling beer and breaking glasses all the way across the front bar of the pub. Eventually, the publican herded them out the door so they wouldn't smash any more of his furniture up, and we all trooped outside for the show.

Evil was elated. 'She fucken goes hard!' he enthused as a puffing Mercedes grabbed two handfuls of Jodie's skeleton-coloured hair and whipped her to the pavement. Mercedes did indeed go hard, but Jodie was certainly no slouch when it came to bitch-brawling either. During the battle she managed to claw several bloody furrows into Mercedes's face, pull out some clumps of frizzy auburn hair and had landed at least six hammer-fists on her face and upper body.

The final outcome was anyone's guess. Unfortunately, the paddywagon returned in a whoop of sirens and a flash of lights and the two girls were roughly hauled apart.

'Piss off home, Jodie!' the policeman who had spoken to me earlier puffed, holding the still-struggling Mercedes in a reverse bear-hug. Jodie wiped her bleeding face, ran her fingers through the mare's nest of peroxided rubbish on her head and peered around the second cop, who had interposed himself between her and Mercedes.

'Fucken slut!' she spat.

'Get home!' the cop repeated. Jodie glared a last time at her protagonist and limped up the street straightening her clothing.

Mercedes had gone limp as Jodie headed home, and the police officers quickly and efficiently bundled her into the back of the paddywagon.

'Oi!' Evil yelled. 'What are you doing?'

The two cops were getting back into their van.

'Oi! Fuck ya! Where are you taking her?' he demanded, walking over to the passenger-side window.

'Calm down, mate,' the policeman said evenly as he put on his seatbelt. 'We're just going to take her to the station and dry her out. We're not gonna charge her. She can sleep it off and we'll take her home in the morning.'

Evil was mortified. 'That's bullshit!' he insisted, but the cop closed the door and they drove off.

Mark walked over to Evil and placed a conciliatory hand on his shoulder. 'Come on, mate,' he said. 'Don't fucken worry about it.'

But Evil would not be consoled. 'Fuck that! I spent sixty bucks on her! I was in! We were all in!'

He then walked out into the middle of the street and stared down the road to where the paddywagon had turned off. 'I'm gonna get her out,' he declared, marching over to his bike and jamming his helmet onto his head.

This declaration was disturbing on a number of levels. First, the police had thus far proven to be quite reasonable about our presence in town. And the impression they gave was that provided we didn't escalate our behaviour and left in the morning, they would leave us alone. Secondly, Evil never made empty threats. In fact, he never made threats at all. He just did what he said he was going to do, immediately upon deciding that that was what needed to be done. Thirdly, he clearly felt he had been wronged and that his investment, for that is how he viewed it, had been compromised by the police. And fourthly, we were all completely wasted and none of us was in any position to be making rational decisions. Which is probably why no one stopped Evil riding off after the cops.

The way it works in outlaw clubs is that your brother is your brother, right or wrong, all the time. When things might go pear-shaped or have already gone pear-shaped is not the time to debate who is right and who is wrong. That is a discussion for another time. The situation at hand, no matter what it is, demands unity.

Instructions were issued to procure more alcohol before the pub closed, and for Terry, Dead Bob, Ankles and Badger to head up the road and set up camp by the river. Mark and I would ride in the opposite direction and behold what evil Evil was planning to wreak.

The police station was only a few hundred metres away and when Mark and I pulled up out the front Evil was already hammering at the front door like a jackhammer. 'Don't be a cunt!' he howled. 'Let her out! Come on, man!'

'Fuck off!' came the muffled reply from within the police station.

Evil redoubled his efforts on the security door. 'Give me the fucken onion back!' he shrieked.

Mark and I walked up behind him, which is when the door was flung open, the floodlights came on and the police officer who had been so pleasant to me before emerged with a night-stick in his hand. 'I have called for back-up,' he declared. 'You all need to piss off right now.'

I might have been drunk, but I knew full well that 'back-up' would be some time in getting to Hay. Griffith, Narrandera, West Wyalong and Balranald, from whence any back-up would conceivably come, were all at least an hour or more away. The off-duty cops in town might get there a little quicker, but it was obvious to everyone there that his threat was a little hollow. If things continued in the shape of the pear, the police station could be on fire and the bikies could be playing football with his head way before his mates turned up.

Of course, despite whatever Evil had planned, which seemed to be nothing much more than yelling and banging, we were not about to torch the cop shop over Evil's sexual imperatives. But the policeman did not know that.

He closed the door in our faces but left the floodlights on, so that whatever impending villainies we undertook would be illuminated.

'He's being a cunt,' Evil declared, aiming a kick at the security door.

'I think he's been pretty reasonable,' Mark observed. 'I would have shot you ages ago.'

Evil looked at him, his feelings clearly wounded. 'Mate, I spent shitloads of money on her. I gave her most of my drugs. I was gonna share her around. She was cool. She was up for it. She was ...'

'She was beating that other slut like a rented mule and she got locked up for it,' I interrupted.

Evil nodded, acknowledging the veracity of this. Then he grinned. 'She fucken goes hard, aye?'

Mark and I both agreed that Mercedes did indeed go hard.

'You reckon he'll let her out?' Evil asked.

'Not before tomorrow morning and probably not while we're out here,' Mark said.

'I'm gonna wait a bit,' Evil stated flatly.

'Do you think there's much point?' I asked him.

'What if the back-up he says he called for turns up?' Mark asked.

Evil considered this for a moment. He might have been impulsive, but he was not an idiot. If we got into some kind of crazy altercation with a dozen sleep-deprived and hugely pissed-off country cops at three in the morning (which is about when back-up would have got there), and this happened because Evil's penis remained un-addressed, the repercussions would have been ugly.

'Yeah, alright,' Evil nodded and we walked back to our bikes.

Just before we started them, Evil turned back and addressed the floodlit police station at the top of his lungs. 'Oi, mate!' he yelled. 'I reckon what you've done is a bastard act! Best grass-cuttin' I ever seen! She likes rum and coke. I'll leave you a couple of cans!' He then produced two pre-mixed cans out of his jacket, set them on the footpath, and we rode slowly back to where the others were camped on the banks of the Murrumbidgee River.

The next morning dawned warm and we were grateful for the shade trees we were passed out under. We had just a touch under 300 kays to go to Mildura – 130 of it across the flat and featureless expanse of the Hay Plain. But as we fired up the bikes, it became clear that two of our party might not be proceeding as planned. Terry's bike, which had started the night before, was not repeating that blessing this morning. It was utterly dead. The black FLH sat there like a block of wood, lifeless and obdurately obstinate, while Terry swore at it. Evil's bike had a flat battery and while its starter motor clicked promisingly, it also refused to start.

We all agreed these issues would be better comprehended and addressed if we got the bikes to the big petrol station and truck-stop on the outskirts of Hay on the Sturt Highway. We all needed petrol, and some breakfast would not go astray either. It wasn't far, so while the rest of us rode there, Terry and Evil were resigned to pushing their bikes those few hundred metres.

After a relatively dire breakfast of shitty coffee, reasonable bacon-and-egg sandwiches, marijuana and a little speed to offset the forthcoming mindless drone of the Hay Plain, we considered our predicament. This did not take very long. We were not deep thinkers, so we decided to fix the easiest thing first. And the easiest thing to fix was Evil's problem. He just needed a battery, so he went and stole one from a truck parked nearby. After some judicious ocky-strapping and hamfisted wiring, his red FXR was good to go. Terry's FLH was a different matter. It just would not go. We tried push-starting it. We tried jump-starting it from Evil's truck battery. We tried replacing the plugs and the points and were on the verge of summoning a priest to exorcise whatever demons had possessed it, when Terry decided upon a course of action.

'You're gonna tow me to Mildura,' he said to Evil.

Evil understood this was not a subject open to debate. He was a prospect and it fell to him to assist a member whenever a member was in need. But we all knew towing a bike for around 300 kilometres was an exercise fraught with the most appalling perils imaginable.

Still, we had promised the police we would be gone by morning, and it was now morning. Evil also had a stolen truck battery tied to his bike, which was not going to contribute favourably to any future discussions with the police when they turned up – and there was no doubt in any of our minds that they would eventually turn up. We implicitly understood that whatever rules applied during the night were always null and void in the harsh light of day.

Dead Bob rolled a fat bunger and we smoked it to help us focus on the problem at hand, which was fundamentally the fact that Evil had never actually towed another motorcycle anywhere. He was not to be blamed for this. Most motorcycle riders had never towed another bike anywhere. This is because towing a bike with another bike is one of the most arduous things you can ever attempt. Everything conspires against either party having any kind of success. The laws of physics hate it when you interfere with them. Both riders have to rely on each other not to fuck up, and the further you have to tow a bike, the more chance there is of something going stupendously wrong. Towing a bike for 200 metres is like holding a cup brimming with battery acid on your head and trying to walk. Towing one for 300 kilometres is 2800 times worse.

We had no choice, however, we had to be gone. So Terry looped a length of rope (also stolen from a nearby truck) around the front of his frame and tied it off. For shorter tows you would simply loop the rope around the handlebar and hold the loose end gripped between your hand and the handlebar so you could release it instantly if things went to shit. But there was no way Terry could hold the rope for 300 kilometres.

While this was undertaken, I offered Evil what advice I could about towing: 'Take off slowly. Do not allow the rope to get any slack in it – keep it taut all the time. Make sure you use Terry's weight as a brake. And take it easy. Seriously. He's tied to your bike, so if you lose it, you'll both go down. Pay attention all the time.'

Evil stared at the ground and nodded solemnly. He knew this was serious business. I knew the chance of him being able to pay strict attention to anything for longer than a few minutes was unlikely, but what I was saying seemed to be sinking in.

By the time I'd finished, Terry had transferred all of Evil's luggage to his bike (Evil's bike could not accommodate both a giant truck battery and his gear) and tied the other end of the rope to the back of the FXR where the top of the shock absorber was bolted to the subframe.

'Let's go!' he declared once he was done.

The rest of us started our bikes, consigned our two mates to the mercies of the Road Gods and set off for Mildura via Balranald. It was pointless for all of us to ride with them. Their average speed for that 300-kay or so journey would not be much over a lunacy-inducing 50 kms per hour. We all agreed it would be better for everyone if only two of our number went mad in the desert and killed each other.

It was 8 am and a bold 29 degrees when the five of us shot

ahead. It was a rude 37 degrees when we hit Mildura three hours later. After establishing we could camp at the Buronga Riverside Caravan Park on the north side of the Murray River, we loaded ourselves into the Grand Hotel to await the umbilical brothers.

Our first news of Evil and Terry came at about four that afternoon when the Let's-Go-See-Where-The-Fuck-They-Are Party of Dead Bob and Badger reported back. 'They were doing so well,' Dead Bob sighed, clonking his lid onto the bar and ordering a beer. After he drank half the glass, he was refreshed enough to tell us what happened. Evil and Terry had made it all the way to within sight of the 'Mildura 10 km' sign. Terry told us later that he could see the sign from where he was lying, but it was a bit blurry because of the battery acid all over his face.

Evil may have seen the sign in his mirrors when he rode past it, but he'd grown sick of checking on Terry about an hour into the trip, and eschewed their use for the rest of the journey. So he also didn't see the truck battery part company with his bike when he went past the sign, with Mildura a few minutes away. Terry saw it though, up close and very personal. It was quite a sight, too, as he recalled. There was no warning. One second it was strapped to the seat of Evil's bike, the next it was a-bouncin' and a-leapin' and a-sprayin' gouts of battery acid as it came tumbling down the road straight at his tethered bike. Terry must have flinched instinctively, which probably saved his eyes being melted in his head when the battery hit his FLH square on the front guard and exploded, dousing him with warm and zesty H_2SO_4. Either way, he instantly let go of his handlebars to claw at his eyes, which then caused his grossly overladen FLH to veer savagely off the road and into the nearest orange plantation.

The first Evil knew of this was when the back of his bike was brutally wrenched two metres sideways, into the table drain by the road and onto its side. Dead Bob and Badger came upon them scant minutes later. Using the puddles by the road and in the orange orchard, they managed to bathe Terry's face, but were unable to save his clothes which had been utterly destroyed by the battery acid. Which was alright, because he wouldn't be needing clothes until he was ready to leave Mildura Base Hospital. And that didn't happen until about 10 pm that evening, when I gingerly pillioned him to our campsite in his hospital gown, burning with gravel rash and nursing several heavily bruised internal organs and a freshly relocated shoulder.

Evil, as it turned out, was remarkably unhurt and his bike was rideable. His hip was a bit sore from where the table drain whacked him, and his bike had a bent footpeg, half a clutch lever, two smashed blinkers and mirrors, and some slightly out-of-whack handlebars.

Terry's badly twisted FLH, with its new acid-etched look, was a different story. Its split petrol tanks had been torn off their mounts, the front guard had been smashed, the forks were twisted and bent, and the orange orchard had claimed the front brake's master cylinder, the speedo, the carburettor (complete with manifold), and one of its footboards.

As we gathered around the campfire that evening we were somewhat subdued. Terry was hurting badly and a little crazy on the pain-killers he was on. Evil felt terrible about what had happened, but when viewed objectively he couldn't be held personally responsible. Sure, the battery came off his bike, but it came off after hundreds of kilometres. Had it come off after ten kilometres, an argument could have been mounted about ocky-strap negligence. But his strapping job, and a few of us did check it (including Terry), was sound. It was just one of those things. Shit happened. It has a tendency to do that, especially when you least expect it. And certainly no one expected it within sight of the finish line.

Terry was having a little trouble standing upright, but since he looked quite hilarious in his hospital gown, swaying in the firelight with a beer in his hand, we did everything we could to prolong his consciousness by feeding him methamphetamines. They had an interesting effect when coupled with the hospital-grade pain-killers he'd been pumped full of, and I was a little concerned he might dislocate his shoulder again when he started jumping over the campfire. But he made three quite wonderful leaps, then simply passed out in the dirt with his hospital gown a little singed around the bottom. The rest of us toasted our good fortune (no one was dead or in jail), toasted Evil (he had towed Terry for nearly 300 kilometres and didn't actually kill him), and toasted our own overwhelming and collective self-beautness, then passed out by the fire.

The next morning we made arrangements to get Terry and his bike back to Melbourne by train. He certainly couldn't ride, and wouldn't until his shoulder had healed enough to allow him to raise his arm. Evil generously volunteered to go with him and look after him, but Terry felt he was better off alone. His brother would meet him at Spencer Street station, unload the wrecked bike for him and see him back to his house.

The rest of us set off for home. Evil had stolen another truck battery, but since he rode at the back of the pack anyway, no one was too fussed about it coming off. And it did. But not until we were only 200 kilometres from home. He swears it didn't hit the car behind him, but since he didn't have any functioning mirrors on his bike, it was kinda hard to believe him.

'HI! WE'RE THE COPS!'

Lots of weird shit went on at the green house in Merrylands. Share houses are like that. But they are especially like that when you share them with pretty much everyone you know, twenty-four/seven. The cops were frequent visitors, but they usually only came around when the music was too loud, the screaming in the back yard became too outlandish, or the perpetual bonfire beside the Hills Hoist was scaring the people in the flats looking down on our yard. Now and again they would come and serve a warrant on someone who had not paid a speeding fine, but since the penniless shitbag always went quietly, the cops never had a reason to come past our front door, or our back gate. They were not stupid ... well, some of them actually were, but most of them weren't, so they knew illegal shit was going on inside that house. Was it the kind of illegal shit that needed search warrants, raids and all sorts of unpleasantness? Well, it was borderline, and we had been threatened with armed intervention a few times, so it was probably inevitable. But did it really have to happen at such an awkward time?

AT THE ALTAR OF THE ROAD GODS

'Policemen so cherish their status as
keepers of the peace and protectors of the
public that they have occasionally been
known to beat to death those citizens or
groups who question that status.'

DAVID MAMET

Having the cops barge into your house angrily barking orders, knocking over your cheap furniture and rudely interfering with the balanced and genial ambience of your life can be an extremely unsettling experience. Having the bastards come through your bedroom window at 18 o'clock[1], bristling with automatic weapons, hard-baked with hatred and black body armour, is somewhere the other side of 'unsettling'. It is, quite frankly, an occurrence that sucks a whole monstrous fridge full of fairly horrible cocks. They know this, which is why that particular hour and that particular method is their preferred *modus operandi*. It is also because 18 o'clock is one of the two times in your life when you are most vulnerable and thus most easily subdued with brute force. The other time is when you've got your pants down around your ankles having a shit. But unless your house is bugged, the police can't usually pin down your shitting time

---

1   For those of you unfamiliar with amphetamine use, 18 o'clock is
    not an actual time – it's more like a state of being brought about
    by two or three days of snorting insane chemicals into your sinuses,
    fucking your girlfriend into a state of mutual madness, then lying
    on the rumpled, sweat-ponged midden that is your bed, grinding
    your teeth and vainly wishing the drugs would just fuck off and let
    you be.

with any accuracy, so they prefer to go with the 18 o'clock visit. And the overtime pay is heaps better.

You also have to understand that the cops do not make social calls. They are not crashing into your bedroom armed for bear because they feel you need to help them with their 'enquiries'. They are in your house and up in your shit because they have either a) been given to understand that you are irredeemably evil; or b) they've made a terrible mistake. Either way, the experience is one of those cosmic paradoxes that assail us from time to time, in that it is very unpleasant for you and very pleasant for them, and thus is balance brought to the universe.

The first time the police came lumbering into my home was during one of the Great Marijuana Famines that would bedevil Sydney now and then in the '80s. Advances in hydroponics eventually made these famines a thing of the past, but there were periods during that decade when dedicated dope smokers would be licking the paint off the walls and threatening to slaughter their regular suppliers with claw hammers when they couldn't 'get on'.

Quite naturally, the police and the judiciary were entirely unsympathetic to the keening anguish throughout the city. As far as they were concerned, the occasional lack of marijuana was a good thing. Society was clearly far better off drinking itself bloody and broken into the back of their police wagons than sitting at home craving highly specific food combinations like green apples and tasty cheese.

So on this general principle the cops would hound and prosecute dope smokers with zeal. Then the judiciary (most notably in medieval Queensland) would impose shockingly lengthy jail terms for the entirely victimless crime of getting stoned, laughing until your spleen burst, eating too much chocolate and eventually passing out in the clutches of a sweaty vinyl beanbag.

The '80s were a tough time to be a dope smoker. Unless you had a regular, reliable supplier or a few crappy plants hidden somewhere in your back yard, you were doomed to trawl through various pubs asking all sorts of dodgy pricks if you could score a stick of half-decent head. Then there were the phone calls that were never returned and the promises that were never kept. I lost entire weeks of my life waiting for some sack of deeply stoned shit to remember to call me back when he said he would, or remain straight long enough to ride to some rendezvous point with my smoko. So much stress for an ounce (and often much less) of usually quite mediocre marijuana.

The stress levels inside the big crazy green house in Merrylands, a suburb in Sydney's west, where I was living with several dozen of my closest friends during one of the longest marijuana droughts in Australian dope-smoking history, were fast approaching the unendurable end of the scale. It was a living arrangement I have previously described as a cross between utopian Marxism and a pirate ship. This unique set-up was entirely fuelled and sustained by the rich spectrum of drugs enjoyed by outlaw bikers, along with cases of hard liquor and an accommodating Lebanese landlord called Abdul. You can thus imagine the prevailing mood in the house after almost a month without the calming presence of marijuana.

So one night when Badger rode home with a quarter-ounce of dope wrapped in Alfoil, it was as if Christ Jesus Himself had come to impregnate a bunch of handclapping church-virgins one sunny Sunday morning. There were five of us lounging about in the large sunroom at the back of the house that evening, disconsolately drinking beer to try to take the edge of the amphetamine jag we'd all been on for the last two days. Liberal inhalations of marijuana were what we normally used to defray the nervy, incondite descent from the speed high, but since there hadn't been so much as a leaf of dope in the Sydney basin for almost a month, we were using alcohol. Now and then we'd have an impromptu motorcycle drag-race up the street or set fire to something in the back yard. The situation was not at all ideal and made us grumpy, snappy and prone to punching each other in the face when we got on each other's tits. Some kind of barbiturate would have helped, but none of us were all that much into pills, and the idea of paying ten dollars per Valium to some jumpy junkie shithead at the local pub was simply unthinkable.

Big Dima and his sexually enslaved girlfriend, Svetlana, were sitting beside me on the couch. She was dutifully clipping his disgraceful yellow toe-claws and he was picking his nose in sublime contentment. Svetlana was always grooming the big Russian ape in one way or another. I suppose it made a change for her from being endlessly fucked, or choking back his penis while he drank beer and watched the television as a break from fucking her. I was entranced by the whole bestial scene and could not take my eyes off them. I knew exactly how Dian Fossey must have felt studying gorillas in the misty hills of Rwanda. But both Big Dima and Svetlana were devoted and brazen exhibitionists, so they didn't ever mind being stared at.

The two of them lived together in the centre of the house in a room we'd constructed out of cupboards when we first moved in.

Big Dima said he found it 'very much sexiness' knowing we could hear him getting whacked on speed and fucking Svetlana's rather sparse brains out almost every day. None of us minded it much, either, so it was a workable situation for everyone.

On the floor beside the couch, Zorro, our resident dope fiend *par excellence*, was studiously cleaning the house bong in anticipation of greener days, and Mark was shuffling listlessly through our record collection to see if he could improve on the Santana that was currently playing on the stereo and driving us all a little mad. Our edgy tranquillity was suddenly shattered by Badger's hot-rod Sportster thundering down the driveway, and a few minutes later he clumped through the back door and dropped a familiar-looking foil package onto the coffee table.

'Tah-dah,' he said, spreading his arms in the universal gesture of showmanship and grinning like a sunrise. Everyone instantly froze in disbelief. It had been a long time (in terms of dope smoking) since we had last seen any marijuana, so we all gazed in cargo-cultish awe at the wrinkled silver stick before us.

Then Mark fixed Badger with a deadly glare: 'That better not be full of fucken poisonous tree bark – I almost died on that shit you brought last week.'

In our increasing desperation to find something to smoke when the drought really started to bite, we had engaged in a kind of escalating retardation. The smelly speckled dregs floating in the ancient bong water were the first THC-impregnated remnants we'd eagerly dried and smoked. Redfern Hash, as the acrid black paste from inside the bong stem was known, was next. It made us hack like terminal cancer patients and the stone it provided was brief and crappy, but we were becoming a touch frantic. Then Badger had come home with a bag of crushed brown plant-matter he'd bought off some bloke in a pub in North Sydney. It didn't smell like dope, but after getting Badger's money, the bloke assured him it was a perfectly good substitute widely used by Bolivian Indians for centuries. We duly smoked it, and spent the next hour retching and coughing up our weeping souls. We were far too ill to even consider riding back to the pub and stomping the opportunistic prick who sold Badger the shit.

Looking back at Mark, Badger's smile became positively beatific: 'I checked. It's all head.'

'You fucken beauty!' Zorro chirped and the whole room suddenly came to life. I levered myself into a more upright and attentive position, Mark decided that Deep Purple's glorious *Made in Japan* album was to replace Carlos, and Big Dima loudly demanded Svetlana immediately get her tits out and make an occasion of it all. In very short order a mull bowl was produced, followed by a small pair of scissors and the foil package was carefully unwrapped by Zorro as if it contained holy Christian relics.

'Smell that!' Zorro moaned, holding the wrinkled silver foil up to our respective noses. I sniffed and was instantly overjoyed that Badger had indeed found some good-quality smoko. That's one of the most encouraging aspects of buying dope, as opposed to buying pills or powders. You can almost always tell how good the marijuana is going to be by sight and smell alone.

'Mull up,' I declared and took a moment once again to admire Svetlana's delicate young breasts, which were right then on their way to the kitchen to help her put fresh water into the bong. Familiarity was never going to produce contempt where those puppies and I were concerned. As my gaze followed her small panty-clad bum down the hall, I saw her turn right into the kitchen and was immediately concerned to see a bright and entirely inexplicable light shining through the smoked glass panel of our front door. As Zorro snipped happily away with his scissors at the dope in the mull bowl, the light was quite suddenly accompanied by a loud and aggressive banging. I could see human shapes and shadows shifting through the heavily opaque glass of the front door and I felt the bottom of my stomach drop a little bit. There's only one type of visitor who comes banging on your door at night with a piercingly bright flashlight.

'This is the police!' came a muffled bellow from behind the front door.

'Fuck!' I yelped, leaping to my feet and staring wildly around the room. Having never been raided before, it seemed like a suitable action at the time. My friends all looked blankly back at me as the pounding intensified, rattling the glass in the door.

'Open the door! This is the police!'

I looked back up the hall and saw Svetlana pulling her top back on and looking over her shoulder at us for further instructions. Big Dima and I moved as one. I was past her and at the front door while he quickly pushed her back into the kitchen and started shoving all the speed we had in the fridge into her vagina. When I opened the door I was instantly blinded by three torches shining into my eyes.

'Does Jeff Walters live here?' a voice behind one of the torches demanded. I blinked and moved my arm up to shade my eyes. I had no idea if Jeff Walters lived here or not. So many people (most of whom were only nicknames to me) came and went and used our address for all sorts of reasons, it was entirely possible.

'What is your name?' a different voice barked.

I stated my name and was informed they had a warrant to search the living quarters of Jeff Walters.

'How many people live here?' the first voice asked.

'What? Right now?' I asked.

'Yes, dickhead,' the policeman sneered. 'Right fucken now.'

I shrugged. It was an honest response. I had no idea how many people lived there at that moment. That morning there were seven of us. But this was now night time. Things may well have changed.

It was not the response he wanted. Soon I was being propelled backwards down the hall and into the sunroom by five hefty police officers.

'What the fuck's going on here?' asked one of them as he beheld Zorro in mid mull, Mark pulling apart a cigarette to add its tobacco to the mix and Badger shoving the remains of the foil down the front of his jeans.

I hoped this was a rhetorical question. It was perfectly obvious what the fuck was going on. But I hadn't done so well on the last test question, so I kept my mouth shut. This being my first police raid, I was completely nonplussed as to what was going to happen next and figured any further input from me could well be counterproductive. Thus far there were no guns being pointed at anyone and it would be good if things remained like that.

'All of you stay where you are,' ordered the officer holding me by the wrist. He then suddenly took a sharp step backwards as

Big Dima and Svetlana came out of the kitchen and down the hall towards us. Big Dima stood more than six and a half feet tall in his underpants and weighed about the same as good-sized bison. He was liberally etched with bizarre Russian prison tattoos, had five gold teeth and a heavily scarred and shaved head. Svetlana was much smaller, impossibly good-looking and invariably dressed like the lead babe in a cheap porn film. This evening she was in her usual lounging-about-the-house outfit – a tiny pair of panties and a tank-top. They were a striking couple by any measure.

'Vot is fucking problem?' Big Dima demanded, pushing Svetlana behind him in a gesture both fiercely protective and unmistakably aggressive. I saw her grimace a little as she tee-tered around his bulk and briefly wondered how uncomfortable it must be to have several plastic bags full of speed packed inside your vagina.

'Are you Jeff Walters?' the policeman asked. He had reverse-mirrored Big Dima's move when he appeared and was now holding me protectively in front of him.

'No,' Big Dima grinned. 'I em Dimitry Vassiliyevich Byelonogov.'

'I'm Jeff Walters,' I heard Badger say behind me.

Everyone turned to look at him. This was not the name any of us knew him by, but right then was not the time to have that discussion.

'Do you live here?' asked the policeman closest to him, moving even closer and taking him by the wrist. I saw a set of handcuffs appear in the officer's other hand. Badger nodded.

'Which is your room?'

Badger inclined his head over the policeman's shoulder to where Big Dima was standing. 'That one with the green door.' Then I watched him sigh heavily, slump visibly and swallow drily. I actually heard his throat click from two metres away and over the sound of Ian Gillan's masterful 'Child in Time' vocals coming through the stereo.

When we first moved into the Merrylands house, Badger had scored the room with the green door. The green door went with the room's green walls and ceiling and was located between the kitchen and the sunroom. Very shortly after he moved in, it became an Aladdin's Cave of stolen goods, dangerous weapons and prohibited articles. Badger worked in a massive freight-forwarding warehouse and like most of the other employees there, would avail himself of the various goods that came through the place on a daily basis. He told me it was the greatest job he'd ever had and while it didn't pay very well, the working conditions were shithouse and the hours crap, the opportunity to acquire a vast array of loot more than made up for these shortcomings. The stuff he would bring home strapped onto the back of his bike would invariably have us all gaping in awe. Massive wheels of exotic cheese, cases of liquor, boxes of ammunition, clothing, cutlery, stationery, haberdashery, stock feed, fertiliser, tools, nuts, bolts, lengths of wire and cable, clothing, footwear, light fixtures – in short, the entire retail range of everything that most Australian retailers stocked, or ever planned to stock, was available to him. He once arrived home with a clothes dryer lashed to the back of his bike. The next day he arrived with a kerosene heater.

None of us sat in judgment on Badger's thievery, since few of us were in any position to adopt the moral high ground when it came to crime. I used to tell myself that since he wasn't actually breaking into people's houses and stealing their personal belongings, it really wasn't all that bad. He'd normally sell the things he flogged very cheaply, or swap them for drugs, alcohol or bike parts; or he'd just hand random shit out at our parties to people he felt might enjoy a twenty-kilogram tub of Bulgarian fetta cheese, a box of 300 Bic lighters or a case of cherry brandy.

His green bedroom was like a great transitional hub for all the gear he acquired: nothing was ever in there for long and the inventory was constantly changing, but there was invariably a lot of stuff in there at any one time. So we could all understand how he must have been feeling when the cops opened the green door, looked inside, then almost came in their pants at what they beheld.

Badger was then pushed brutally into the wall next to his green door and we could all hear the sharp, metallic rasp that indicated handcuffs were being applied.

'Now then,' said the policeman holding me and looking down at the mull bowl. 'Whose marijuana is this?'

'It's mine!' Badger sang out from the hallway. 'I just fucken bought it!'

My policeman (well, we had been together for a while now and I was getting a little possessive) grunted and shook his head. Then he reached down, grabbed the mull bowl and handed it to another officer, who produced an evidence bag and dumped it all into that.

'That saves lots and lots of paperwork,' he explained, letting go of my arm.

Big Dima put his arm around Svetlana and spat loudly onto the floor. 'Sveta, look vot big pizda[2] dis vun iz. Even det KahGehBeh sabaka[3] I kill in Novgorod voz not ez big pizda ez dis.'

Oh no! I thought. That mad Russian bastard getting his cop-hate on was the last thing this situation needed at that moment. Big Dima had done a few years' hard time, first in some woebegone Russian military prison, then in some dire Siberian gulag for an assortment of violent crimes, before finally being released – whereupon he contrived to escape across the then Soviet border to Finland and somehow made his way to Australia and into my life. And while he made a truly magnificent and loyal friend, he was about as terrible and grim an enemy as you could ever find. I've known lots of hard men in my time, but Big Dima was an order of magnitude harder than almost all of them. Soviet prisons made our penal institutions look like Christian volleyball camps. The men who came out, if they ever did, were either broken, or unbreakable. Big Dima was very much the latter. He was utterly fearless and of the informed opinion that in comparison to the Soviet cops who gave him many of his scars our entire police force was nothing but a vapid herd of mealy-mouthed, soft-bellied man-bitches.

The man-bitches all quite suddenly tensed up and the atmosphere in our sunroom changed very quickly. Since this was before cops carried capsicum spray and Tasers, there were only a few outcomes possible now.

Outcome One: The cops shoot us all.

---

2   The Russian word for cunt.
3   KGB dog

Outcome Two: The cops try to shoot us all, fail in the attempt and shoot themselves and probably wing a few of us.

Outcome Three: The cops attempt to arrest Big Dima, who is certainly not going to be alright with that, and which will then require us not to be alright with that either. This would quickly bring matters back to either Outcome One or Two.

Outcome Four: We all calmly discuss how to move forward in a positive and productive manner.

After a long and impossibly tense thirty seconds, my cop relaxed, shook his head and sighed. 'Look,' he said, glancing at each of us in turn. 'We have what we came for. We're now going to take all those stolen goods out of your mate's room and then we're going to leave.' He gave Big Dima a lingering look. 'We don't want any fucken shit out of any of you. If we get any fucken shit, we can always come back another time and see whose cocks are bigger then.'

The smart police officers always know how to back off without backing off.

'There's no chance of you leaving us some smoko, is there?' Zorro asked plaintively.

The policeman actually smirked. 'None.'

It took two of the cops two quick trips out to their cars to empty Badger's room of all the stolen goods – three cases of El Toro Tequila, a box of Hawaiian Tropic suntan oil, one box of railway detonators, two boxes of Brut 33 deodorant and two plastic bags of Chinese-made thongs. While they did that, my cop was methodically searching Badger by the front door, clearly not planning on putting him in the cop car unless he had been thoroughly searched. When he finished, I saw him deposit

Badger into the back seat of the police car – exactly like I'd seen them do in the movies.

And so my first police raid came to an end. As I was about to close the front door after they left, I noticed something shiny lying on the dirt, just off the broken concrete path that led to the front gate. It was the foil Badger had hurriedly stuffed down his jeans when the cops pushed me into the sunroom. And it was still half full of dope.

I found out later that it wasn't Badger who dropped it there.

SHIT

Yeah ... um, look, sometimes really horrible things happen on a motorcycle. There's nothing you can do about these things. You just have to deal with them as they present themselves.

```
'When suffering knocks at your door
and you say there is no seat for him,
he tells you not to worry because
he has brought his own stool.'
```

CHINUA ACHEBE

Pissing and shitting and motorcycle riding are not a happy threesome. They are, for the most part, hateful flatmates – two of whom gang up on the third and try to slash him with broken beer bottles and dance in his blood. While it's possible to mount an argument for pissing yourself astride a motorcycle ('Look, it was raining, I was wet and cold, I'd drunk a million beers and that last bump was massive and don't fucken look at me like that …'), it's not at all possible to find a world where shitting yourself on a motorcycle is in any way acceptable. It's just not.

Urine is relatively benign. I've used it as brake fluid in a pinch, I understand people drink it for a variety of health reasons and it washes off pretty easily. Shit? Shit is a whole other universe of yuck.

Suddenly realising you're 'touching cloth' when you're stuck in traffic or on a freeway with nowhere to pull over will quickly enable you with riding skills you never imagined you possessed. When that smelly brown turtle starts to nudge its way out, respect for the *Motor Traffic Act* is suddenly something other people have. You will ride like a thousand Valentino Rossis, and break every speed limit and several laws of physics in your efforts to find a suitable place to squat and void. Such is the compulsion of shit.

A man can make a fist of having a wee pretty much anywhere if he is creative, clever and his bladder's teetering on the knife-edge of catastrophic failure. But finding somewhere suitably private to have a shit … well, that's an entirely different story of swinish shame and ignominy.

All of this is compounded astride a motorcycle. I can assure you there is not a single riding position that helps. Each and every one of them, from racer's crouch to cruiser's slouch, only conspires to make the need to shit (or piss) all the more urgent. Once you have added in the motorcycle clothing factor, as anyone who has ever struggled to get out of racing leathers, wet-weather gear or long underwear on the side of some rain-splashed road or box-sized servo toilet will attest, you are in a dire, smelly, nether circle of Hell.

I have contended with the shit demon many times in my riding career. And on all but two occasions I have triumphed against the brown bastard. The other two occasions ... not so much.

My great friend Brother Silverback still refuses to speak of the second episode. He was not present at the first incident, but he was certainly there at the second. Other than rendering me some much-needed assistance and saying 'Catch!' at the appropriate time, he has remained stolidly and stoically silent about the whole thing. Which, I hasten to add, is the only right and proper course of action between friends. He knows I would be entirely within my rights to stab him if he ever brought it up. But to tell you about my first episode, I must first break you in with my second. Trust me. It's better this way ...

My second descent into Shit Hell began quite innocently. I'm sure passengers on the *Titanic* were all sweetness and light as they set sail, too. This particularly splendid and bright Monday morning, immediately after the MotoGP at Phillip Island in Victoria, Brother Silverback and I were wending our way vaguely north. Our aim was to rejoin the Hume Highway at the town of Euroa and grind our way home to Sydney that same day.

We were both hungover, which was not at all unusual for the Monday after the MotoGP weekend. What was unusual was that I was hungover on a much deeper and more reprehensible genetic level – a level that Brother Silverback simply could not achieve.

My chromosomes felt like flecks of spiked vomit lurching through my abused body. Each bump and curve on the road only served to amplify my physical misery, which was deep and ill and cruel. I was nursing the kind of hangover that comes along only rarely in a man's life – the kind of hangover that shortens and shames his time upon this earth – but somehow, perversely, also enriches it.

Brother Silverback felt better than me. He always did. Whenever we managed to pollute ourselves with excess, he invariably fared more successfully. I put this down to his much larger mass and iron-clad intolerance for any solids while drinking.

On this occasion, he had more than matched me drink for drink over the preceding five days. It was a truly heroic effort by both of us. The only difference was that Brother Silverback had, wisely as it turned out, refrained from venturing into the abyss of substance abuse I had so eagerly descended into. And he'd certainly had nothing at all to do with the family-sized pepperoni pizza with double cheese and an entire jar of dried chilli poured on top – because that was one of my brightest ideas the night before we left for home.

To his eternal glory, he made no comment as I explained my dietary needs to the appalled man in the stained apron behind the pizza counter. For reasons I can only put down to a massive and very much self-inflicted chemical imbalance, I had a craving for spicy food in general and pizza in particular.

The next day, as we approached Euroa, I realised the pizza had not been such a great concept. Things were happening in my lower bowel that filled me with panic and despair. Bizarre and unnatural noise from my abdomen could be heard clearly above the 140-kms-per-hour wind-noise, and each time I shifted my weight to negotiate a bend in the road, a spasm would signal that the unspeakably toxic garbage I'd enjoyed over the last five days was now planning its coming-out party.

Euroa was still some 40 kilometres away. I had now begun to sweat and nudged the bike up to 180 kms per hour. I was desperate and becoming more unhinged by the second. There was no question. I simply *had* to make toilet in Euroa before the log-jam of sigmoidal putrescence came a-geysering out of my ruthlessly clenched clacker.

But it was not to be. Critical mass had been reached and Brother Silverback was suddenly treated to a massive back-wheel lock-up as I desperately tried to avoid colossal self-befoulment. The bike was still running and the dust from the road shoulder on which I had somehow managed to stop was still swirling as I scuttled into a paddock of thigh-high grain. And there, among the gently swaying crops, commenced The Horror.

I now need to point out there are few things in a man's life as complex as trying to squat-poo in a field while dressed in track boots, leather racing pants, long underwear and a three-quarter-length touring jacket. The logistics are nightmarish. First, my pants could not be lowered sufficiently due to the height of the boots and the pants' massive knee-padding and knee-slider arrangement all conspired to prevent me dropping my pants anywhere lower than mid-thigh. Mid-thigh is not where you want your pants to be when the devil-bog from colo-hell is on its unstoppable way out of your shrieking rectum. Secondly, there was nothing to hold onto for balance as I swayed and stumbled and squatted, other than nettle-filled clumps of beige-coloured grass. Thirdly, I should have taken my jacket off, because its tail was now folded under me, precisely where I did not need it to be folded at this crucial juncture.

And then, with a suddenness that beggars belief, I, as a man, was taken out of the equation. The searing jet-stream of a million beers, untold amounts of criminally crappy trackside food, a dizzying assortment of nose-scorching chemicals, heavily polluted bong-water inadvertently ingested, and the hottest pizza in all of southern Australia erupted from my puckered bunghole like pressurised caramel sauce from a fire hose. The smell was crippling. I clung to the grass with the brute desperation of a man made utterly wretched, debased, in pain and completely scandalised by his bowel.

I opened my tear-filled eyes but dared not to look down. I could see Brother Silverback peering at me from his vantage point on the road. He knew, on a very basic level, what was going on in that field, but luckily he wasn't privy to the sheer scale of the all-encompassing grisliness going on south of my belly-button. The grass was just long enough to hide my disgrace. And I was grateful there was a wind from the north. It was helpfully blowing the stench away from Brother Silverback and effectively masking the pathetic keening noises I had been making since my ordeal began.

I dry-swallowed and breathed through my mouth. The wind was good, but not good enough to spare me from the thick miasma of backdoor evil that pervaded my immediate vicinity. Then I felt the spasms passing, and I trembled a little with gratitude. My bumhole felt like someone had taken a burning heat-bead and poked it just inside the opening. But that was bearable when compared to the grotesque apocalypse I saw when I finally mustered the courage to look down. My awkward quarter-squat in the field had ensured that not only had I covered the tail of my jacket with my noxious, oozing cack, but I had also managed to splatter the waistband of my pants and the backs of my boots. And my inability to spread my legs properly had ensured a generous coating for my shuddering buttocks.

'I need toilet paper, water, some rags and a clean pair of jeans, please,' I informed Brother Silverback, and threw up a little into my mouth as the stench made its way down my throat.

The items were bundled and thrown to me with remarkable accuracy, with the word 'Catch!' assisting their flight. I was immensely glad that I was able to do so.

———

A decade before that dark and dreadful time in the field outside Euroa, I had an even more appalling experience. I have told very few people about this incident and despite the distance of many years separating me from it, the memory of what happened between Kong and me on the frozen steppes between Sydney and Thredbo still raises the hair on the back of my head. Because no matter how unspeakable dealing with your own shit is, dealing with someone else's is several orders of bastardry worse.

Kong came into my life when I was living in the crazy green house in Merrylands in much the same way so many of my friends and acquaintances at that time came into my life. He just appeared one day, introduced himself as the cousin of one of the club members and helped me sort out the back brake on my Shovelhead.

I was instantly in bro-love with him. He was a big man, almost as big as Big Dima (who was the very definition of 'big'), bearded like a Viking, and carried an unimpeachable outlaw heritage having once been a member of another outlaw club. He was nicknamed Kong because his surname was King and his physical presence resembled the movie monster in more ways than many people were comfortable with. But like most big men (and Big Dima was one of the few exceptions) Kong was essentially gentle, though there was a lurking madness in his eyes which promised a veritable smorgasbord of destruction if required.

He would come around now and again, and since neither party was interested in him joining our merry band of psychopaths, he was always a most welcome and valued guest.

Until the day he fell in love with Big Dima's girlfriend, Svetlana. Fortunately for peace in our time, Big Dima was becoming even larger and more horrible while he spent a year in one of Her Majesty's prisons, and was not around when Kong lost his nuts over his girlfriend. Never the sharpest knife in the drawer, Svetlana was nonetheless fanatically faithful to her man, and quite nonplussed when Kong declared his undying love for her. He stated he would leave his wife of ten years, forget his three children, damn his burgeoning construction company to buggery and spend the rest of his days brushing his teeth with her sweet-scented shit, if only she would agree to the union. And he would state this *ad nauseam* every time he came over to visit, which had now become almost daily. I'd started thinking of hitting him up for rent, but since he always brought over vast quantities of alcohol and drugs, threw them onto our communal drug-snorting table and proceeded to get as baked as a thrice-glazed ham, I tended to defer that conversation. Besides, it's not like he actually ever slept or ate at our house.

Quietly, I sympathised with him. Svetlana was certainly the kind of girl a man would shamelessly ruin himself over, but she was devoted to Big Dima and that, in my social milieu, was pretty much that. We would look after her until he returned, and if that meant shooting Kong if he decided to take his affection for her to the next level, then we would shoot the big bastard, making sure we used the heaviest loads in the shotgun.

As it was, his love for her manifested itself in an altogether benign and really rather pathetic way. We would hear his big Harley-Davidson Ultra Glide rumble down our drive, then hear him unpacking his drugs and booze from the cavernous top-box. When that slammed shut, we would hear his heavy tread clump up the back stairs, followed by an 'It's me!' bellow, and within seconds, a giant bag of speed would land on the table, followed by a case of beer and two casks of Kong's favourite booze – the unspeakably vile piss called Fruity Lexia, a sour-sweet white wine blend obviously made from the fermented urine of tortured cats who had been force-fed polluted grapes from birth.

Svetlana would dutifully appear in her usual lounge-about-the-house outfit of panties and singlet, say hello by pecking him on the cheek then cart the beer off to the fridge and return, plonking a big glass in front of Kong. Subsequently she would go back to the room made out of cupboards she normally shared with Big Dima and resume waiting for him to be released from prison.

Next, as if following a script, Kong would sigh deeply, his eyes trailing her ridiculously perfect arse as she left the room. He

175

would open the cask, fill the glass, dump a vast amount of speed onto the mirror we'd affixed to the top of the table for just that purpose and proceed to cut lines the size of cigarettes.

'Fuck, she's beautiful,' he'd murmur as he expertly shaped and chopped the methamphetamine with a knife. 'Fuck, I love her. Fuck.' Then he would proceed to fuck himself – alternately snorting lines and swilling Fruity Lexia with a determination that always left me breathless.

He was a big man, but the amount of gak he would inhale was truly epic. After each line (and he would always have four in one go because, as he explained, four lines at once was what 'separated the men from the poofters') he would glug down some wine. So it went: 'Snoorgh! Gulp. Snoorgh! Gulp. Snoorgh! Gulp. Snoorgh! Gulp. Snoooooooooorgh, hack, sniffle, sniffle.' His eyes would bulge even further and he would list Svetlana's manifold charms, how much he adored her, how he would joyously lick the toilet bowel she relieved herself in, eat her toe-nail clippings and permit her to tread on his private parts with her high-heeled shoes. We were used to it, and while I would commiserate with him, I would repeatedly point out to him that Svetlana was off-limits – we were prepared to indulge his madness for her while Big Dima was in jail, but he had to understand there was no hope his love for her would ever be requited.

'I'll kill the cunt!' Kong would declare. 'Fuck him. I'll get myself locked up, find him and kill him!' I doubted that was possible in a face-to-face confrontation with Big Dima, but Kong was not averse to shanking people in the back, so his threats could not be totally discounted.

Whenever he started on this tack, I would remind him that if he got himself locked up, his almost daily sessions of Svetlana-worship, drug abuse and Fruity Lexia would end, and I'd have no one to help me out with my Shovelhead's mechanical foibles. Which, much like Kong's love for Svetlana, were unending.

Kong would acknowledge my wisdom in this regard and our snorting and drinking sessions would continue until the first cask was empty, whereupon Kong would belch, chop up a few more lines, and declare himself reconciled with his lot in this life. He would love Svetlana from afar, he'd say. His love would be pure and chaste and he would content himself with masturbating furiously in our toilet while holding a pair of her dirty panties up to his nose.

He had stolen these panties from the floor of her room one day and guarded them with the tenacity of a junkyard dog, refusing to surrender them and begging us not to let the issue come to knives.

'Please,' he yowled when we confronted him clutching the pale-yellow scrap of underwear in his vast fist. 'Let me keep them. Don't be bastards about this, she's got lots of undies. I just want this one fucken pair. Let's just have a line and move on.'

He was persuasive in this regard, and seeing as Svetlana shrugged it off as being nothing more than one of the bizarre man-things she was constantly exposed to, we snorted the proffered lines and duly moved on. Then, as these things invariably do, it all came to a head and shit, quite literally, happened.

The incident shook me to a core I didn't even know I had and Kong and I parted ways not long afterwards – which was the only honourable thing either of us could do. It began one Thursday afternoon in late autumn and Kong arrived as usual, dumped an indictable amount of drugs on our table and cracked his first cask open. Svetlana was all dolled up and on her way out with a few of the other girls, and when she appeared with Kong's glass, we all caught our breath. She was, by any definition, a walking wet dream that afternoon. And the noises Kong started making in his throat when he clapped eyes on her were quite alarming. She clicked into our shabby speed-snorting room on wicked fuck-me heels, a tiny top and a tight leather skirt so short it was pornographic. She had sprayed herself with Big Dima's favourite perfume, which on any other girl would be a noxious blend of cheap flowers and vaguely musky chemicals, but which managed to smell like sweet damnation when she wore it.

'You look fucken beautiful!' Kong wheezed.

'Thank you,' Svetlana smiled cautiously. Kong made this declaration almost every time he saw her, and her response was always guarded and polite.

'Where are you going?' he asked.

'I'm going to the pub with the other girls,' she said.

'Which pub?'

Svetlana's eyes darted towards me in supplication. No doubt she had visions of Kong turning up to join her on the dance floor – and no one wanted to experience that again after the last time it happened and the police had to be called to stop Kong murdering the entire clientele of the pub after a few of the locals started to applaud his moves on the dance floor. I can't blame them. Seeing a man that large and fierce on his knees in front of a girl dressed like a porn star while shimmying his shoulders like an Iranian bellydancer was certainly worthy of applause.

'Just the local, mate,' I lied. 'Management will look after them there.' I actually had no idea where the girls were going and didn't much care. They could look after themselves and I knew that one or two of the members would probably ride herd on them to make sure they actually *could* look after themselves.

'Fuck, you look so beautiful,' Kong repeated. 'Wanna line?'

Svetlana leaned over the table and her tiny skirt rode up as she shnorked back half of one of the massive lines arrayed on the table's mirror. I think that was the moment Kong went insane.

'Oh fuck ... fuck ...' he gagged, jumping up and rushing off to the bathroom to abuse himself. Svetlana wiped her pretty little nose, shook her head and left.

Mark, Badger and I sat there quietly for a few minutes listening to Kong masturbating savagely a few metres away. He returned, his face shiny with sweat, had four quick lines, then another two and demanded we bring him tequila.

'Fuck it!' he roared when he'd slammed down three shots. 'Fuck it, fuck it, fuck it! I can't go on like this!' The three of us exchanged concerned glances.

Kong then poured himself a full schooner glass of tequila, grabbed a teaspoonful of speed between his sausagey fingers, dumped it into the glass and made a concerted effort to scull it. Getting the concoction down his neck took him two goes, but when he'd finished there was an awe-filled silence in the room.

'You okay?' Badger asked quietly.

Kong's watery red eyes roamed the room for a second as if looking for the source of the voice. Then they locked onto Badger. 'No, arsehole,' he slurred. 'I'm not fucken okay. I'm fucked. And I'm gonna get more fucked. And then I'm gonna die and this bullshit will be over.'

We all exchanged more meaningful stares. This did not sound promising, and a pleasant evening of drinking and partying was starting to look doubtful. Kong was making a growling sound in his throat and his hands were twitching. His face was so suffused with blood it was almost brown and his eyes were unfocused and red with despair and madness.

'Who wants a fucken line?' he demanded through gritted teeth. When there was no immediate response from us, he barked contemptuously, upended his voluminous bag of methamphetamine onto the mirror and proceeded to carve the fattest lines I had ever seen. They were like white pencils of disaster.

'Got any bourbon?' he growled. 'The fucken tequila is giving me a gut-ache.'

Mark went to his room and returned with a bottle of Jack Daniel's.

'Fucken Jack!' Kong cheered. 'I love fucken Jack.'

He poured himself a glass of the amber fluid, shovelled another chunk of speed into it and sipped at it like it was hot tea. Three sips later, half the glass was gone and Kong was clearly hitting his stride. He snorted a pencil and passed me the straw.

'Have a fucken line, you cunt,' he grinned. 'Don't be a cunt.'

I made an effort, but the pencil defeated me about a third of the way along. My brain felt like it was going to ooze out of my right eye.

'What about youse cunts?' Kong asked, snatching the straw off me and pointing it at Mark and Badger. They shared the rest of the pencil between them while Kong looked on and sipped at the remaining Jack-and-speed in his glass.

'Fuck, I love her,' he intoned to the room. 'I love her so fucking much.'

'I know, mate,' I said gently, putting my hand on his massive shoulder.

'No, you fucken don't,' he breathed, and then he started to cry. Great hacking sobs rocked him and snot tinged with blood dribbled out of his nose as he wept.

Mark, Badger and I watched him in silence. We didn't know what else to do. Then, as if someone had flipped a switch in his head, he snuffled back the ropes of gory snot dribbling down into his moustache, grabbed the straw, shnorked back two massive lines in quick succession, guzzled the rest of his drink and fell off the chair. He convulsed once or twice then lay still.

'Check his pulse,' Badger suggested and I put my hand to his neck. His pulse was rapid but strong. His blood pressure must have been 480 over 200, given the amount of speed he'd ingested in the last hour, but it did not occur to any of us to call an ambulance. Our own respective sky-high blood pressures were preventing any serious clarity of thought, so we just let him lie there for a while.

When his beeper went off, we all jumped. Kong woke up, fumbled for the beeper at his belt, brought it up to his face, peered at it intently then crawled along the floor to where the phone was. He swept it off the table, reassembled it and dialled.

'What?' he growled into the mouthpiece. He listened for a few seconds, his eyes closed and his breathing ragged and uneven. 'What? Now?' he rasped and listened again. 'Fuck!' Dropping the phone to the ground, he started to lever himself upright. 'Chop some lines,' he snarled at me. 'I'm going to Thredbo.'

'There's no way you're going to Thredbo,' I said. 'You're so fucked you're probably going to go to hospital at some stage. But sure as shit you're not going to Thredbo.'

Thredbo, in case you're wondering, is a ski-resort town about 500 kilometres from Sydney – at the time a six-hour ride on a good day, with the Road Gods smiling upon you. It was now about six o'clock in the evening and looking like rain.

Kong eased himself back onto his chair and poured himself a glass of Fruity Lexia. 'I'm fucken going to Thredbo,' he stated flatly. 'I have to sign off on the work contract I have down there. It has to be signed and witnessed by 9 am tomorrow. I have to go.'

'Fine,' I said, standing up. 'I'm going with you.'

Kong looked up at me, his eyes flickering with alarm and craziness. Then he grinned crookedly. 'You'd best have a line then,' he said and began moving the remaining speed into more human-sized lines.

An hour later, we were geared up and I was reminding Kong how to start his bike. He had entered some realm of purely divine and disjointed madness, and while he could walk and talk (more or less) he seemed to have forgotten important things. 'That's the gear lever, isn't it?' he mumbled, pounding the brake lever with his boot.

'No, that's on the other side,' Mark told him. 'And do up your top pocket. You don't want that shit blowing all over the road.'

'Right, yes, thanks,' Kong said, scrabbling at his jacket where he'd tucked his bag of speed. He then licked his finger, dipped it into the bag and popped the coated digit into his mouth, grimacing.

I lit a cigarette and considered with not a little alarm what awaited us on the ride south.

'You really should give those things away,' Kong observed, fastening his battered helmet and making strange shapes with his mouth as the speed worked its way around his maw. 'They'll fucken kill you.'

I felt his concern for my health was sweet, but his timing in offering it somewhat misplaced.

We started our bikes and headed off into the night. Our pace was measured and I rode a few metres behind Kong, amazed at his ability to function on any level, let alone ride a giant Harley, after what I had seen him ingest. I was extremely concerned about a whole range of issues as we made our way onto the expressway and the cold started to make itself known. It was autumn, we were heading into what is known as 'snow country', the sky was obscured by cloud, and I was mildly drunk and buzzing furiously on speed. My companion was catastrophically pissed and had enough methamphetamine in his blood to fly fighter jets into battle for a month. What could possibly go wrong? My question was answered when I felt rain hitting my face.

'Great,' I muttered, mentally steeling myself for a difficult ride. We had just passed Campbelltown on the outskirts of Sydney and the rain seemed to ease every few seconds, only to fleck me again. Then I realised it wasn't rain.

I sped up and came roaring up beside Kong. 'Pull over!' I shrieked, waving my arm at him and gagging. In the glow of my headlight, my horror was confirmed. Kong had befouled himself, massively, and was sitting in his own filth. His jacket had ridden up and I could see liquid shit working its way up his back and being blown backwards by the wind.

We eased onto the side of the road, Kong crabbed off his bike and collapsed in the breakdown lane. He had shit and piss and who knows what other bodily fluids all over him. It had seeped down both his legs and up his back. It was as if he had been submerged in excrement up to his waist. The stench was insane. He smelled like a plague-corpse. I could feel dried bits of shit on my face, and I could see flecks of it on my sunglasses and on the front of my jacket. There were spots of it all over my headlight and forks. Some had probably gone into my mouth as I rode. I threw up next to him.

'Errrggllgh,' he moaned and rolled helplessly into my vomit. I immediately threw up again, and by the sounds I could hear over the odd passing truck, Kong was still spasmodically evacuating his bowels.

This was it, I thought. I had reached rock-bottom. My life was piss, shit, vomit and this giant, bearded, love-struck, drug-fucked, shit-smeared bastard, who was my companion in this lunatic purgatory I was in.

'I feel sick,' Kong groaned.

'Fuck you,' I rasped. 'Fucken die.'

I was completely at a loss. Being covered in someone else's shit was an entirely new experience for me and I was unmanned. I remember slowly spinning in a circle as cars whizzed by, their occupants cheerily oblivious to my despair.

'Have you got any water?' I demanded from the prostrate Kong.

'In the top-box,' he moaned.

I opened his top-box and saw he had another cask of Fruity Lexia in there, but no water.

'There's no fucking water in here, you fucker!'

'I thought there was,' he muttered.

I pulled out the cask of wine, tore off my jacket, jumper and sloppy joe, then pulled my T-shirt off. I used the wine and my T-shirt to clean my face, glasses and jacket as best I could. My world now smelled nauseatingly of cheap wine, vomit and shit, which was marginally better than just smelling of vomit and shit.

'What are we going to do?' Kong wanted to know.

'We have a choice,' I said heavily. 'I can ride off and leave you here to fucken die in your own shit, because there's not enough wine on earth to clean you, or you can get up, get on your bike and we're going to ride to the Pheasant's Nest servo and deal with it there.'

'How far is that?'

'Not far,' I said.

And it wasn't. The all-night truck-stop and service station was maybe twenty kilometres up the road.

'I don't know if I can get that far,' Kong said plaintively.

I glared daggers at him. 'Then we're left with option one.'

'Please don't tell Svetlana about this,' he moaned. 'Please. Promise me.'

'I promise. Now get up, fuck ya.'

'Help me up.'

'You're on your own there.'

'Fuck,' he groaned. Then he moistened a finger, reached into his jacket pocket, pulled out a dab of speed and put it in his mouth. He shook his big head as the drug worked its evil sorcery on him, and a few seconds later he was upright. He was a sight to behold. There were literally litres of liquefied shit inside his pants and, now that he was standing it was oozing down his legs and pooling at his feet, except for the stuff leaking into his boots. When he threw his leg awkwardly over the bike, flecks of it splattered across the freeway and I felt my gorge rising again.

'You go first,' he said, like there was some choice in the matter.

We rode off into the night, and a few minutes later we rolled into the neon-lit oasis. I idled around the back to where the trucks were parked and it was dark enough so that affronted drivers wouldn't recoil in horror and call the police when they beheld the two shit-coated bikies. We stopped the bikes and I told Kong to wait while I checked to see if the toilets were occupied. It was still relatively early, so there were only a few big rigs parked up and I figured the drivers were either inside eating or in their cabs sleeping. If the Road Gods were kind, the toilets would be empty and I, and a billion litres of running water, could start to deal with things.

The omens were good. The toilets were deserted. I offered a silent thanks, splashed water all over myself and used the paper hand towels to clean myself as well as I could. I really needed a hot shower, but that was not an option. Once I was as clean I as I could get, I made my way back to Kong who, to my unending dismay, had not been idle in my absence. He had contrived to take off his unspeakable jeans and underpants, which lay in a noisome pile a few metres away, and was leaning on his bike furiously masturbating with one hand while holding Svetlana's panties to his face with the other. The big motherfucker was nothing if not hardcore and consistent.

'Get into the fucken shitters now, you mad fuck!' I hissed.

He stopped jerking off and we skulked into the toilets, where I watched the door while he clumsily cleaned himself. I did my best not to look and stayed by the entrance, since the smell was still overpowering, but my own drug-addled consciousness could not help but find the whole scene obscenely funny. It was like being in some lunatic director's D-grade road film.

Kong was quite unsteady on his feet, so he was on his knees in front of the hand-basin, spurting water into his shit-filled boots and muttering under his breath. There were piles of wet, cack-smeared paper towels all over the rest-room and the acrid pong of sour excrement was thick. There was no doubt in my mind the servo staff would be dialling triple zero the second someone ran up to tell them about the holocaust going on in the toilets. But luck remained with us and no one needed to use the facilities while Kong washed himself as best he could. When he finished we went back to the bikes and considered what to do.

'I still have to go to Thredbo,' he said flatly.

'You're in no fucken state to go anywhere,' I observed.

'Fuck,' he said suddenly and scuttled off into the nearby trees.

I heard him squirting poison out of his arse and swearing.

'Can you get me some toilet paper?' he called.

What could I do? Say no? I walked back to the toilets, excused myself as I edged past the truck driver who was standing in the doorway wondering what obscene ritual had recently taken place in there, grabbed a roll of toilet paper and walked back out.

'Here,' I said, tossing Kong the roll. 'Look, maybe if we got to Goulburn, found a motel and lay up for a few hours, we'll be able to get there in the morning.' Despite everything, I was still not about to let him ride off on his own.

'I can't sleep,' he burped, stumbling out of the bushes, clutching the toilet paper. His penis jiggled maniacally from side to side. It was a most disturbing sight.

I doubted he would ever sleep again, given the amount of speed he'd had; I was certainly not going to get any shut-eye for at least the next week myself. 'You need to do something about the fact that you have no pants,' I said. 'That would be my first priority.'

Kong looked at the noxious mound of his former jeans a few metres away. 'I don't think I can wear pants at the moment,' he said, rubbing a hand over his belly. 'My stomach problems aren't over.'

I figured his stomach problems were just beginning, but the fact remained that it was going to be awkward to ride anywhere if he had no pants. There was still a long way to go to Thredbo and it was starting to get seriously cold. That aside, if the police happened to stop us, any explanation I might be prepared to offer them would probably get us shot.

We walked over to his jeans, looked at them, then looked at each other. 'You're gonna have to wash them out,' I told him.

'I can't,' he whined. 'I just fucken can't.'

'They're your pants – I'm not washing them.'

Kong just stared at the disgusting heap of cotton and crap on the ground.

'Look, I'll help you, okay?'

His look of plaintive gratitude was overwhelming. 'Wait here,' I said and walked off into the bush. I returned with a metre-long branch and handed it to him. 'Here ya go. There's a hose over there.'

Kong took the stick, hooked it into his jeans and carried them over to the hose. Thankfully it was at the side of the servo, so his pants-less penis-out shame would not be on show in the brightly lit forecourt.

He spent the next five minutes firing a jet of water at his jeans, while I smoked and watched with amazement at just how much shit was being hosed out of them. He must have emptied both intestines of everything he'd eaten for the past year. When he finished, he wrung out the water, then dropped the pants, grabbed the toilet roll from his bike and ran off into the scrub again, his bare arse reflecting the small amount of light coming from the front of the servo. When he returned he was pale and waxy. 'I feel fucken terrible.'

'I'm sure you do. But if you want to go to Thredbo, we need to make some miles. Put your pants on and let's go.'

He was not about to be pressured into pants. 'I'm going,' he said, digging around in his bag of speed again. 'But I am not wearing pants.'

What could I do? He had decided not to wear pants and I was old enough to know that arguing with serial drug fiends who don't wish to wear pants is a zero-sum game.

I fuelled up both bikes while Kong waited in the dark, then we mounted up and headed south. It was certainly cold, but not unbearable. At least, that was my view and I was wearing jeans. Kong, on the other hand, must have been feeling the bite. But his headlight remained a steady ten metres behind me. Now and again I would notice his headlight veer off to the left and weave. After the third time this happened, I realised he was actually taking a shit. He explained to me later that when he felt it coming on, he would lever himself upright, place one knee on the seat, arch his back and just let it spew, hoping that the wind would carry it off. And for the most part, the wind did just that. But when we stopped for petrol on the outskirts of Canberra it was obvious the wind did not do a great job. There was a smear of dried foulness that ran from the seat, across the top of the right pannier and up the side of the top-box.

Once again I fuelled up the bikes while Kong wandered off into the sparse scrub of the median strip to spew his venomous shit into the grass. It was almost midnight, and the traffic coming into Canberra via the Federal Highway was pretty light. Provided the service station manager didn't see my no-pants mate and his horrid cock bobbing across the road, and provided he didn't wonder too much about why I was fuelling two bikes when I could really only ride one, we were sweet.

As we made our way down Canberra's deserted Northbourne Avenue, approaching the main city centre of Civic, Kong suddenly roared past me, veered hard left, went up onto the footpath and disappeared between some pine trees. We'd just gone past the Rex Hotel and there was a large green space running perpendicularly away on both sides of Northbourne Avenue. It was into this park-like area that Kong had disappeared.

I figured he needed to shit again, so I pulled up and waited. And waited. And waited. Then I started up my Harley and rode after him. About a hundred metres in, I saw Kong's bike lying on its side and him lying on his back beside it. I slid to a halt and jumped off, thinking he had crashed, but then I realised that's not what had happened. For starters, the bike was switched off. Then there was the fact that there were no skid-marks in the grass. The big bastard must have decided he needed to lie down, stopped, turned the bike off, got off it, then laid the bike down on its side and lain down beside it.

But he was not asleep. I could see his big bug eyes staring at me. 'You're not asleep, are you?'

'Fuck no,' he said. 'I just needed to lie down for a bit.'

'What about Thredbo?' I asked.

'I just need to lie down for a bit,' he repeated.

I figured that was fair enough. 'Do you wanna put your pants on? Seeing you lying there without your pants is freaking me the fuck out.'

Kong thought about this for a bit. 'No, I don't think I'm ready for pants yet,' he said, then he rolled onto his side and proceeded to shit himself. Again.

I took a step back. Wow, I thought. He is seriously fucked up. If he can shit while lying on his side, this is pretty special.

'Can I have some wine?' he asked when his arse had finished doing what it had been doing pretty much since we left Sydney.

'Sure,' I said, levering open his top-box and pulling out the half-full cask of Fruity Lexia. 'Can I have some speed?' I asked him as I handed over the cask. 'I think my edge needs sharpening.'

'No problem,' Kong smiled weakly, digging in his jacket pocket and handing me a rumpled plastic baggie still containing a respectable amount of goey. I dipped a wet finger in and popped it into my mouth. The acrid metallic taste made me grimace and my gorge rose, but the Fruity Lexia helped my gag reflex to relax a little. I plonked wearily down on the grass on the opposite side of where he'd shat, and we sat quietly for a few minutes.

'Want me to pick up your bike?' I asked.

'That'd be cool, mate. Thanks.'

I levered up the big Harley, leaned it on its stand and sat back down next to Kong, who was once again lying on his back. He had squirmed a metre or so away from the puddle of his fiend-ish arse-juice, and the breeze was blowing the stench away from us. So all things considered – the soft green grass, the brisk snap in the air and the fact that neither of us were in jail or hospital but rather in Australia's capital city – we weren't too badly off. At least we weren't on the road spraying rancid bum-liquid at the cars we passed.

We sat in companionable silence for a while, then Kong spoke. 'I don't really have to go to Thredbo, you know.'

'What?' I was gobsmacked.

'I lied. I don't have to go to Thredbo. There's no contract I have to sign.'

For a few lunatic seconds, I considered pulling out my folding Buck knife and plunging it repeatedly into Kong's belly, chest, neck and face. It seemed, given my mental state at the time, an entirely reasonable thing to do. I felt that even he would under-stand as he bled out on the dewy grass.

'Mate, seriously, what the fuck? I don't get it. Why are we here? Why have we ridden all this way?'

Taking a deep breath, Kong levered himself up onto an elbow.

He looked bizarre. The top half of him was still dressed in his riding gear; the bottom half was naked, pale and largely hairless, apart from the bush of dark pubic hair surrounding his shrunken cock. His eyes were wide and staring, but his breathing was even and I could sense he was probably not as insane as he was an hour ago.

'It's Svetlana,' he said. 'It's all about Svetlana.'

'Svetlana is not here, you prick.'

'Yes, but she's at the pub.'

I looked at my watch. It was almost midnight. Svetlana and the girls would certainly still be at the pub. They were all so full of Kong's methamphetamine, they would probably be in the pub until it closed, whereupon they would all go home, turn up the stereo and dance like crazy in their underpants until the sun came up. And instead of being there to admire them, I was lying on the ground in a Canberra park with a certifiable lunatic bullshit artist and a puddle of his noxious shit.

'I don't understand. Please make me understand.'

'You know when my pager went off?'

I nodded.

'That was my wife. And you know when I made that phone call?'

I nodded again.

'I didn't actually call anyone. I just pretended to call.'

'So what was this bullshit about Thredbo and contracts?'

'I wasn't thinking clearly. It was the first thing that popped into my head.'

I sat up. Then I stood up. 'Listen,' I said evenly. 'I understand you are fucked up. I am also fucked up, but I am not as fucked up as you. You are not making any fucken sense to me at all. I have just ridden 300 shit-splashed kilometres with a half-naked, dysentery-riddled arsehole who has left a trail of his demonic shit all over two major highways, a truck-stop, his bike, my bike, himself and fucken me! I did this because I did not want to let this drug-fucked pisshead, my mate, ride off into the mountains at night. And now we are here, with 200 more kilometres to go, and you're telling me we don't have to be here? What the fuck?'

Kong was staring at the grass, still up on one elbow. His other hand was wiping the speed-sweat from his bearded face. The wind had dropped and the smell of shit was once again cloaking us both.

'I was going to go to the pub and put it on Svetlana,' he finally said.

'Put fucken what on fucken Svetlana!' I shrieked.

'I was gonna ask her to go away with me.'

If my jaw had not been clenched with methamphetamine abuse, it would have dropped. 'Go where?'

'I don't know. Just away. To be with me. I love her so much. I know we would be happy.' There were actual tears in his eyes when he said this.

'And what were you going to do when she told you to fuck off and leave her alone?'

He blinked the tears away and they ran down his face. 'I was gonna kill myself,' he said, his voice breaking with emotion.

But I wasn't letting him off the hook just yet. Too much shit had literally gone down for me to just shrug all this off and move on. 'So why the bastard-fuck did we just ride all this way?'

'That's your fault. I just said I had to go to Thredbo so you wouldn't tell me I couldn't go to the pub and be with her. Then when you said you'd go to Thredbo with me ...'

'You cunt,' I said. 'You fucken stupid crazy fucken shitting cunt.'

'I'm sorry,' he moaned. 'I wasn't thinking clearly.'

That was the first thing he had said in recent times that made any sense. I'm sure he wasn't thinking clearly. Hell, *I* wasn't thinking all that clearly myself at the time.

'Fuck,' I said.

'I'm sorry.'

'Fuck.'

'I'm sorry.'

I walked off. If I couldn't smell his shit, it would probably help me to think. And if I wasn't looking at him lying there with his pants off, I might not give in to the urge to stab him a million times.

In reality there was really not all that much to think about. The bottom line was that Kong and I were still in a Canberra park at midnight reeking of shit. We had maybe a quarter cask of Fruity Lexia left, a few grams of speed, and about 200 dollars. There was not all that much open at this hour; no motel or hotel would admit us, but thanks to the drugs, neither of us was hungry and neither of us was cold. We were both probably certifiable, but Canberra being Canberra, we were hardly alone in that regard.

I went back to where Kong was still lying on the ground near our bikes and his personal little shit-pond.

'I'm sorry,' he keened when he saw me.

'I know. Shit happens.'

He nodded. 'I think my guts feel better.'

'There's probably nothing left to shit.'

He nodded again. 'You wanna line?'

I nodded and reached for the proffered bag.

If you're gonna be a bear, you might as well be a grizzly. Albeit one that smells like shit.

'HI, IT'S US AGAIN – THE COPS.'

This time, when the cops came to visit, they came with all their toys and hatred in their black hearts. I cannot blame them. They thought they were fighting crime and bringing evildoers to justice – and if that meant sifting through a girl's underpants drawer, then so be it.

I was trying to make a fresh start after moving out of the green house in Merrylands following an orgy of drug-fuelled destruction. So there was actually no crime and no evil going on at all in my new place. Still, karma has a way of catching up with you and all your firearms.

> 'There's only two people in your
> life you should lie to. The police
> and your girlfriend.'
>
> **JACK NICHOLSON**

Being raided by the police is fundamentally dissimilar from them calling over for a chat. Having them turn up at your door with a warrant for your arrest over unpaid traffic fines is quite different from them entering your bedroom in a shower of broken glass, crazed flashlight beams and harshly barked and usually contradictory commands.

For the first few years of my outlaw motorcycle career I was quite blissfully ignorant of the difference. Sure, I'd had innumerable chats with various cops on the side of the road, or at my front door, or even when they were executing a warrant on one of my mates. I had been handcuffed and arrested numerous times and even batoned about the legs and kidneys quite enthusiastically one balmy summer evening on the side of the Old Pacific Highway when a young Highway Patrol officer took umbrage at me explaining how I viewed him as 'a thoroughly worthless fuck with nothing better to do than pull over innocent tax-payers going about their business'.

That my business that day was steadfastly doing just under 160 kms per hour with no helmet on my head and an M1 carbine strapped to the handlebars of my Shovelhead was what was at issue. Apparently. And fair enough.

But he didn't need to be rude about it or approach me with his baton held at port arms. I'd pulled over the second I'd realised he was behind me and I could hardly be blamed for not being able to hear his stupid siren over the thunderous, antisocial explosions booming from my exhaust pipes for, according to him, the last five kilometres. If he knew anything about Harleys, he'd have known that the mirrors vibrate so much that looking into them, even briefly, gives one a sense of vertigo and nausea, and we only kept them on the bikes to prevent being issued defect notices. Is it any wonder I thought he was simple-minded when he kept asking me how it was that I couldn't see him behind me? So we had this brief discussion on the side of the road, then he gave me a bit of a touch-up with his flogging stick, and we went our separate ways. He drove off with a squeal of tyres and I lay there after my flogging for a few minutes trying not to cry like a girl after a bad date.

I was no stranger to the normal bikie–police interactions – I'd had plenty and was to have plenty more, but the morning the Special Operations Group (or the 'Sons of God' as they like to refer to themselves) came swarming into my house like black hatred manifest was a whole new and quite seriously alarming bowl of cornflakes.

Their arrival at my house came about as a result of a series of seemingly disconnected events beginning with a teenage dirtbag breaking into a car and making an amazing discovery. This was rapidly followed by a totally unhinged celebration of sex, drugs and building demolition, succeeded by an eviction, a move, a new neighbour ... and well, I guess I should just tell it as it happened, huh?

At the time I was living with my girlfriend Rachel and my mate Badger in a small fibro house in the western Sydney suburb of Granville, in a new but pretty futile bid to inject some normality into my rather shambolic, drug-enriched, crazy bikie life. I had moved out of the vortex of insanity that was the green house in Merrylands after deciding I didn't really want to live aboard the land-based equivalent of a psychotic pirate ship anymore.

The event that drove me to this decision was a delirium-filled sledgehammer wrecking fest that began as a perfectly normal four-day drug-and-booze-charged party held when Big Dima and I returned from our South Pacific cruise. Everything was fine at first and it was good to be home in the loving, tattooed arms of my extended family, but sometime during Day Two an obscenely large amount of cocaine had found its way into our normal happy party mix of methamphetamines, dope and cheap booze. And when I say 'obscenely large', I'm talking about almost two pounds, which is an amount of cocaine most people see only on televised drug busts and Hollywood movies.

This vast pile of sinus-stinger was brought to the party by Preacher Tom, who had never seen cocaine before but figured someone in the green house was sophisticated enough to confirm his suspicions about the densely packed brick of neon-white powder he had obtained from his younger cousin, Binky. A most horrid fifteen-year-old, Binky spent every available moment with his equally appalling mates, breaking into rich people's houses and cars on some Robin Hood-like ethical principle – except Binky and his mates considered themselves poor enough to be the sole beneficiaries of their thieving.

One evening, as they were eagerly ransacking parked cars in the ritzy suburb of Bellevue Hill, they came across the cocaine in a BMW's boot. Now, according to Preacher Tom, Binky hoped that what he had found was drugs, but he wasn't really sure. He was a street-kid from the western suburbs – he knew the basics (speed, hash, Valium, LSD), sold some killer dope, but was completely at a loss when it came to cocaine. He had only ever seen it on TV, knew it resembled speed in appearance and application, but that was it. Australia has never been a classless society, and coke being the party drug of the well-heeled it is not often used by flanno-wearing fuckers with mullets.

Binky and his mates tasted some of their find, felt their lips and mouths go almost instantly numb, panicked a bit and made their way to Preacher Tom's place too scared to try any more. Preacher Tom was likewise a bit at sea when it came to cocaine. He'd only ever seen it on TV too, but he had a few more kilometres on his clock than Binky did and he knew that what they had brought him was drugs. He also knew it wasn't speed and it wasn't heroin. By default, he hoped that meant it was cocaine.

'Surely these teenage fuckwits couldn't have found this much cocaine?' He looked, wide-eyed, at Mark and me as we examined the crumbly brick in our garage, the party raging on outside to the appropriate sounds of George Thorogood's 'Gearjammer'.

I'd experienced cocaine a few times, and knew the taste and the effect. Mark, being from the States, was far more familiar with the drug and, apart from being insulted and appalled at how ridiculously expensive it was in Australia, admitted to being quite a fan. I liked it a lot, too, but was simply not prepared to pay the $300 per gram asking price, when $60 would buy an equivalent amount of speed that would be more than adequate for almost two days of partying, whereas the coke would be gone in two hours then there would invariably be tears before bedtime. The rude truth was that cocaine, as much as we liked it, was out of our price range.

Mark and I tasted Preacher Tom's offering and exchanged

meaningful looks. Those teenage fuckwits had indeed got their dirty little hands on a stupid amount of cocaine – and pretty much the purest, most brain-squirming coke Mark or I had ever encountered.

'What do you want for this?' I asked Preacher Tom, as Mark immediately began racking up lines on the work bench.

'Ah man, I don't want any money,' Tom shook his head and grinned. 'I don't know what it's worth anyway. I didn't pay for it. You blokes have always been good to me and my missus. Just kick it into the mix, aye?'

'What about Binky?' I asked.

'What about the arsehole?'

'Is he gonna kick up a stink?' The little bastard was evil enough to slash all our bike tyres and poison my dog if he figured he'd been ripped off. I knew that much about him.

Preacher Tom's grin got a little wider. 'He's gonna consider himself lucky if I don't smash his fucken face in for trying to poison me and my mates with strange, unknown chemicals he found in a car boot.'

The deal was sealed when Mark snorted a massive line and went crashing and reeling around the garage holding the side of his face, barking 'Fuck! Fuck! Fuck!' over and over again. Things went rapidly downhill after that. Well, initially things went in a wonderful, upward direction. We were all snorting coke like Miami gangsters, slamming back tequila, declaring a deathless love for each other and loading our guns for reasons none of us could remember afterwards. The girls were taking off their clothes and dancing like the coked-up sluts they had all suddenly become. Big Dima insisted Svetlana suck his tattooed cock as he stood pants-less on the coffee table so that everyone could see what a great porn star she would make.

We then began mixing the coke with speed, declaring it to be the greatest narcotic combination in the history of humankind, and started up Mark's bike – which was one of the finest ideas any of us had ever had. We shrieked like the damned as he did a burn-out that saw the tyre explode and the back wheel seize in the swing-arm after showering us in sparks and chunks of concrete as he kept the throttle pinned in second and gouged a huge rut in the garage floor. When the engine finally died with a metallic bang and the whole bike caught fire, we only cheered more loudly. Mark then took a twelve-gauge shotgun and emptied seven rounds into the flaming bike and I thought I would explode with bestial joy and actually kissed him on his bearded mouth. Then we snorted more chemicals, drank more impossible amounts of piss, performed the most heinous public sex acts with our girlfriends, threw live rounds into the bonfire, then decided (as you do when you've had industrial amounts of mind-altering stimulants) that the garage walls and roof contained hidden caches of cash – certainly stashed there by our Lebanese landlord, Abdul.

Yes, yes, I know. But I cannot tell you how much sense this made at the time. There was just no way Abdul had *not* hidden shitloads of cash in the garage walls and ceiling. The bastard. And he was using us, his pet bikies, to guard it, even though we didn't know we were guarding it. That night it all became clear. There was nothing else we could have done at that time. We racked up some more lines, sent the more 'together' girls to the bottleshop for more alcohol, and began demolishing the garage.

We had the presence of mind to move the bikes out first, then stripped to the waist and armed with sledgehammers, pry bars, shovels, fence palings, bits of shopping trolley and lengths of tree, we began to demolish the structure.

It took until dawn. The police arrived, some time not long after we had begun, in response to the gunshots some appalled neighbour had reported. But we explained that what they had heard was obviously us wrecking the garage. The police accepted this. There was certainly enough hammering and banging going on.

'Why *are* you wrecking the garage?' asked the senior constable who had been out to the house several times over our tenure there, and who was, all things considered, a most reasonable chap.

'We're putting in a pool,' I said.

'You have a nosebleed,' the policeman observed.

'I must have bumped it,' I sniffed, wiping my sweat-and-blood-smeared face with the back of one filthy hand.

'Look, it's three in the morning. It's not really the time to be doing demolition work, is it?'

'We're almost done,' I grinned. Experience had taught me to always try to avoid directly answering a policeman's questions, and instead offer him some kind of hope for a positive outcome.

Behind me the smashing and crashing continued unabated. The garage was half gone and we weren't actually breaking any law, though the way Big Dima was using the sledgehammer to powder mortared bricks ('Because derti Arab maybe hez put gold in dem!') was quite frightening.

'Please try to keep the noise down,' the policeman directed, completely without any confidence any of us would comply, and left.

I immediately went back to looking for Abdul's hidden money and snorting cocaine. Just like the other blokes crawling through the rubble, I was at that obsessive-compulsive stage. I would probably not sleep for the next week and would be shitting blood and bile for days. But I was gonna find Abdul's money if I had to turn the whole garage into dust.

Of course there was no money. By 10 am the following morning all that remained of the garage was a pile of pulverised timber, mortar brick, corrugated iron and asbestos – before it was deemed to be a danger to collective humanity. All that remained of us was barely human. We were impossibly filthy, dangerously unbalanced with exhaustion and madness, and spiralling down off the massive coke jag. We had heaps left, but none of us could even contemplate snorting any more. Badger had lost the vision in his left eye, my nose was clogged with dried blood and caked drugs, and Mark had taken to eating it because his sinuses had collapsed. But then he had managed to gnaw a big, weeping ulcer into the side of his numb tongue and could no longer form words. Big Dima had wandered off with the sledgehammer over his shoulder and the outcome of that was quite indeterminable at that stage. Zorro had simply fainted when some of the roof had hit him in the face, and now appeared to be in some kind of coma near the back fence. We knew he was alive because he kept wetting his pants and squirming, so we weren't too worried. Our own lack of any type of well-being was keeping us well occupied.

'Fucker must have buried it,' Badger groaned, his voice husky with chemical burns and his eyes gleaming with red insanity.

'I don't care anymore,' I grunted, throwing down my sledge-hammer and trudging off into the house to take a shower.

Over the next few days, surveying the damage and counting the cost only reinforced my view that I didn't care anymore. The pirate ship was clearly out of control and it was only a matter of time before something truly horrible happened. I resolved not to be a part of that. I had just come back from a rather astonishing cruise and the travel bug had bitten me. There was a trip to Europe in my immediate future and I did not want to jeopardise my passport or various visas by getting arrested and charged with an assortment of gelatinous bastardry, which is precisely what would have happened had I remained in the green house. Thankfully, Abdul, our landlord, pulled the pin on us all.

'What you fucken do to garage?' he demanded a few days later, standing in the back yard and surveying the pile of rubble.

'I'm sorry, Abdul,' I said. 'I really am. Shit just got out of hand.'

'How this happens?'

How could I explain that to him? 'I'm not really sure. One thing led to another ...'

'What I do now?'

I spread my arms in a futile gesture of empathy and ignorance. 'We'll pay to build you a new garage,' I offered, figuring we could probably sell the remaining cocaine and fund the building in that way.

Abdul shook his head slowly. The gold chains around his thick brown neck flashed in the sun and he fixed me with his dark criminal eyes. 'How you pay?'

I asked him to wait a second, went into the house and came back with the remaining coke. I held it out to him.

He looked at it intently, wet his little finger and had a taste. His eyes flashed and widened. 'Okay,' he grinned and nodded.

The next few days were somewhat muted and numb. The frenzy of those days of drug-madness had left its mark on all of us. We all knew this particular party was over for good. What had been seen and done and said could not be unseen, undone and unsaid. Cocaine doesn't grant amnesia. It was time to move on.

I duly found a neat little joint in an adjoining suburb and persuaded Rachel of my iron-clad intent to live a quieter, less communal-based lifestyle. I was somewhat successful in this, at least initially. Badger moved in with us to help pay the rent, and for the first few weeks things were pretty quiet. Then we had a barbecue and most of the usual suspects turned up. It was a great weekend – not as crazy as some of the green house parties, but it certainly made an impression on the neighbours. Then a few quiet weekends went by, and we had another party. After a while, things settled down into a kind of manageable rhythm of almost non-biker normality.

Svetlana and Big Dima had moved into a townhouse a few suburbs away, Zorro had moved back home, Mark was living with his brothers reasonably nearby, Badger was paying his rent on time, and we were all pretty much cruising through our various lives now that the maelstrom of insanity that was the green house was no longer the epicentre of our universe.

Then Jed came into our lives. He lived across the street from where we had moved in, and when we were unloading the truck he came over to lend a hand. I thought this was most neighbourly of him, offered him a few beers, a bong, then another bong, and by sundown we were all moved in and Jed was staying for dinner.

Jed wasn't a biker, but he loved motorcycles and the whole outlaw lifestyle with a feral, all-encompassing madness. He drove a rumbling matte-black Holden panel van and would accompany us on our runs, carrying beer, tools, drugs and guns and producing whatever was required whenever it was required. A big, broad-shouldered and immensely good-humoured bloke, his favourite pastime was getting mindlessly drunk and roaring with laughter at our war stories. He was completely without pretence, staunch as an iron bar, seemingly honourable, devoted to what we had going on and delivered mail in Gosford for a living.

I was working as a telegram delivery boy at Chatswood post office at the time, so we had a common employer. One morning I was surprised to see him striding out of the loading dock at the rear of the post office with a sack of mail on his shoulder.

'What are you doing here?' I asked.

'I got transferred,' he grinned. 'I'm a Chatswood postie now.'

I was a little nonplussed by this, but figured he would fit in rather well with the other fifteen or so local mailmen, who were almost without exception sleep-deprived drug addicts, alcoholics and socially inept imbeciles who had found a safe anchorage in the tolerant bosom of Australia Post.

As it turned out, Jed's idea of being a Chatswood postie was to neck half a bottle of Jim Beam before starting work at 4.45 am, haphazardly sort his mail, then lurch aimlessly about the streets of Chatswood randomly delivering letters into whatever post box he felt could do with some input. His lunch hours (note the plural) were spent augmenting the breakfast bourbon with a dozen or so schooners, which ensured the afternoon's mail deliveries were even more random and creative.

Of course, this farce didn't continue for long and Jed was eventually sacked. The next day he loaded all his worldly possessions into his panel van, bid us a fond farewell and headed off to Queensland to sell cars, as he explained it. A few weeks later the post office was held up and robbed. Or more accurately, the senior postal clerk and I were held up at gunpoint on the street and robbed as we were taking a briefcase full of cash and money orders to the nearby bank. Was it Jed? Who knows. All I saw out of the corner of my eye was a big guy in a parka and balaclava who came up behind us, pointed a handgun at the senior postal clerk's mullet and demanded the briefcase. The postal clerk immediately handed over the briefcase and the bloke ran off up the street. It was all over in literal seconds and we were left to stumble back to the post office and have interviews with the police, who arrived shortly afterwards. In retrospect, it could well have been Jed, but it could also have been anyone who had made the effort to stake out the post office and observe the briefcase being walked to the bank at pretty much the same time each day.

The senior postal clerk and I were offered counselling to help us get over our trauma, but we chose to medicate ourselves with beer at the local pub and talk over what happened instead. Neither of us felt particularly traumatised – it all went down so quickly we didn't have time to fear for our lives. One second we were ambling to the bank, the next second some bastard had robbed us and was legging it up the street. Just quietly, I was a little disappointed that it wasn't more of an ordeal. I was given to understand that people who have been at the pointy end of an armed robbery are paid compensation and can spend years being counselled. The postal clerk and I got drunk that afternoon, laughed ruefully, shook our heads in disbelief, went home and told all our mates what had happened, then came back to work the next day and got on with our lives.

A month later, seemingly apropos of nothing, at Stupid O'Clock in the morning, the cops came crashing into my house bristling with guns and bad manners. Why they came to be in my bedroom at Stupid O'Clock in the morning, crunching shards of broken window glass into the cheap carpet and admiring my girlfriend's quite attractive and utterly naked arse as she lay on the floor beside the bed not liking me very much at that moment, was a mystery to me. And one that was not solved until many hours had passed and the handcuffs I was slapped in were finally removed.

I was also spreadeagled naked on the floor, but unlike Rachel, I had a large tactical boot creasing the side of my face ensuring my complete compliance with any further instructions. Up until then I had done quite well, I felt, thus far un-shot and un-bashed.

I had not even really had time to react heroically to the simultaneous sound of the bedroom window breaking and both the front door and back door being splintered off their hinges. What I did do was lurch upright out of bed, goggled-eyed and breathless in fear, then promptly fell to the ground in confusion and chaos. So much for my Jason Bourne fantasies. There was contradictory yelling, concurrently instructing me to 'Get on the ground!' and 'Don't move!' and the sound of what appeared to be lots of very large, heavily armed bears moving angrily through my house. Doors were being slammed open, drawers pulled out and lights turned on in every room.

I remember Rachel whimpering in abject terror and confusion and I felt terrible for what she was going through. Getting rained on for being a horrible bastard comes with the turf of being a horrible bastard, and horrible bastards generally understand that. But when those you love get caught in the rain, it's a bitter pill to swallow.

That aside, I was still completely ignorant as to why it was even raining at that moment. I had done nothing to warrant this kind of attention from the police: the rent was up to date, the power bill had been paid, the hose in the back yard, as far as I knew, was off.

From my vantage point on the floor, I saw two pairs of non-combat boots walk into my bedroom and I swivelled my eyes upwards. Two medium-sized detectives had their business faces on and one was holding a small sheaf of papers. 'Are you Boris Muchaluchuk?' he asked sternly.

I figured this was not a good time to ping him about pronouncing my name properly and asking him if English was his second language. 'Yip,' I mumbled from under the sole of the tactical boot flattening my vowels for me.

'Who are you?'

Rachel identified herself.

'Can you let her put some clothes on?' I wheezed.

'Oh, I kinda like her like this,' the detective leered, as the other one started emptying the contents of my bedside table onto the floor near my face.

I was then roughly and very tightly handcuffed, hauled to my feet and led off into the lounge room. Rachel remained terror-frozen on the floor in the bedroom, but I noticed one of the SOG blokes drop a blanket over her nakedness.

I was deposited on the lounge and the grinning detective informed me that I was under arrest and that he had a warrant to search my premises, which he then waved in my face. 'Do you understand?' he asked.

I nodded. 'What am I under arrest for?'

'You have an outstanding warrant.'

'What for?' I blinked. I truly had no idea why a warrant would be issued for my arrest.

The detective consulted another sheet of paper and his grin widened. 'It's for an unpaid fine for parking on a footpath,' he chortled.

My jaw dropped. 'Are you fucken serious?' I asked.

He dropped the warrant beside me. 'Dead fucken serious,' he said. 'And don't fucken swear at me.'

There was an armed SOG officer in the lounge room with us, and I could see him trying to stifle a grin. Clearly he hadn't been told his crack team of black-clad life-takers, heartbreakers and door-smashers had been deployed to deal with such a heinous bikie gangster. His expression changed as the second detective came into the room carrying three shotguns, followed by another SOG cop carrying my other seven firearms cradled in his arms.

'These were all in the bedroom, boss,' the second detective said.

'Fucken nice,' the first one smiled, nudging the pile of guns on the floor apart with his shoe. 'Any of them loaded?'

'Only the silver pumpy that was by the bed.'

He was referring to my beloved Ithaca twelve-gauge, seven-shot roto-forged riot gun, for which I had saved up and bought from Mick Smith's gun store with my father's blessing a month after leaving school. You see, back in those lawless, halcyon days, it was perfectly legal to own all sorts of wonderful firearms. All it took was a shooter's licence, freely and easily available from any police station for, from memory, about ten dollars. I did, of course, have such a licence, because buying guns and ammo without one was just not possible. I had had one since I was seventeen – my father insisted upon it. Over the years I had acquired a nice collection of shooting irons, which were now on my living-room floor, along with a water pistol that vaguely resembled an Uzi with an orange-tipped barrel, with which I used to squirt my dog into a barking frenzy when the mood took me.

It was, in retrospect and by today's standards, quite an arsenal. There was the aforementioned Ithaca, a Remington Wingmaster five-shot pumpy and an altogether marvellous twelve-gauge double-barrelled Baikal coach gun. Next to them was a 303.270 my father had given me as a gift; a 30.30 lever-action that had sent many a razorback to its maker; a .30 M1 carbine that always jammed; a hefty .243 I used for goats; a gorgeous .222 that was the bane of kangaroos and foxes the breadth of western NSW; a well-used .22 Magnum mainly used for plinking at cans when there was no game about; and a .300 Magnum leopard gun I had recently acquired in case dinosaurs ever made a resurgence.

Several boxes of the commensurate ammo were subsequently deposited on the floor beside the guns. 'Do you have a current shooter's licence?' the first detective asked.

'In my wallet,' I replied.

'This wallet?' he asked, producing my rather battered, but still ruggedly handsome biker item, complete with belt-chain and decorative edge-braiding.

I nodded and he opened the wallet and started tossing bits of folded paper onto the floor until he found the creased blue licence, which he unfolded and studied with great intensity. He then put it in his pocket and tossed my wallet onto the carpet beside the guns and ammo. Stooping, he picked up the Baikal coach gun, which he cracked open and shut a few times, hefting it in his hands, then ran his thumb across the business end of the twin barrels and nodded.

'Good fucken job shortening this,' he grinned and handed it to his mate, who likewise rubbed his thumb across the ends of the barrels.

'I didn't shorten it,' I grated. 'They come like that.'

Which was true. Twelve-gauge coach guns were all stubbier versions of normal-length shotguns, and the name was coined in 1858 when Wells, Fargo & Co issued them to its stagecoach drivers and guards (who were called 'shotgun messengers' and 'rode shotgun') for their protection.

'Bullfuckenshit,' the detective spat. 'This firearm is not of a legal length.'

'I think you'll find it is,' I said. I was certain of this. Like most of my shooters, I had also bought this gun from Mick Smith's gun shop and the barrel was of a legal length. By one quarter of one inch, sure. But what's legal is what's legal, as the police were often fond of telling me, and theirs was not to question the law, but merely to enforce it.

Right about then, as I was sitting nude on my cheap-shit vinyl lounge surrounded by men all of whose penises were doubtlessly bigger than mine, I was wondering whether that still applied. By the looks of the grinning idiot strutting about my lounge room, it would not be beyond him to produce a file and grind that pesky quarter-inch off my Baikal's barrel.

The second detective had taken the gun and left the room and I could hear Rachel answering muffled questions from the bedroom, her voice strained with fear and anger. 'I don't know ... no, I don't know ... ask him, I don't fucken know!'

And she didn't know. We didn't tell our girlfriends anything about anything – precisely for just such an occasion as this. You can't tell the police something if you don't know anything. Some girls bitched about being kept in the dark, but the smarter ones understood it was for their own good. Rachel was one of the smarter ones. I couldn't hear what she was being asked, but she knew no more about my unpaid 'park on the footpath' fine than she knew about my gun collection, so her answers were going to be quite consistent.

The SOG blokes had mostly all left by now and been replaced by a few uniforms, and through the window I could see my neighbours, all dressing gowns, pyjamas and suburban curiosity, gathered in gossiping clumps across the street from my house. The second detective returned to the lounge room, had a whispered exchange with the first one, then took two of the uniformed cops standing aimlessly near my front door and proceeded to conduct a search. This mainly consisted of them emptying the contents of every drawer in the house onto the ground and kicking the spilled contents around with their boots – including the kitchen drawers and my ancient fridge's vegetable drawers. They spent some time at the fridge emptying all the ice trays, opening all the crusty old jars of tomato paste and foil-wrapped chicken corpses and pizza slices. They then moved into the room where my girlfriend kept her clothes (our bedroom cupboard was too small for anything but my jeans and T-shirts, and nothing I owned needed hanging anyway), and amused themselves going through her underpants, bras and miniskirts.

They then proceeded to Badger's room, which was thankfully devoid of anything incriminating – and in fact looked like it had been stripped. There was nothing in it but a small pile of dirty laundry, a bare mattress, some vile mouldy boots and an old crash helmet. Badger had been staying at his new girlfriend's place for the last fortnight (he called it a 'breaking-in period') and had taken most of his stuff with him.

'Whose room is this?' the detective sang out.

'Badger's,' I replied.

'What's his real name?'

'Badger,' I repeated.

The detective in the lounge room bent at the waist and peered intently into my face.

'What's his fucken name?' he growled.

'That's the only name I know him by,' I said flatly, staring past him.

'Bullshit!' he barked and his spittle flecked my face and went into my eyes.

That wasn't a question, so I had no response. The other detective and the two cops with him came back into the lounge room and joined the other two uniforms and my detective. The two plain-clothers had another whispered exchange and behind them I saw Rachel appear in the hallway dressed in a short dressing gown with her arms crossed over her chest the way all women cross their arms when they're pissed off, affronted beyond measure and beholding the piece of shit responsible for their innumerable woes. But at least she wasn't in handcuffs on the couch beside me. That she had been seen naked by half a dozen cops was not going to bother her much. The girls we were hanging out with were not the kind to be troubled by being seen without their clothes, and generally wore very little anyway.

I gave her a rueful grin and she sighed and I could see a tiny spark of pity in her eyes. She knew this kind of shit sometimes came with her boyfriend's turf. That it had not come up till this point was fortunate, but now that it was here she would deal with it. Even if she wasn't entirely sure yet what it was she had to deal with.

I was also still completely at a loss to understand why all this was going on. I'd been arrested for outstanding warrants before, and it was invariably a far less intense operation. It usually occurred by the side of the road when, after performing a licence check, the police officer discovered an outstanding warrant for some unpaid traffic fine (there were times when these came so thick and fast, it was not at all surprising that some of them slipped under the payment radar), and usually said: 'Look, you have an unpaid fine that's turned into a warrant. What do you wanna do?'

The options were either to go to the police station and pay it, or serve it out at $50 a day. And since this was the era when even the most dastardly speeding fine was usually around $200, you could pop into your local police station on Friday evening, spend an enervating weekend eating take-away food and leafing through old *Penthouse* magazines in the cells, then go to work on Monday, warrant free.

I figured I had nothing to lose by enquiring if any such options existed on this occasion. 'How much is the warrant, detective?' I asked.

The detective spun on his heel and glared at me as if I had just asked to hold his gun. I was all innocence and earnestness.

He rifled through the papers. 'One hundred and seventy dollars,' he said.

'I'm happy to pay that,' I said.

He glared at me in naked hatred. 'Yeah? Well, you know what I'm happy about? I'm happy about dragging your fucken arse back to the station.'

Hmmm, I thought. This was obviously not about my parking fine.

'Which station would that be, officer?' I asked.

'Chatswood,' he replied.

After a few more moments of whispered discussions, the uniforms stood me up, helped me on with some jeans and a T-shirt, and led me outside to a waiting unmarked car. Another two uniforms followed with all my guns. I managed to tell Rachel to call Mark as they led me out. Mark would call a lawyer if one was needed and we would proceed from there.

The trip from Granville to Chatswood was full of meaningful silences, accompanied by meaningless-to-me updates from the in-car police radio. I tried to be funny by asking them to turn on the sirens so that I could feel important about being hauled off to jail, but my quip was met with a stony silence.

Once we arrived at Chatswood police station, I was placed in a featureless interview room and left alone for more than an hour. I had watched enough TV to understand this as a standard police interrogation tactic meant to soften the resolve of the accused, but since I had no idea why I was even there, apart from not paying a fine for parking on a footpath, I really had no resolve that needed softening. So I tilted my chair back, rocked back and forth, tried not to think about how fucked my wrists were going to be when the super-tight handcuffs were removed, counted the carpet tiles on the floor, thought about how fine Rachel's arse looked that morning, and wondered what had become of my guns.

Then the door opened and the two detectives came in and sat down. They were all business, but they did undo my handcuffs.

'I am Detective Sergeant Miller and this is Detective Clemens. We would like to ask you a few questions about an incident that occurred on the twenty-third of March this year.'

'Was that the day I parked on the footpath?' I asked, rubbing my wrists.

Detective Sergeant Miller slammed his hand on the table. 'Look,' he snarled. 'This is all going to go a lot better if you stop being a smart-arse and co-operate.'

I nodded. It had finally dawned on me what this was all about.

'On the twenty-third of March this year you were involved in an armed hold-up outside Chatswood post office. Is that correct?'

I nodded.

'What can you tell us about what happened that day?'

'I made a statement the day it happened,' I said. 'It's all in that statement.'

'Well, I want you to tell me again,' Miller rasped. 'From the beginning.'

So I did. It took less than five minutes. Then we all looked at each other.

'Do you know Jed Crossman?' Miller finally asked.

'Jed?' I chirped. 'Yeah, I know Jed. I didn't know his surname. Is it the same Jed?'

The detectives exchanged what I am sure they felt were meaningful glances. But I actually didn't know Jed's surname.

'Where is he now?'

'He told me he was going to Queensland.'

'When did he go?'

'Ages ago.'

'Has he been in touch with you since he left?'

'Nope.'

He hadn't and I saw no reason to state otherwise.

'Why do you think that might be?'

I shrugged. 'Maybe you should ask him.'

Miller shuffled through his notes. The other detective, Clemens, stared at the wall behind my head. He seemed to be in some kind of trance.

'I am asking you,' Miller finally said after putting his notes down.

I sighed, put my arms on the table before me, and cleared my throat. My body language was no longer that of the beaten, eager-to-please cur. Enough was more than enough. I had been roughly woken up before dawn, showered in broken glass, had my face stepped on by a large policeman, had my naked girl-friend shamed and insulted, and had provided my neighbours no little amount of intrigue and gossip.

'And I'm fucken telling you that I have no fucken idea. He's been gone for ages. He hasn't called. We weren't that close.'

Detective Sergeant Miller was not easily put off; he glared right back at me, rose out of his chair and pointed his finger in my face.

'I fucken know you had something to do with that post office hold-up!' he snapped.

I stood up as well. 'You're a fucken genius!' I roared back at him. 'Of course I had something to do with it! I was one of the fools who was held up!'

'You set the whole thing up with Jed Crossman!' he barked back.

It had occurred to me this was where everything was leading. I sat back down again and tilted my chair back onto its hind legs.

'Fair enough,' I grinned. 'If that's what you reckon, then I suggest you fucken charge me.'

Miller looked as if he was about to erupt and shower the room with his brain-lava. 'Oh we're gonna charge you alright!' he howled, waving his finger at me.

'Then get the fuck on with it!' I yelled back. Miller grabbed his sheaf of papers and he and Clemens left the room.

Another hour went by. I re-counted the floor tiles. I was not really concerned that I would be charged. If they had enough evidence to charge me I would have already been charged, but a small part of me was concerned what the pricks could possibly be fabricating out of my sight. After all, it's not like people being fitted up with make-believe evidence was unheard of when it came to the NSW police force.

The door opened and a middle-aged uniformed senior sergeant came in with a junior constable. 'Your mate is out the front and he's paid your warrant,' he said to me.

'Where are my guns?'

'They're at the front desk.'

'I'm good to go?'

The sergeant nodded, po-faced.

I walked out of the interview room and around a bunch of desks. I was on the first floor of the police station, which is where the detectives did their work. I saw no sign of either Miller or Clemens as I followed the sergeant down the stairs to the reception desk. The junior constable followed me.

Mark was waiting for me at the counter. 'You okay?' he asked.

'Yep,' I nodded then turned to the constable. 'Give me my fucken guns.'

He looked like he wanted to say lots of things to me, but instead he commenced piling my artillery onto the counter.

'I need you to sign this,' he said when the last rifle had been placed on the stack.

It was the standard warrant discharge form. I had signed many of them. I scrawled my name on the line, then Mark and I picked up my guns and walked out of the police station.

'Where's the car?' I asked.

Mark looked confused.

'What car?' he said. 'I didn't bring a car. I don't have a car to bring.'

This was true. None of us actually owned a car. The car we had relied mostly upon was Jed's and Jed was gone. Svetlana had a car, but she was probably at work.

Mark and I stood there for a few minutes wondering what to do. Chatswood police station is in the middle of the busy Chatswood shopping precinct. Our arms were full of guns and people walking by were looking rather alarmed. That we were standing outside the police station was probably the only thing that prevented mass panic and screaming. We could clearly not stand there forever – eventually the cops would come out and unpleasantness would doubtlessly ensue.

'Reckon you can carry them on the back of the bike?' Mark asked.

I shrugged. My choices were limited.

He put the five shooters he was holding on the ground and went to get his bike. In short order, I had arranged myself on the pillion seat with the ten guns on my lap, and we slowly moved off. Lane-splitting was impossible due to the extra width of the guns, so our journey home took far longer than it should have.

Along the way, people stared. I'm sure some of them even called the cops.

PARANOIA

It is not possible to know what is enough until one grasps what is more than enough. William Blake understood this when he penned his 'Proverbs of Hell'. But I am not William Blake. And because I am not gifted with his immense wisdom, I have been testing the validity of his brilliant observation most of my life. That testing is now over: I hold Mr Blake's reflection to be true. I can also offer an accompanying observation. If you wish to find out what is more than enough, Surfers Paradise is a pretty appropriate place to do it. It seems designed for just the kind of mentally damaging excesses motorcycle-riding drug fiends enjoy exploring. William Blake didn't ride a motorcycle, but I'm sure he would have loved Surfers Paradise nonetheless.

'Sometimes paranoia's just
having all the facts.'

WILLIAM S BURROUGHS

Fuck knows why my mate, Two Flared Nostrils and I suddenly felt we had to go to the Indy car race on the Gold Coast. We don't give a shit about cars. We do, however, have an abiding affection for the tawdry bogan glamour of the Gold Coast. So that was probably the prime motivator.

It being Indy and all, we figured a lot of that glamour would, in the weeks leading up to the event, be snorting its bodyweight in methamphetamine and cocaine, so as to best fit into the gold lamé hotpants it would be wearing when the race crowds came to town. It would also need to be taking its clothes off on high-rise balconies and shaking its wondrous tits at the world. Because that is what the local glamour does when it's full of drugs and alcohol and the race cars come to Surfers.

Our local source had assured us this was very much the case. 'Man, you gotta see this shit,' the source had said. 'All the clubs and venues hire every good-looking babe for a thousand kilometres, dress them up in bikinis and shit and make them walk around the streets holding up signs advertising the venues. The bitches all go mad because it's hot, they have to wear heels and walk everywhere, and punters yell at them and try to grab their tits. So they all snort bulk coke and speed to deal with it, and then they go off like sex-weasels. They get naked and fuck on the balconies!'

Two Flared Nostrils and I exchanged meaningful looks when this information came out of the loudspeaker on his office phone. 'Do not lie to me, fucker,' Two Flared Nostrils intoned. 'I doubt you even know what a sex-weasel is.'

'Look,' the source wheezed out of the speaker. 'All I know is that the bitches spend a month before Indy dieting and gym-ing like mad, they buy all the powder I can get my hands on, they wax themselves smoother than surfboards, and they book up every fake tan and nail salon from Tweed to Maroochydore. Then come Indy, they fucken go off! It's a fucken madhouse!'

After the source hung up, Two Flared Nostrils and I discussed the intelligence we had just received. He was of the view that it would be hugely remiss of us not to be on hand when all that crazy shit started strutting around the streets in seven-inch heels, all orange, cranky and crazy. I was not convinced the intelligence was at all sound.

'How reliable is that bastard?' I asked.

'He pays his legal bills on time,' Two Flared Nostrils replied. As a lawyer, he measured his clients' reliability in terms of when his invoices were paid.

'Is he full of shit or not?' I demanded. 'It's a long way to ride to be swallowed up by car freaks or beaten to death by cops.'

'Do not be paranoid. I do not think he's lying,' he replied. 'His trial is coming up. He doesn't need to upset me by lying to me.'

This was cheering news. 'Besides,' Two Flared Nostrils went on. 'We could do with a holiday. It's a beaut ride up if we do some of the back roads, and an old high school mate has a holiday house in Broadbeach, right across the road from the beach. If he's not using it, I reckon he'll lend it to us.'

The alternative was to go to the World Superbike races at Phillip Island, but both us were fed up with the endless police harassment, the shitty trackside facilities, the insane weather changes, and the mindless drone back up the Hume because we were invariably too ill from substance abuse to take any other route. A few days in the sun on the Gold Coast, when the Gold Coast is in party mode, sounded like a much better idea.

So we made our plans, plotted our route, packed our bikes and headed north the week before the race cars started their engines and Surfers Paradise was transformed into rev-head and coke-slut central.

It's worth reiterating that neither Two Flared Nostrils nor I were the kind of motorcyclists who also shared a passion for cars. He liked cars more than I did, but only in a kind of vague, half-hearted, yeah-if-I-had-money-I'd-like-an-Aston-Martin kinda way. Being a lawyer who predominantly dealt with dire criminal matters and who preferred to spend his 'argument cash', as he called it, on whores, drugs, extravagant lunches and motorcycles, it was unlikely he would ever amass that kind of money any time soon, so he confined himself to loving motorcycles. They were cheaper, faster and offered far more bang for your buck, in more ways than one ...

As far as I was concerned, people who were into cars and actually paid large sums of money to watch cars race needed to be chemically neutered, herded into caged compounds, and made to repair roads and till the soil for the good of the motorcyclists who would rule over them with a stern benevolence. But I understood that when the Gold Coast was going off because cars were there, and the women had spray-painted themselves orange, filled their heads full of marching powder and were committed to large-scale copulation, it was a place I needed to be.

We planned to head up the New England Highway, intent on turning right at Tamworth and heading for the coast via the

Oxley Highway. The twisty goodness of the Ox would allow us to cleanse ourselves spiritually, and thus arrive in Queensland refreshed and ready to howl at the moon. I was wedged upon my beloved Triumph Speed Triple and Two Flared Nostrils was riding his pimped Suzuki GSX-R, which he had, in a fit of drug-induced madness, caused to be airbrushed to look like the head and genitals of some kind of dragon. It wasn't entirely his fault. I had assisted him in this endeavour by sketching out various snarling reptiles on scraps of paper while he toasted my efforts with expensive bourbon and endless lines of very high-grade methamphetamine. By the end of that two-day bender, we were both convinced I was an artist of rare skill, and that our mutual friend Brush would be able to transfer my sketches onto Two Flared Nostrils's bike. Brush was polite enough not to laugh too loudly at my rubbish and in a few weeks returned the bike painted up to Two Flared Nostrils's satisfaction. In the interim, Two Flared Nostrils had organised for the Suzuki to have all sorts of meaningful engine work done and the suspension upgraded, and ended up with a bike that was not only visually striking, but also went quite hard.

We took our time, left mid-morning, scrubbed the edges of our tyres on the Putty Road by adopting the advisory speed shown on corner signs as a challenge to double, stopped for a few bracing whiskys outside Cessnock, then once again near the green horse pastures and white wooden fences of Stroud, and again just the other side of Murrurundi. Since we had consumed the best part of a bottle of Canadian Club by this stage, we felt it would be sensible to get off the main highway, so we chucked a right the other side of Wallabadah, and took Fossickers Way and Lindsays Gap Road to the small town of Nundle, where we stopped for lunch.

Shrugging off our jackets in the warm sun, we took one of the tables on the pub's front verandah. It was a weekday, so the place was empty, and I headed to the toilet while Two Flared Nostrils made for the bar. When I returned, water dripping from my smiling face, Two Flared Nostrils had acquired another bottle of Canadian Club to replace the one we'd mostly drunk, and a bottle of red to go with the lunch we had yet to order.

'What are you gonna have?' I asked.

'I've had lunch,' he said, emptying the wine into two schooner glasses, and rubbing his nose.

'You're kidding!' I hissed. 'We need to eat. We can't be snorting that shit now, we'll run out before we get to Queensland!'

Two Flared Nostrils smiled bashfully. 'No,' he said. 'We shall not run out.' He showed me what was in his pocket and I had to agree we would not run out of drugs any time soon, or even any time this side of Christmas. The following year.

Clearly, one of his drug-fiend clients had been unable to pay his legal fees in the traditional manner, and had given him a shitload of product instead. We were thus well-provisioned against the rigours of the road and the unknowable variables that awaited us in Surfers Paradise. So I had some lunch as well, ordered another bottle of red which we drank as dessert, and we snuck into Tamworth via the back way and into a motel.

It was a messy afternoon. It turned into an even messier night, some of which was spent screaming at the TV as Two Flared Nostrils indulged his passion for gridiron.

'Tom Brady is a cunt!' he howled as his beloved Patriots quarterback threw another shit pass. 'Take him out and shoot him in the fucken face!'

I poured him another whisky. It only made him angrier.

'Bring Bledsoe back, you worthless fucks!'

Eventually the madness passed from him and he settled in to watch a replay of an old Rugby World Cup match in which the Wallabies spent an hour stomping the hapless Springboks into paste.

I took seven showers and worried about how we were going to meet the challenge of the Oxley Highway the following day after a sleepless, madness-fuelled night. Two Flared Nostrils was unperturbed. As the sun rose, he had some eye-watering nose-breakfast, and made me have some too. We then repacked our bikes and headed for the Oxley.

We managed the first section, which is mainly fast sweepers, without too many issues, and once we hit the long straights on the Tamworth side of Walcha, Two Flared Nostrils let the big Suzi have its head and steadily gapped me with his extra fifty horsepower. I was grateful that he had to slow down as he entered Walcha and as we fuelled up I told him I was starting to feel like garbage.

'Do you need some morning tea?' he asked, his nostrils flaring and eyes sparkling with delight and anticipation.

'Fuck, no,' I shook my head. 'I might just drink some water instead.'

My mouth tasted like a nightmare. There was some kind of poisonous moss growing along the back of my tongue and I found it hard to swallow. Also, some type of insane volcanic bullshit was going on in my guts, which had not experienced any solid food for at least thirty hours, and had been dealing with nothing but chemicals, whisky and red wine since I left Sydney. But my mind was clear and sharp, which was helpful given what awaited us.

Bugger it, I thought as I headed out of Walcha, the sooner I get this over with, the better. So I jammed the throttle open. With Two Flared Nostrils on my rear wheel we flew with intent and purpose towards the rainforest and the eight million corners that led down from the range to the coast.

Things were going really well, and then they suddenly weren't. I was starting to see black fluttery things at the edge of my vision. I slowed down, but they were still there. When I turned my eyes to the right or left, they weren't there. But when I stared straight ahead, my view was framed with a bizarre flapping blackness. I pulled over.

'I'm seeing shit!' I yelled at Two Flared Nostrils.

'Is it bad shit?' he yelled back.

'I don't know.'

'Can you ride on?'

'I don't know.'

Two Flared Nostrils considered this for a few seconds. 'We should have some coffee,' he said, and rode off slowly.

I followed as best I could, my vision spasming with darkness, and my heart filled with hate for the coffee-wanting arsehole ahead of me.

The nearest coffee was at Gingers Creek, which was still a way off and in the middle of all the really difficult twistiness – twistiness that made demands on me when I was on my game,

232

rested and in the zone. The way I felt now, it was highly probable I would go sailing off the first cliff and spend an hour or so bleeding out among the pretty green ferns.

But Two Flared Nostrils only rode a kilometre or so up the road and turned left onto a dirt track. I followed and a hundred metres or so in, he stopped and switched his bike off.

'Coffee?' he asked genially. I stared at him in total incomprehension, lurched off my bike and went to have a piss. My urine was a strange colour and felt thick and gluey coming out. But I was more concerned about the fact that Two Flared Nostrils had clearly gone insane. I was expecting him to smash the back of my head in with a tree limb at any second and run gibbering off into the scrub. Instead, when I turned around, he had produced a small gas-operated coffee-maker from his Gearsack, placed it on a lump of sandstone and was adding water to it from a large bottle he'd packed. I watched in fascination. In all the time we had been riding together, this was the first time he had ever done anything like this on the side of the road.

In a few minutes he had brewed up some great-smelling coffee, and I had hauled out my bag of beef jerky and managed to gag down a few pieces. The black flapping at the edge of my vision was gone. I felt very tired, and I was looking forward to the coffee.

I closed my eyes for a minute or so, leaned back against my bike and enjoyed the silence of the bush. The day was warm, the sky was blue, the bikes ticked as they cooled and the whole world smelled of spring, holidays and fresh coffee.

'Here you go,' said Two Flared Nostrils. I opened my eyes and he handed me a small cup of hot coffee. I took it gratefully and sipped at it gingerly. It tasted fine – a little metallic, but that must have been from the steel pot.

'I think we should have some of this,' Two Flared Nostrils said as he pulled out a small green bottle from his bag. 'I understand it is medicinal and full of healthy and exotic herbs.'

I stared at him and the bottle in horror. 'That's fucken Jägermeister.'

Two Flared Nostrils agreed that it was indeed Jägermeister. 'It has fifty-six different herbs and spices,' he said to me, peering at the label. 'And it's seventy proof!'

'Do you really think we should be necking that stupid German cough-syrup at a time like this?'

Two Flared Nostrils looked aghast. It was the same expression he used when a hostile witness provided an answer Two Flared Nostrils did not want the court to hear. 'Of course,' he said. 'It will help us deal with the speed I put into our coffee.' That accounted for the metallic taste, and the fact that I had started to chew the insides of my mouth again.

'The herbs are meant to be very healthy for you,' he said, proffering me the bottle.

'The alcohol would have murdered any health those herbs might have had,' I said, but I took the bottle off him and had a swig. It tasted indescribably appalling. I understand Jägermeister enjoys a certain popularity among the trendy young clubbers of the world – but they all hold their hands in the air when they dance too, so it's not like they can possibly understand anything about good taste.

Still, it was the first alcohol I had ever tried that could override the bitter-brass taste of speed. I took another belt and passed the bottle back to Two Flared Nostrils. 'It's just fucken awful,' I grimaced.

He peered at me closely. 'But you're getting your colour back,' he grinned.

I was feeling better. I knew, however, that my well-being was nothing but a Potemkin village: eventually, the shit would all fall down and what would be revealed was not going to be pretty.

That was a problem for Later-Borrie, though. Right-Now-Borrie had only one problem. His bike was some fifty horsepower down on his mate's, so he would have to make up that deficit in the corners. 'Let's go,' I said, zipping up my jacket and tightening the strap of my helmet.

Two Flared Nostrils took a good, long belt of the evil German booze, got on his bike and we pulled back out onto the Ox buzzing like bees in a bottle. Riding with a head full of speed is quite unlike riding with any other drug. Get the dosage right, and you'll be rewarded with god-like levels of focus and aggression. Get the dosage wrong, and you'll high-side yourself into the nearest trauma ward.

You'll remember that methamphetamine was widely used during World War II by both the good guys and the bad guys, but mainly by the bad guys, who called it 'pilot's salt' or *Panzerschokolade* (tanker's chocolate). The Nazis produced more than thirty-five million three-milligram doses of speed for its army and air force, and were enjoying a good deal of military success until Russian stubbornness and climatic issues came into play.

For their part, the Japanese government made one billion speed pills (known as Philopon) to assist its soldiers to hack off heads and its pilots to fly their planes into Allied warships. It was still feeding them to its workers in the 1950s as they hurried to rebuild a country, ironically devastated by speed-filled US pilots.

More recently, half the US Air Force was hopped up on Dexedrine (dextroamphetamine) and bombed its Canadian allies in Afghanistan with the same happy determination it had bombed the Taliban's forces of evil.

In my experience, successfully operating a motorcycle on any drug was a question of dosage. Lots of blokes reckon they ride faster with two schooners of beer in their guts. Others swear by a double-shot of rum. Still others find that a joint centres them wonderfully and allows them to focus better. Two lines of cocaine have been known to put a bold heart into many a weekend scratcher, and a fat line of good speed has seen men ride with tooth-grinding ferocity and grace.

Problems arise when fools begin to combine various drugs and then add alcohol. This plays all sorts of havoc with previously workable and established dosages. And havoc was what was going on inside my foolish head as I hammered up through the gears and prepared to engage with the Ox. Two Flared Nostrils was a metre from my back wheel as our speed climbed and we began to enter the first of the many, many corners that would eventually spit us out at the base of the Great Dividing Range and from there to the coast near Port Macquarie.

Things were happening very quickly, and a glance at my speedo showed me why. I should so not be doing that speed on this road, I thought. It's just fucken silly. But I was entering the corners at the right place, apexing them cleanly and exiting them sweetly. By all rights I should have been overcooking them, standing the bike up under panicked braking, then wobbling along to the next one. But I wasn't. And then suddenly I was.

I had gone in way too hot and way too hard and I felt the front-end juddering as the tyre lost traction and I was no longer in control of the bike. Somehow, I didn't go down. I do not know why I didn't. I just didn't.

I took the next few corners at a much reduced speed as I tried to get my head right and my pulse-rate down. I checked my mirrors. Two Flared Nostrils was nowhere to be seen. Ha! I thought, he must have shitted himself when I almost crashed and backed off.

I continued on my way past the Gingers Creek shop, and a kilometre or two past the end of the thick forest. Then just as the road started to descend more steeply, I pulled over at a road-side lookout to wait for him. I waited and waited and waited. I smoked several cigarettes. But he was nowhere to be seen. I really did not want to ride back and look for him: clearly, he was either dead or horribly maimed – if he wasn't he would be here with me. Arsehole.

I lit another cigarette. I decided I would smoke it slowly, and when it was finished I would consider going back to look for his body. The speed was making paradoxical things happen to my thought processes. Part of my mind was convinced he was impaled on a dead tree. Another part was wondering how I would deal with that. Yet another section was wondering if he maybe wasn't actually in front of me somewhere, that I was so whacked that I hadn't seen him pass me. And then I heard his engine gearing down and he hove into view. For some reason, he had my wet-weather gear stuffed down the front of his jacket and the metre-long chain and padlock I used to secure my bike draped over his head like the collar on a plough horse. Turning off his bike, he glared at me through the gap in his helmet.

'Where the fuck have you been?' I shrieked, relief flooding through me. 'I thought you were dead!'

'Thanks to you, I almost was,' he snarled, taking off his helmet, then throwing my wet-weather gear at me and tossing the chain on the ground at my feet.

'That came off the back of your bike. The chain and padlock first, it hit the road, bounced up and slammed into my front guard.'

I looked at his bike. There was no front guard where there should have been a front guard.

'It's back there,' he said evenly, jerking his head over his shoulder. 'In many pieces. It scared the shit out of me. Which was exactly when your wet-weather gear hit me in the face. That scared the rest of the shit out of me. I am now entirely empty of shit. You bastard.'

I was speechless. In all of the years I had been riding, and with all the kilometres I'd travelled, I could count on the fingers of one hand how many times I'd had stuff come off the back of my bike and still have some fingers left over. I was obsessive about strapping shit to my bike. In this case, though, it looked to be materials failure rather than the imbecile effect. I had attached my swag roll to the rack on the back of my bike, and sat the heavier Gearsack on my rear seat. I had then shoved my wet-weather gear under the ocky straps securing my swag so that I could get to them if it started to rain. To prevent them from flapping, I had weighted them down with the chain and padlock, which I had also passed under the ocky straps. I had done this many times before; it had never failed. Except this time it did. One of the ocky straps just gave way, and … well, I now owed Two Flared Nostrils a new front guard. Presumably airbrushed like a dragon's erect phallus as the last one was.

Still, he wasn't dead and he wasn't hurt, and therefore it was funny. So he retold the tale of his near-death experience, and by the end of it we were both in hysterics. When we had calmed down enough to ride, we idled our way to the town of Long Flat at the bottom of the range, and stopped at the appropriately named Traveller's Rest hotel. We rested a while and I ate a bag of salty potato chips. Two Flared Nostrils ate nothing. He gave me to understand that eating food at this juncture would only convince his body that it was weak. He ordered another glass of red instead.

An hour later we were on the Pacific Highway and making good time. We were travelling at just over the posted speed limit, traffic was light, and my brain was a rich gruel of empty white noise. I needed sleep and I needed food, but I needed sleep more. My eyes felt like dried fish-skin, and when I sighed with suffering into the bandanna wrapped around my face, my breath was the exhalation of a sewer full of rotting corpses.

The kilometres clicked by and when we stopped for petrol in Ballina, I managed to push a packet of fruit-flavoured Mentos lollies into my mouth as I paid for the juice. Two Flared Nostrils was already riding out of the servo as I rushed to put my helmet on and follow. We were only maybe two hours from Surfers Paradise now. Maybe a bit less if we threw caution to the wind and turned the wick up a notch. It was hard not to do that in the hills just near Byron Bay, but the flapping black shit had come back to the edges of my vision. I was struggling and by the time we hit Surfers, it was dark and my vision had been entirely overcome by bats. Happily, the lollies had improved my breath a bit, and I had been burping fruity stomach-acid bubbles into my mouth for the last hundred kilometres.

Once we arrived in Broadbeach, Two Flared Nostrils, who has the direction-finding capabilities of a headless bat, led me in an endless succession of turns and twists and stops and starts, until I finally lost my mind and screamed at him to stop.

'What's the address?' I demanded. He pulled out a bit of paper and handed it to me.

'Oi!' I yelled at a bloke with a skateboard who was rolling past. 'Can ... [gasp] ... tell where ... [mumble] ... address is? We lost fuck.' It was all I could do to form words to ask for directions. I felt like I'd been dragged through a rocky field chained to an angry bison.

He dutifully kicked his board up into his hands, looked at the scrap of paper, and told us to ride around the corner.

'That's the street there,' he said. 'The house is the third one from the corner. You mates of Carl's?' Carl was Two Flared Nostrils's friend and it was indeed his holiday house we were to stay at. We had ridden past it three times.

I nodded.

'Cool,' said the skateboarder. 'You here for Indy?'

I nodded again.

'Cool.' And as he skated off, I agreed with him. Yes, everything was pretty damn cool.

The evening was luscious: warm and soft and salty with the proximity of the sea. I could hear waves gently breaking to my right. There were palm trees. In the high rises around us, towels were drying on balconies and faint music and laughter was wafting from a dozen different places. Surfers Paradise is radiantly enticing on a warm evening, but the way I felt, a piss-stained mattress by the side of a freeway would have been enticing right then.

We rode slowly to the house, a huge Queenslander, which was also home to several thousand pot plants of all shapes and sizes, parked the bikes by the front door amid the profligate potted greenery, found the key and started our Indy holiday by passing out on the floor of the upstairs lounge room.

We woke up about 11 am the next morning, having slept for fourteen hours. There was no food in the house, so we had a bracing Jägermeister, two lines of speed and rode the short distance into Surfers Paradise for lunch. We cruised straight up The Esplanade, the road parallel to the beach, amazed at the amount of people wandering around. Indy was clearly a big thing up here and the footpaths were crowded with humanity – most of it in swimming costumes and much of it staring at Two Flared Nostrils's growling, reptilian motorcycle.

As we approached the pedestrian overbridge that extends from the mall at Cavill Avenue across to the beach, the road was blocked off. The actual racetrack was beyond the barrier, and we understood that if you wanted a free look at some of the cars turning left onto the straight (which was an extension of The Esplanade), it was a good idea to stand on this overbridge during the race.

A police officer standing on the footpath where the overbridge descended on the beach side waved us over. My paranoia went into overdrive. I considered running, had already down-shifted into second and was plotting my U-turn, or failing that, a quick dash through the pedestrian mall and then off west into the mountains. But Two Flared Nostrils pulled over. I stopped behind him, leaving enough room to escape in case the cop hauled him off his bike and started baton-ing his kidneys.

'You blokes can park them here in the shade if you like,' the cop said, smiling at us and indicating the footpath area under the overbridge. 'Nice bikes.'

'Thank you, officer,' Two Flared Nostrils nodded, hopped up onto the footpath with a raucous little rev, and I followed him.

'That sounds great!' the policeman enthused, nodding at Two Flared Nostrils's bike. 'You must have paid a bit for that paint job. It's spectacular!' I was now starting to wonder if the bloke was actually a real cop and not some street performer dressed up as one.

Two Flared Nostrils took off his helmet and spent a few minutes chatting to the police officer while I glared at them both suspiciously. 'Have a lovely day, officer,' Two Flared Nostrils grinned at him, walking off with his helmet in his hand. 'And thanks.'

We sat down at an outside table at a seafood restaurant almost directly across the road from where we left the bikes and ordered beer. 'That's a real cop, isn't it?' I asked.

Two Flared Nostrils nodded.

'Why is he being so fucken nice to us?'

'I imagine it has something to do with the tourism dollar,' Two Flared Nostrils replied. 'We're tourists and they've been told to be nice to us. I'm sure if we started behaving like arseholes that would change.'

I was astonished. For the past few years Two Flared Nostrils and I, along with every other motorcyclist visiting Phillip Island for the MotoGP, had been subjected to nothing but hostility, rudeness and blatant revenue-raising by the Victorian police. And tourism be fucked. Despite the many millions of dollars motorcycle riders brought into Victoria each time they visited the Phillip Island racetrack for the MotoGP or the World Superbike races, the cops did nothing but torment them from the moment they crossed the border until the moment they left the state. To be greeted in such a friendly fashion by a member of the Queensland police, who was even now warding our motorcycles while we sipped cold Coronas in the shade, was utterly unreal.

The other unreality was the view. From where we sat, observing the crowds milling around and constantly crossing and recrossing the road from the beach to the mall and back again, we were amazed by how many girls there were. Not only normal bikini-clad girls, but groups of girls dressed up in various outlandish and revealing costumes holding up signs advertising nightclubs. It was indeed precisely as we had heard.

'This is a good place,' Two Flared Nostrils observed, his eyes following a conga-line of hotpanted bleach-blondes clicking through the crowd holding up small placards advertising nearby happy hours.

After we'd sat there for a while sipping through four beers, I had come to the conclusion that every single hot blonde in Australia had been hired to strut around this immediate vicinity, advertising some kind of hedonistic beautness. There could not have been another explanation for such a proliferation of talent. It was highly impressive and immensely promising.

'Look at that,' Two Flared Nostrils breathed, inclining his head to my left.

Two stunning examples of bikini-clad, orange-sprayed, totally bleached and waxed beach-chick tottered along the footpath holding signs saying: 'Want to shoot a .44 Magnum?'

'Ladies!' Two Flared Nostrils called out. 'My friend and I would very much like to shoot a .44 Magnum!'

The girls look momentarily confused at being called 'ladies', but identified Two Flared Nostrils as the bloke who yelled at them and came mincing over.

'Hi, guys!' they squeaked at us, emitting such a fake amount of friendliness I felt compelled to shove a five-dollar note into the nearest one's pants to see if she started dancing around the nearest pole out of reflex.

They gave us a pair of brochures, smiled like their drugs were better than anyone else's and clicked off on their towering heels while Two Flared Nostrils and I watched their impossible bottoms chew gum. We examined the brochures they'd given us, and a few minutes later had made our way to a nearby indoor shooting range, hired a couple of big handguns and were merrily blazing away at paper targets. That we were full of beer and drugs made this ever so fulfilling – with each pull of the trigger I was righting wrongs, kicking arse, taking names and bringing justice to the downtrodden and death to all of those who had pissed me off in recent times.

I know why the government doesn't want anyone to have handguns. I get it. I'm not sure I want people to have handguns, either. Handguns are ridiculous amounts of fun to shoot, they must be banned and kept from the general public forever. It just cannot be permitted to have such fun, for the general public is simply not equipped to be rational about handguns. Given unfettered access to .357s and .44s and 9mm hand-cannons, the general public would quite simply go batshit crazy. And no one wants that. Not even the general public.

As we rode back to our house, I was grinning like a fiend. My day had been a blast: I had fired off a heap of big-calibre pistol rounds; I had seen more hot, near-naked girls in the last few hours than I'd seen in the last two years; I had stood on the overbridge and been blown away by the apocalyptic scream of an Indy car being fired out of a corner during practice. I didn't see much due to the crowds, but the noise was jaw dropping. I had actually managed to eat some food, and had talked Two Flared Nostrils into eating some, too. I had stood on the beach and had seen a girl sucking a man's penis as he stood on a third-floor, glass-aproned balcony, watching some low-flying acrobatic planes buzzing the beach. Two Flared Nostrils and I applauded him. He saluted and waved at us, and so did she. The sun was shining, the evening promised much, and the air was warm and smelled a bit like coconut oil, fairy floss and holidays.

The Saturday night promised to be big, so back inside the house, Two Flared Nostrils and I prepared ourselves for all and any eventualities. We did this by drinking four bottles of red wine, seven beers apiece and far too much methamphetamine than was probably, in retrospect, wise. We even belted down a few Jägermeisters, citing the recently observable benison of its manifold herbs. And then we tried to ride to Surfers.

Our plan was to ensconce ourselves in one of the strip joints, take a leisurely and gentlemanly view of whatever happened to be swinging off a pole in her sweaty G-string, and see what the evening brought. We were on holidays, Indy was in town, girls were fellating men on balconies and Surfers was going off. But Two Flared Nostrils's bike would not start. No matter how many times he pressed the starter button, the Suzuki just sat there, mute and indifferent to his mutterings. Because we were both so insanely wired our eyeballs were vibrating in their skull-sockets, his mutterings and my questions were becoming more and more frenzied.

'Why won't you fucken start?' he mumbled, thumbing the starter button over and over, then stepping back to peer at the bike.

'Maybe it's the battery?' I offered.

'Come on you, fucken thing,' he stated, his thumb mashing the starter button, ignoring my battery question.

'Maybe one of the terminals has come loose?'

'Start, you fucken shit!'

Mash.

'I reckon it might be a fuse.'

'Fucken stupid piece of fucken stupid shit!'

Mash.

'Do you have a multimeter?'

'NO! I DO NOT HAVE A FUCKEN MULTIMETER!' he shrieked, finally acknowledging my presence. 'I have a fucken piece of shit that won't fucken start! That is all I fucken have!'

'Maybe we should try to push-start it?' I said through gritted teeth. I wasn't gritting them because I was angry. I was gritting them because the industrial quantities of speed I had recently ingested made me feel like I was an explosion trapped inside a vault. Gritting my teeth was one of my coping mechanisms. Beating Two Flared Nostrils to death with one of the nearby flowerpots was also starting to look like a viable coping mechanism if he kept being insane and unreasonable.

'Let's push-start it,' he agreed.

Given that the bike showed not a single sign of life, not an instrument light, not a single pathetic whirr or click from its electronic bowels, it was doubtful any amount of push-starting would be successful. But we had to do something. If he kept pressing that starter button and ignoring my very helpful observations when the bike refused to respond, we would end up gutting each other with broken pottery shards.

Methamphetamine is a dastardly and bestial drug in that regard. It is mood-specific. If you're in a great mood and things are proceeding in a cheery and positive manner, then you are the avatar of chatty bonhomie. When things start going to shit, however, being deeply fried on gak is not what you want to be. There are so few positive outcomes when that happens.

Two Flared Nostrils climbed on the bike and I pushed him out onto the road. People were watching us from balconies across the street. I prayed they would watch quietly. Any laughter, smart-arsery or catcalls would result in Two Flared Nostrils and me immediately scaling the side of the high rise like a pair of Spidermen and throwing them into the ocean.

'Second gear,' I stated, as if I was talking to an imbecile, not a bloke who had been riding for thirty years and had been push-started a thousand times.

'I know!' he spat. He clicked his gear lever into second and I pushed.

Because speed is not a drug that encourages patience and commonsense in its users, he dumped the clutch two metres into the pushing, which caused the back wheel to lock and me to smash into the back of his bike. My sternum struck his luggage rack like a mule-kick.

'AAAGH!' I yelped, falling to my knees and wrapping my arms around my chest.

'Push harder,' he yelled back.

'Wait until I get some speed up, fuck ya! Don't just dump the clutch the second I start pushing.'

I got up and started pushing again. This time we got about ten metres along, when he once again dumped the clutch, locked the back wheel up and tore the thong off his foot when it came off the peg and scraped along the road.

'Cockfuck!' Two Flared Nostrils wailed, getting off his bike and limping in circles.

I could see little half-footprints of blood left in his wake. 'You're bleeding,' I noted.

He bent his knee and stared down over his shoulder at the sole of his left foot. Even from where I was standing, and even by the soft glow of the streetlight, I could see it was missing a lot of skin.

'Shit,' he breathed, hopping awkwardly on his right foot.

'Does it hurt?'

'No,' he panted, limping a few steps on the heel of his injured foot. That was another great benefit of speed. It was a supremely effective pain-killer.

I pushed his bike back to the house, helped him up the stairs and used some of his T-shirts to clean the injury with

Jägermeister diluted with a little water. I felt I did a pretty good job, and after I had rolled him a joint and poured him a glass of red, we were the best of mates again.

'Fuck going out,' he said.

'Yeah, fuck going out,' I lied. I really wanted to go out. Hell, I was so wired I wanted to go to the moon, and there was nothing wrong with my bike. But my companion was hurt, and his bike was dead, and if I went out on my own in the state I was in, I was pretty sure things would not end well. I was really in no fit state to be interacting with people who were not as drug-fucked as me.

So we sat on the old lounge and talked and talked and talked until our jaws hurt. We drank all the alcohol we had in the house, and while we knew we would ultimately pay for that madness with a hangover that could turn the tide itself, with all the speed we had taken we remained relatively sober.

'We should try to get some rest,' I said as the clock crept past midnight.

'You're kidding,' Two Flared Nostrils chortled. 'I may not sleep for a month.' I didn't think his estimate was too far off for me, either.

I shook my head. 'I didn't say "sleep". I said "rest". The human body is not designed to remain upright for days on end. It must, at least once every thirty-odd hours, be placed in a horizontal position so the internal organs can de-stress themselves.' I had no idea if this was true or not, but it sounded authoritative.

'Makes sense,' Two Flared Nostrils nodded. As he limped off to his bedroom and lay down, I turned off all the lights and made myself as comfortable as I could on the couch. I closed my eyes and tried to relax. Of course my mind, freed from keeping me upright and mobile, immediately went spiralling off into speed-fuelled insanity, looping from thought to thought without pause and without sense.

I might have been 'resting', but I was hyper-alert and aware. Every noise was amplified – I could hear cars roaring past, people laughing in the high rises across the street and even the waves breaking on the beach some 200 metres away. I looked at my watch. It was just after 1 am. I needed to piss. I got up and padded to the bathroom, had a squirt and was making my way back to the couch when I decided I needed to look out the front window of the house. I duly swept the curtain aside and gazed into the street. Off to my right, where our street ran into The Esplanade, I saw a sight that chilled me to the bone: police cars, marked and unmarked, their lights switched off. Their contents, which consisted entirely of very large police officers, were standing around in clumps staring at the house I was in.

'Fuck!' I spat, twitching the curtain closed, convinced that they'd seen that movement and aware that I had only seconds in which to do something before they kicked in the door and changed my life forever. So I just stood there, shifting manically from foot to foot, completely at a loss. And then, as if a something threw a switch in my head, I was a blur of movement and purpose.

'FUCK!' I screamed at Two Flared Nostrils as I ran into his bedroom.

'What?' he intoned. He was lying flat on his back in the middle of the double bed, his arms folded on his chest, wide awake and staring at the ceiling.

'Cops!' I shrieked.

He jack-knifed into a sitting position like the trained athlete he was twenty-five years ago. 'Where?' he demanded.

'Outside!'

'Where outside?'

'Outfuckingside outside!'

He stood up but seemed dazed, shifted from foot to foot, wincing with pain, his head arcing from side to side in confusion. I was not in the slightest bit confused. I knew that at any second there would be a thunderous hammering on our front door, followed by 'Open the door! This is the police!', followed by a massive smashing noise as the door was kicked in and the cops trooped in mob-handed and stared beating us with their clubs.

I knew exactly what I had to do. 'Give me all your drugs!'

Two Flared Nostrils hesitated for the briefest of seconds, then moved with a will. He got his bag of speed and gave it to me. I ran back into the living room, hauled all the dope I had out of my bag, and paused to peer out the window again. The cops were still there, milling around with rifles and putting on what looked like flak vests. The raid was clearly imminent. I was on a clock.

I hammered down the stairs and out the back door of the house. The garden was dark, but there was enough ambient light for me to do what I had to do. I ran to a corner of the yard, grabbed a plant by the stem, yanked it out of its pot, dropped the big bag of speed into the bottom of the pot, and jammed the plant back into the pot. It wouldn't fit. It was obvious something was stopping the root-ball from sitting snugly in the pot. Fuck! My mind was screaming, hyper-aware of the time ticking away. Any second now armed police would come storming into the yard and find me with a bag of goey in one hand and a pot plant in the other. They would know instantly I was not gardening and shoot me in the face. I grabbed another plant, a bigger one, and yanked it out of its pot. I scrabbled madly at the knotted root-ball with my fingers and gouged out a small hollow. I jammed the bag of speed in there, vaguely alarmed that the space I had made in the root-ball was nowhere near big enough and the bag of powder was still bulging arrogantly out, then pushed the plant back into its pot. The pot broke. I made a brief mental note not to half-heartedly gouge out any more root-balls. Then I went insane. I must have pulled another ten plants out of their pots, tried them for drug-stashing size, discounted them, broke a few, and then eventually found one that was suitable. Now to do the same with the marijuana. What?! It was gone. I'd been holding it in my other hand and I must have either dropped it or put it down in my frenzy to hide the speed. I got down on my hands and knees and started patting the back yard. I had a fair bit of ground to cover. I had been all over the place, from one side to another, and the dope could be anywhere. The cops, on the other hand, were probably marching down the street right now and would shortly be deploying their anti-drug crusade in my face. I wondered briefly if they had dogs, and hoped the smell of the soil would put them off.

My hand found the bag of dope and I grabbed the nearest pot plant, tore it out of its pot, deposited the dope, put the plant back, and sprinted back into the house. As I was going up the stairs, the house was suddenly illuminated by blue and red flashing lights. It had begun. The raid was now.

I suddenly remembered that I also had gunshot residue all

over my hands. Why the police would be testing me for that I wasn't sure, because it wasn't like I was thinking clearly, but I knew that if they did, they would find that I had recently been firing a handgun. This realisation froze me like a feral animal staring into the beam of a spotlight. I stopped in the middle of the lounge room and wondered if I should maybe not just lie down on the floor now. It would certainly save me from being brutally thrown there in a few short minutes. Once again I was gripped with drug-induced indecision, when Two Flared Nostrils emerged from the bedroom.

'They're coming!' I wheezed, my eyes wide with terror and madness.

Two Flared Nostrils looked a little spooked, but seemed more together than me. Of course, he hadn't just been manically trying to hide a stupid amount of drugs in the back yard, so it was understandable. The blue and red flashing lights continued unabated; I could see them through the curtains and their muted flashes swirled around the living room. Two Flared Nostrils went to the window and peered cautiously through the small space between the curtains. Smart man, I thought. Thinking tactically. Never make yourself a big window target in case the police sniper took his shot. He stared out the window for a few long seconds, twitched the curtain closed, and looked at me. 'Come with me,' he said.

'Where?' I demanded to know.

Surely the mad freak was not about to hole up in the bathroom and make the cops yell at us through bullhorns? Maybe he was thinking of barricading the front door and forcing the cops to shoot their way in behind a bulldozer.

He walked to the stairs and went down them. 'Come on,' he said.

He's giving himself up, I thought. Genius. That was being proactive. The cops didn't always shoot those who surrendered. I would follow his example and give myself up, too. I clattered down the stairs and went out the front door with my hands on my head and despair in my heart.

Two Flared Nostrils was standing on the footpath in front of our house, staring up the street at the cops. I lowered my hands and went to stand next to him. We stood there for a few seconds, not speaking. We just looked at the police on the corner, and all their cars and all the flashing lights.

'It's a random breath-testing set-up,' Two Flared Nostrils finally said. He pronounced it quietly and calmly, which made the statement all the more powerful.

He was right, of course. That is exactly what all those cops were doing on the corner of our street. For the last half-hour, as I rushed madly about the back yard hiding drugs, they had been setting up a booze-bus. The flak jackets I had seen were nothing but reflective safety vests. The guns and battering rams were light-wands and 'Stop Police' signs.

'What did you do with the drugs?' Two Flared Nostrils asked, lighting a cigarette and offering me one.

'I hid them in the back yard.'

He nodded. 'Good. It's better to be safe than sorry.'

'Look,' I said. 'I really thought we were gonna get raided. I saw all these cop cars and all these cops and ...'

Two Flared Nostrils put up a hand to silence me. 'I would have thought the same thing.'

I dragged heavily on my cigarette, utterly deflated both emotionally and physically. The last half-hour had been intense. Coupled with the stupid amount of drugs and alcohol we'd had, not only last night (it was now early morning), but over the course of the last two days, our excesses were really starting to take their toll on me.

'It'll be light in a few hours,' Two Flared Nostrils advised no one in particular. 'We should probably try to rest a bit more.'

I agreed and we trooped back into the house. I lay back down on the couch and he went back into the bedroom. Then I must have fainted, because the next thing I knew, it was daylight and there was an unfamiliar man in a shirt and tie asking me if I was awake.

My gummed-up eyes flew open and I was instantly awake, my heart thudding in my chest. 'Who the fuck are you?' I growled, levering myself unsteadily to my feet and preparing to do battle with this nicely dressed intruder.

'Hi,' the man beamed, sticking out his hand. 'I'm Josh, and I work for Glitterbeach Realty. We manage this property. The owner asked me to call by and see if everything was ... erm, okay. People get a bit worried about their rental properties during Indy weekend.'

I felt like throwing up on his chest, but I knew that would probably be counterproductive this early in our relationship. Thankfully, Two Flared Nostrils emerged from his bedroom so Josh stuck his hand out and repeated who he was. Two Flared Nostrils identified himself then asked Josh what I was just about to ask him: 'What are you doing here?'

'I'm sorry,' Josh smiled shyly. 'But I came by two hours ago and knocked and knocked and there was no answer. So I went around the back to see if you might be in the back yard and I saw lots of damaged pots and ripped-up plants. It looked like a hurricane had gone through the place.'

Two Flared Nostrils and I exchanged looks, and Josh went on. 'So I knocked again. I thought maybe you guys had gone out, so I went down to the shopping centre and made some calls and had a bite to eat and then I came back and started knocking. There was still no answer, and I was a bit worried, what with the back yard looking like it was, so I let myself in with the key and saw your friend here asleep on the couch. And then he woke up.'

'We had a late night,' Two Flared Nostrils stated flatly.

'What happened to the back yard and all the plants?'

'I have no idea,' Two Flared Nostrils shrugged. 'We were out most of the night and we haven't been out there at all.'

Josh looked at me. I felt I really needed to throw up on him and probably on myself, but managed to shrug instead.

'It's pretty bad,' he said, wincing expressively.

'Let's take a look,' Two Flared Nostrils said, and the three of us marched down the stairs and out the back door.

It was, as Josh had said, pretty bad. In my insane fear-frenzy the night before, I had uprooted dozens of plants, knocked over dozens more and broken more pots than I could count. There were shards of pottery, leaves, stems and potting mix everywhere. It did indeed look like a small localised cyclone had torn through the yard.

'Fucken kids,' Two Flared Nostrils rumbled, shaking his head.

'Do you think?' Josh said, nudging a large shard of clay pottery with his shoe.

Two Flared Nostrils looked imperiously at Josh. 'What else could it be? Surely you don't think my friend and I decided to come into the back yard and vandalise all these lovely plants apropos of nothing?'

I was pretty sure Josh did not know what 'apropos' meant because he looked a bit frightened and confused, but he did put his hands up defensively. 'No!' he gushed. 'Not at all!'

'There are drunks and drug addicts running wild all through the streets here,' Two Flared Nostrils continued. 'The police are simply not doing their job.'

Josh nodded nervously, which is when I promptly bent forward and geysered a rancid stream of sour vomit onto the ground beside him. I think a little probably splashed onto his trousers.

'My friend is unwell,' Two Flared Nostrils explained as Josh back-pedalled, his face pale with shock and disgust. 'It is probably food-poisoning. I'm going to take him to the medical centre if you're finished here.'

Josh nodded. 'I really have to report this to the police ... and I'll ... I'll ... um, let the owners know what's happened,' he stammered, walking out of the back yard.

'Tell them that a good fence and front gate would certainly help in keeping feral drug-addicts out of their yard, and that if they ever plan to rent this property to us again, then there had better be some security measures in place. We could have been murdered by these criminals last night.'

Josh left and I threw up again, only not as violently. Two Flared Nostrils brought me a glass of water. 'I thought you said this was your mate's place,' I muttered as I gingerly sipped at the glass, half-expecting the bastard had added a teaspoonful of chemical horror to it, but then remembered I had hidden all of that in the yard somewhere.

'It's actually his mother's,' Two Flared Nostrils sighed. 'She would be the one who would have asked that prick to look in on us. The woman's hated me since high school. Says I've always been a bad influence on her son.'

'She sounds like a total bitch,' I said.

'An utter sow,' Two Flared Nostrils agreed. 'Where are the drugs?'

I looked around the back yard. 'I have no idea.' And I didn't. They could have been in any one of the dozens of still-intact pots. Two Flared Nostrils sighed, then we started looking. As it turned out, we didn't have to look for long. I found the dope in the fourth pot I upended, and the speed shortly afterwards.

'Shit,' I said, peering into it.

Two Flared Nostrils came and looked over my shoulder. 'Shit,' he agreed.

When I had jammed the plant back into the pot, I had pushed it straight through the bulging plastic bag full of powder I had half-tucked into the root-ball. It would seem that in my panic, I had been somewhat forceful and the speed was now part of the potting mix clumped around the root-ball.

We went back inside the house. 'The omens are bad,' Two Flared Nostrils said.

I nodded. Our holiday in the sun had indeed taken a turn for the worse. It was certain the police would be around at some stage, and neither Two Flared Nostrils nor I wanted to spend any time answering questions or assisting them with their enquiries. Two Flared Nostrils dealt with police in the course of his work, and felt that each time he did a small part of his soul died. He was certainly not about to engage with them on his holidays. In my case, few positive outcomes had ever been reached in my dealings with them over the years.

'Maybe we should take the long way home,' I suggested. 'And maybe we should take it now.'

Two Flared Nostrils nodded. 'I do believe it is time to get out of Dodge.'

And so we did. But we first had to turn his bike's kill switch to the 'On' position. Which was probably something we should have considered the night before. Among many other things.

RACE ME OFF

My wife is a highly observant woman. Whenever I skulk home after having committed some odious offences against humanity, shamed my ancestors or threatened to bring ruination upon my family, she looks at me with her wonderfully liquid eyes, observes my cur-like demeanour and says: 'You're a fucken idiot.' It's not like she even knows any details of my corruption yet; she can tell by the way I look, or smell, or something, that I have done shit I am regretting with every fibre of my being. Probably. Happily, her supernatural powers of observation are backed by the patience and tolerance of a saint. And not one of those new-fangled modern ones, either. Her patience is that of the old-time saints. Hell, a mountain range could take patience lessons from my wife. But I still manage to test her reserves of it from time to time.

> 'Racing is life. Anything before
> or after is just waiting.'
>
> **STEVE McQUEEN**

The wages of sin are manifold. And my sins, being more sinful than most people's, usually command an executive-level salary, with bonuses. So when I committed the sin of unalloyed stupidity and added to it the sins of hubris, arrogance and overweening pride, the price I paid was both suitable and commensurate – and included smashed ribs, bruised organs and a wife who took great delight in my inability to wipe my own arse for a fortnight.

How I had been reduced to lying on my couch for two weeks and whimpering like a scabby yellow dog is a cautionary tale of middle-aged dumbness and conceit, and like many such tales began one evening in a faux German beer hall in Sydney's Rocks area. I had just completed a two-year stint as editor of *The Picture* magazine, which was at that time the highest-selling weekly men's magazine in Australia despite its staff of genius misfits, brilliant substance-abusers, and a gigantic bow-legged Nazi who looked like he tortured animals in his kitchen. In the time-honoured tradition of tabloid journalism, whenever a staff member departs it is incumbent upon the remaining staff to replace as much of his blood with alcohol as they can manage before the paramedics are called and proceedings shunt to an unpleasant halt. The beer hall was chosen because the staff knew of my fondness for good beer and loathing of German oompah-pah music, the confluence of which, after I had consumed a few litres, was hugely entertaining for everyone. Except the hapless musicians, who nonetheless heroically struggled to play Cold Chisel every time I demanded it.

Of course, being immeasurably full of my own self-worth and having convinced myself I could easily drink a few litres of beer with my staff and still ride home in perfect splendour,

I rode down to the Löwenbräu Keller and parked my bike out the front. About five hours later, I sailed unsteadily back into the street, past the two po-faced bouncers and a smiling waitress in a pretty dirndl that pushed her big tits upwards to the heavens in a most enticing fashion, and navigated my way back to my waiting Triumph.

I was no longer drunk. I had been drunk an hour or so before, but the five sour apple schnapps shots I had necked since becoming drunk had ensured that I was now in the state known as Beyond Drunk. It is a state when all things seem possible, nothing is forbidden and you are the lord of all you survey. It took me three goes to stutter my key into the ignition, and I considered going back inside for a quick schnapps to steady my nerves.

'You okay to ride?' a voice said from behind me. It was my chief-sub, a talented young woman called Amelia, who had followed me out and was clearly seeking verbal confirmation as to my immense and obvious well-being. I turned, somewhat majestically as I recall, fixed her with a beaming grin and winked slowly with both eyes because I was strangely unable to do so with one.

'Fuck, yeah!' I enthused.

'You sure?'

I nodded. 'Mate, if I can't throw my leg over her, I can't ride her,' I explained, and promptly smashed my knee into the seat as I went to demonstrate. 'That was practice,' I explained as she reached out to steady me.

I succeeded on the next attempt, performed a slow but mostly proper U-turn, and with her quite unnecessary instruction to 'Be careful!' sounding in my wake, headed off. Home was almost forty kilometres away over the Harbour Bridge and down the M2 tollway, and since I was well-acquainted with the fact that the cops did not normally erect their brightly lit roadside random breath tests on fast, multi-laned roads like tollways, expressways and freeways due to their well-founded fear of being run over by the very drunks they are meant to be catching, I felt I was on safe ground. Provided I didn't do anything strange and attract attention to myself, I should be able to get home without interference. But I did understand that I needed to get home rather quickly, rationalising that the longer I was on the road in my enhanced state, the greater the odds were of terrible shit happening to me. I may have been full of beer and schnapps, but my powers of higher reasoning certainly seemed sound.

So as I crossed the Harbour Bridge, I twisted the throttle open a bit more and found that 170 kms per hour was a perfectly suitable velocity for the conditions – both mine and the Gore Hill Expressway's. A few minutes later, I was in the zone and commencing my run up the M2. I only had a few kilometres to go until I was safely home, the traffic was sparse and the night was warm. I was burping schnapps into my mouth and thinking that it, of all the various alcohols I had tried, seemed to retain its taste-integrity even when it was coming back up. Snuggling my arse further back into the Speed Triple's seat, I checked my speedo which told me that 170 was still being provided, then looked into the tiny, almost dentist-sized mirror I had fitted to the bike to replace the hideous but effective stock items.

I saw blue and red flashing lights a fair way behind me. My stomach lurched, then immediately settled. Blue and red – it was obviously an ambulance. The cops had all-blue flashers. I was cool. But I checked my mirror again. Fuck, I thought. That ambo is really moving.

The flashing lights were now close and getting closer. I was already in the left-hand lane, so I fully expected the vehicle to pass me with a wail of sirens at any second. I even slowed down to about 150. But he just sat on my arse. And my stomach fell into my ankles. The realisation that the vehicle behind me was not an ambulance came at exactly the same time as my recollection that the police, and indeed all emergency vehicles, were adopting uniform blue and red flashing lights.

For a few brief seconds I considered doing a runner. My runner score at that time stood at one-all – twice before I had run from the police, and my success rate was 50 per cent. And I was stone-cold sober on both of those occasions. So while the sour apple schnapps coursing through my veins insisted I stop being a bitch, screw the throttle to the stop and give the Highway Patrol a chance to earn its wages, whatever small amount of commonsense remained told me to pull over and try not to get pepper-sprayed. I throttled off, put on my blinker and eased to the shoulder of the M2.

The Highway Patrol car pulled up behind me, and I turned off my bike and dismounted as steadily as I could, desperately trying not to tumble over the Armco railing and into the deep drainage ditch on the other side. Much like Napoleon at the onset of the Russian winter, I was still confident – reckoning there was still a chance I could bluff my way out of this with only a speeding ticket. I stood beside my bike and faced the approaching Highway Patrol officer with schnapps-fuelled bravado and my jeans full of terror.

When he was two metres away from me, he spoke. 'Bit quick, Borrie,' he said cheerily.

Borrie? Fuck. He knew who I was. This had happened to me now and again and was purely as a result of my columns in *Australian Motorcycle News*, which the police doubtlessly read with interest and concern.

When he got within a metre of me he stopped and recoiled. 'Fuck me,' he said, waving his hand in front of his face. 'How much have you had to drink?'

'A lot,' I shrugged. The jig was as up as a jig could ever be. There was clearly no chance of bluffing my way out of this, and no point in pretending otherwise. There was also no point in antagonising a seemingly friendly cop with a litany of lies, half-truths and schnapps-powered bullshit – experience had taught me that performances of this kind result in over-tightened handcuffs, baton-enriched kidneys and some facial scuff-marks from when they place a boot on the back of your head and press your face into the ground to enhance your co-operation.

'I'm going to need you to do a roadside breathalyser,' the policeman said, somewhat sadly, I thought. He produced the hand-held device, and while he was inserting the disposable white tube he asked me why I was riding so fast.

'I just wanted to get home as quickly as possible,' I replied truthfully.

'You know I wouldn't have stopped you if you weren't going so quick?' he sighed, putting the breathalyser to my face. 'Breathe into the tube until I tell you to stop. You were flying. Stop.'

'Was I weaving?' I asked while he waited for the machine to confirm what he and I both knew.

'Nah,' he grinned, peering at his machine. 'You were track-ing true. I'm now going to place you under arrest and take you back to the police station where you will be required to undergo a breath-analysis. Have a seat on the Armco.'

I sat down and he went to call a paddywagon. When he came back he asked me if I was alright. I nodded. Physically I felt fine. Mentally, not so much. I knew I was in several worlds' worth of shit and strife and it was only because I was still extremely drunk that I wasn't wailing and howling and beating my chest in self-loathing.

'I'm going to have to book you for Speed Dangerous, too,' he said gloomily.

'Really?' I asked.

He nodded ruefully. 'Yeah.'

'Fuck.'

'Yeah.'

The paddywagon arrived, and I stood up. 'Do you have to handcuff me?' I asked.

'I think we can do without that,' he smiled. 'In you go. Mind your head.'

This was the first time I had entered a paddywagon in this fashion, so not everything in my life had turned into total shit. Just most things.

Before he clanged the door shut, I asked him what police sta-tion we were all going to.

'North Ryde,' he said. It wasn't far and a few minutes later I was off-loaded at the back of the station and taken into the charge room.

'I want to call my lawyer,' I suddenly said.

Both the Highway Patrol officer who had arrested me and the senior sergeant who was about to charge me looked at me in surprise. 'You're being done for DUI,' the sergeant said, 'not fucken murder. You'll be out of here in an hour.'

'I want to call my lawyer,' I repeated.

The sergeant shrugged and asked the Highway Patrol bloke to prepare the breathalyser machine in the next room while I made my phone call. I called Brother Silverback, my best friend and, coincidentally, one hell of a criminal lawyer.

'I'm fucked,' I said when he answered.

'Where are you fucked?' he asked.

'At North Ryde police station.'

'What are you fucked with?'

'High Range PCA and Speed Dangerous.'

There was a brief silence, which did much to reinforce my view of my dire circumstances, then Brother Silverback spoke again. 'I'm on my way.'

While he did that, I was taken next door to do some more breathing into a much larger machine, which informed everyone that I was well over the bottom level of High Range Prescribed Content of Alcohol in my blood (which was 0.150). From memory, I was 0.172, so those last few schnapps shots really worked a treat.

'Nice,' the sergeant nodded, peering at the paper on which my score was inked, then showed it to the Highway Patrol officer.

'Nice,' he agreed.

Following that, Brother Silverback appeared with another police officer. He looked at me with pity, then fixed his gimlet gaze upon the two cops. Now Brother Silverback was, by any definition, a magnificent specimen of a lawyer. Suitably grey-haired with a small, neat beard, he stood an imposing six and a half feet tall and possessed an intellect that literally seared you with its scope and might. He was a dour and grim opponent. Not only was he physically intimidating – to his opponents he was the intellectual equivalent of a NATO airstrike on an Afghan village. When he was done explaining to you why you were wrong, there'd be nothing left but wailing, smoke, horror and people going: 'What the bastard-fuck happened there?'

On this occasion the fact that he was also rather drunk and filling the room with the sour tang of some doubtlessly fine vintage red was entirely overlooked by the cops, who gazed upon him with quite suitable awe.

'I represent him,' he said, indicating vaguely in my direction with a large hand but keeping his gaze on the cops. 'Might I have a word with the arresting officer?'

The Highway Patrol officer immediately obliged and they left the room while the sergeant fingerprinted me and typed up the charge sheet. As I sat in the holding dock I burped the last of the schnapps into my mouth. More than an hour had gone by since my arrest, but I did not seem to be sobering up. If anything, I was drunker now than I had been when I was pulled over. Part of me wanted to lie down and another part of me wanted to go to a strip-club and throw money at strippers. While I was working out how much I would need, and how I could explain such a late night ATM withdrawal to my wife after being charged with such criminal offences, Brother Silverback returned.

'Are you finished, Sergeant?' he asked politely.

The sergeant nodded, handing him a small sheaf of papers. 'Just get him to sign those and he can go.'

'Thank you so much,' Brother Silverback smiled, opening the gate of the holding dock and leading me over to a desk. 'Sign here and here,' he said, handing me a pen.

I signed and the crushing reality of what had just happened began to assert itself in my muddy head.

As he drove me home, he wanted to know why I was so inordinately stupid. I wanted to know what we were going to do about my bike sitting on the M2 all by itself in the middle of the night. He wanted to know if my wife was going to drive a kitchen knife into my face the second I told her what I had done, or if she was going to wait until I passed out. I wanted to know how many years' jail I was looking at and when, if ever, I was going to get my licence back.

The only question we could answer at that moment was the one about the bike. After dropping me home, Brother Silverback would ask my wife to drive him back to get my bike, thereby delaying, possibly, any stabbings she might want to deliver in the heat of the moment of my revelation. Which is pretty much what happened.

I passed out on the couch seconds after my wife and Brother Silverback went to get my bike and woke up the next morning without a steak knife in my neck. But that was the only positive thing that could be said about that day. My licence was gone. For how long was yet to be determined by a court, but it was looking pretty dire. The guideline judgment from the NSW Court of Criminal Appeal – which Brother Silverback explained to me was an instruction manual from some senior justices for the scummy magistrates who were, in the justices' learned opinions, far too lenient with people who operated motor vehicles while drunk – stated that I should lose my licence for three years. Add to that another six months' suspension for the Speed Dangerous charge and ... well, immigrating to South Africa was starting to look like a viable option.

Seven weeks later my case was due to be heard. Brother Silverback was on fire with determination and messianic purpose. He understood what was at stake. He was my best mate and the bloke I rode everywhere with, and we had shared some wild old times. On that day, however, he was my lawyer and I was his client, and that was exactly as it should have been.

'Why aren't we going inside?' I asked him as we waited outside the courthouse, chain-smoking cigarettes and not really talking about anything, except how it was impossible to get a good cup of coffee anywhere near Ryde Local Court.

'We don't need to go inside yet,' Brother Silverback explained.

'But court started an hour ago,' I blinked.

'Yes, it did,' he nodded. 'I had a word with the prosecutor. Good bloke, I played cricket with him back in uni. We agreed that Her Honour is not the sharpest knife in the drawer and that when the time is right, she may benefit from my explanation of the guideline judgment.' I had no idea what he was talking about, but if my lawyer didn't think I had to be in court, then I didn't have to be in court.

At precisely a quarter to twelve, Brother Silverback declared it was now time for us to be in court. His reasoning was that Her Honour would be keen to go to lunch soon, and that immediately after he had explained certain things regarding the

271

guideline judgment and how my crimes needed to be viewed within the spirit of that judgment, he was sure her lunch would be one relatively free of concerns regarding the social impact of my criminality.

When we entered the courtroom, Brother Silverback and the police prosecutor, a severe-looking, dry-skinned axe of a man, consulted in whispers for a few minutes while Her Honour read stuff on her bench. Neither she nor the prosecutor so much as glanced at me, which was somewhat disappointing as I had made every attempt to look as upstanding as I possibly could. I had let my hair grow out so as not to appear like the shaven-headed bikie thug people would normally imagine me to be. I was wearing my only suit, a cheap, shapeless item some Lebanese con-artist had sold me out of his van in a car park one evening. I'd taken off my rings, covered up my tattoos, and instead of contact lenses I wore thick glasses. I'd also brought a veritable phone book of character references from every respectable human being I knew. Brother Silverback had told me that providing good character references would assist Her Honour in not imposing the death penalty, and I knew he was only half-joking.

'Yes, counsel,' Her Honour intoned, looking at Brother Silverback and the prosecutor over her glasses. In case you were wondering, the word 'Yes' is not used by magistrates and judges as a form of permission, assent or agreement. It is normally an instruction to proceed, but it can also be a request to shut up, or an order for hostilities to cease while His or Her Honour reads something or consults a legal text.

'If I could be excused, Your Honour,' the prosecutor stated

flatly. 'The prosecution has nothing further than the facts on the brief of evidence to tender.'

The judge accepted the brief he offered, excused the prosecutor, read the brief, then looked at Brother Silverback. 'Yes,' she said.

This was my cue to look as contrite as it was possible to look without turning into an abattoir animal.

'Good morning, Your Honour,' Brother Silverback began, and after identifying himself, he launched into a learned, wide-ranging and utterly brilliant legal oration. Every movie lawyer I had ever seen looked like a blundering, stuttering, half-baked shyster by comparison. Brother Silverback was more than just a simple criminal solicitor: he was licensed to practise as a barrister, and was able to perform that function as well as many of the best be-wigged and black-robed learned counsels in the country.

Her Honour was clearly as impressed as I was. The prosecutor would have been impressed too, but he had mysteriously left and had not returned, and thus there was no one to press the prosecution case, demand that I be crushed by the full weight of the law, or dispute Brother Silverback's insightful interpretation of the intent of the guideline judgment.

He spoke for about half an hour. His tone was measured, polite and mellow, his observations were erudite and his manifest understanding of the issues was authoritative. His performance was utterly mesmerising to me. I had seen him do his court thing before and I had seen how utterly devastating he could be when cross-examining a witness who wasn't providing the answer he required. But this was my arse on the line that day, and it was obvious that what he was doing was simply charming the magistrate in order to save it.

'Thank you, counsel,' the magistrate interrupted him. 'I have heard enough. Stand up, Mr Mihailovic.'

I stood up.

'I trust you understand the gravity of your offence?'

'Yes, Your Honour,' I nodded.

'You endangered yourself and other road users by being so heavily under the influence of alcohol, and I acknowledge there is a great deal of concern within the community about drink-driving and it is the court's job to reflect the concerns of that community.'

My heart sank. She was clearly going to smash me to pieces.

'I have read your references and I have listened with great interest to the submissions of your counsel.' Here she paused and smiled at Brother Silverback, who respectfully and gallantly inclined his head, in much the same way a musketeer might bow before Marie Antoinette.

'I feel,' she continued as I mentally tried to prepare myself for my doom and failed, 'that all things considered, a licence suspension of no less than sixteen months is warranted in this instance.'

'Thank you, Your Honour,' Brother Silverback quickly said and, taking me by the arm, led me out of the courtroom, making sure we both stopped at the door and bowed respectfully to the bench.

'Did she say sixteen months?' I demanded as we stepped out into the sunshine.

'She sure did,' Brother Silverback beamed at me.

'Do you want me to suck you off here or in the car?' I asked, struggling to understand what had just happened.

'I might get you to pay for someone else to do that later, but yes, it's a pretty good result.'

'What are you talking about?' I gushed. 'It's a fantastic result! I thought I was gonna get three and a half years off the road!'

Brother Silverback's satisfied smile could have warmed a homeless child. 'Good thing the Speed Dangerous charge disappeared, huh?' he winked.

I blinked at him in confusion.

'When I spoke to the prosecutor this morning, we agreed that you were in enough shit as it was with the High Range PCA and another six months' suspension on top of the three years you were probably going to get was just … well, just not necessary. He agreed not to proceed with that charge.'

I wanted to fall to my knees and worship him as the Risen Christ.

A few days later, as I climbed aboard a train to go to work, the dour reality of my situation hit me in the guts like a frozen chicken fired out of a cannon. Certainly an appalling catastrophe had been avoided by Brother Silverback's legal brilliance, but there was still a medium-level catastrophe that needed to be dealt with. Sixteen months off the road was just unthinkable. I could not wrap my head around it. I had lost my licence by running out of points several times over the years, usually for three-month stints and once for a six-month period. It was certainly onerous, especially during the summer months when all your mates were out riding and you were at home slamming cones and drinking yourself into a stupor as quickly as possible so as not to be tempted to go for a quick spin just to ... um, keep your eye in, as it were. But three months was doable with some crying, and to be perfectly honest, I did ride during those suspensions. I just picked my time and place, and was very careful.

But sixteen months ... That was an age. Yes, it was much better than three and a half years, and yes, it was certainly all sunshine and lollipops outside the courthouse that day, but as I sat in the train carriage bathed in the eye-watering bodily fug of my fellow passengers, my soul began to die.

In this instance, I simply did not dare ride on the road during the suspension. Brother Silverback went to great lengths to make me understand that my licence was not simply suspended as it had been in the past, it was actually cancelled. It had ceased to exist. And riding while suspended for using up your licence points does not carry the same death-by-firing-squad type of punishment as riding around when your licence has been thrown into the garbage because you were criminally drunk and cracking the old ton down the freeway one warm spring evening.

Brother Silverback was adamant in this regard. 'Don't do it,' he said. 'Just don't fucken do it. If you get caught they will put you into a pit with vipers and diseased lunatics will shit upon your stupid head. I will not be able to help you. No one will be able to help you.'

So I started doing my time. With each lurch of the train carriage, a small shining piece of my motorcycling spirit turned black and perished with a silvery little squeak of anguish. The sheer and insufferable inconvenience of not being permitted to ride or drive impacted my entire family every day. My wife stopped glaring at me after about a month and I think she started to feel a little sorry for me, because she genuinely understood how much being able to ride meant to me. She never actually said anything, but I knew there was pity in her heart for the shambles of a man I was becoming. I was a train and bus commuter. I was an *Untermensch*. A prole. A peon. A snivelling, scuttling insect at the mercy of public transport, which is a hate-crime industry run by and staffed by lobotomised lizards who have recently learned to walk upright and who actively despise commuters and their endless need to commute.

Then my mate Ian had an idea. And it was a beauty. 'You need to go racing,' he said to me one evening.

'Racing?' I blinked stupidly at him. 'What kind of racing?'

'Motorcycle racing,' he chirped. 'The best kind of racing there is.'

This racing thing had not even occurred to me before. I'd never had any kind of desire to race on a track, and while I was certainly competitive on the road and would chase other motorcycles like a dog chases balls, it was always for shits and giggles. Racing, from what I had seen and understood about it, was serious. It required racing bikes and special leathers and full-face helmets and testicles that were enlarged and hefty with masculine zest. I certainly believed I owned such a pair of testicles, but was bereft of all the other requirements.

Once again Ian had an answer. 'You can race the Manbike,' he grinned.

This was true. I could. It was, after all, a purpose-built race bike. Ian had raced it, with scant success, but I imagined that was more to do with Ian's skill-set than the Manbike.

His Manbike was ever so aptly named. It was in essence a

Suzuki GSX1100 motor from about twenty years ago, when Suzuki would fill their engines with the shrieking souls of the damned, searing hate and naked horsepower in equal measure. Added to that was some high-performance sorcery from the high priest of Japanese speed, Pops Yoshimura himself, whose factory had contributed cams and an assortment of other internals in an effort to stop the donk detonating like a Taliban IED when you opened the taps. This whole bundle sat within the cradle of an English-built Harris frame which, much to the consternation of Ian's fellow members of the British, European and American Racing and Supporters (BEARS) club, made the Japanese monster eligible to race among them.

As a genuine, purpose-built race bike, and a rather budget-based one, the Manbike made no concessions to comfort or glamour. In the dip on the body-work behind the home-painted tank which was the space allotted for a seat, there was a centimetre-thick square of black rubber foam. It was where you sat. But only at those times your arse took a break from being puckered in horror and needed something softer to help spread the shit evenly throughout the backside of your leathers.

The Yoshimura exhaust system was held on with disparate bolts and a few hopeful prayers, the controls were minimal and mismatched, the clutch-action heavy, the throttle-action heavier, the steering ponderous and the whole bike looked brutal, meaningful, old, nasty, and like it was built in some bloke's shed – all of which it was. But it went like a missile. It had no choice. That motor certainly provided a significant amount of ponies and the brilliant Harris frame did everything in its power to make the thing handle. It was let down a little by its suspension, its brakes and its not inconsiderable weight. The end result was much like riding an angry fridge down a mountainside. It was quite hard work on a tight and technical track – at the end of ten laps you felt like you'd spent a few hours debating your bizarre views on democracy with the Egyptian riot police.

Of course, I did not know any of this the evening Ian suggested I go racing. Nor did I know it a few weeks later when a bunch of us got together at his house for the unveiling of the finally finished Manbike and the announcement that I would be contesting two 'Formula Three' BEARS races at a forthcoming race weekend. And I would be doing this at the tight and technical 'Creek', Sydney's Eastern Creek Raceway, which is today grandiosely named the Sydney Motorsport Park.

That fateful day was four months away. In that four months I had some hoops to jump through before I was allowed to endanger myself and my fellow racers on a racetrack. I had to join an accredited club, acquire a racing licence and, most crucially, reduce my disgraceful lap-time around Eastern Creek from an all-together sleep-inducing two-minutes-and-who-gives-a-shit-how-many-seconds to something much less shameful.

The lap record around Eastern Creek then stood at around the one-minute-thirty-second mark. Anything in the high one-thirties and you were probably wearing sponsorship on your leathers. Times in the mid one-forties were what blokes who raced regularly and on pretty quick bikes were pulling. A normal street-riding monkey like me was considered 'okay' if he could manage his shit-heap around the circuit in under two minutes. Anything in the high one-fifties was shrugged at by the fast boys and deemed unremarkable, but not sailor's-penis-in-the-mouth-gay like times over two minutes. Of course, no one said anything to your face about being slow or scared or shit, but because it's racing, everyone always asked you about your lap-times. You could decide for yourself how you were doing by their reaction to your reply.

So if I was to make a vague fist of racing in the BEARS Formula Three Class – and not being lapped during Lap Two of a five-lap race would be a good start – my kung fu had to be much mightier than it was.

Formula Three is an interesting and wide-ranging class in BEARS (who are a fabulous bunch of blokes, but should more rightly be known as BEARP, for 'British, European and American Racing Psychopaths') and featured bikes such as the screamingly intense Aprilia RS250 two-stroke, any of the BMWs (both staid Boxer and vicious K), Husqvarnas, Harley-Davidson XR1200s, two-valve Buells and a selection of the lesser race-oriented Ducatis. And of course, anything with a Harris frame.

In hindsight, this might not have been the most ideal class in which a bloke in his mid-forties would commence his racing career. There are any number of other classes and other clubs where you can virtually idle around the track on old dungers with nervous women, doddery pensioners and deodorant-needing enthusiasts, and pretend you're racing.

Then there're the BEARS. Like I said, fabulous blokes to a man. I could not have asked for a friendlier welcome to their ranks or hoped for more moral support the day I came to race. But they take their racing very seriously. Like mourners by a grave seriously. Like men in SS uniforms coming to your synagogue seriously. Like visiting your dying mother in hospital seriously.

In the pit garages it's all shit-stirring, laughter, advice and all the help you could ever ask for if you need parts, tools or know-how in getting your bike out onto the racetrack. But it is only so they can then murder you on that racetrack like a cold beer on a hot day.

I knew none of this when I first committed to racing. It was one of the steepest learning curves of my life – and one of the fastest. It's only a few seconds between the start line and Turn Four, but I absorbed the information being force-fed to me like a canyon drinking a waterfall. But before I did that, I had to stop riding like an idiot and start riding like a racer, or someone who was going to pretend he was a racer.

To achieve this, I needed race leathers and a full-face helmet, all of which I was given thanks to the fact that I sold *Australian Motorcycle News* the story of my transformation from mere mortal mugwump to motorcycle-racing sex-god, and the editor and some advertisers figured it might be amusing to see me make this attempt. I got the same reaction I would think a fat cake-eating chick would have got had she declared her intention to summit Everest.

So the gear wasn't the problem, and I had the bike, though I had not yet ridden it. The biggest obstacle remained me riding around Eastern Creek like a walrus on a pushbike, so I called my mate Steve Brouggy, a former world-class 125cc MotoGP racer who runs fantastic superbike schools at Eastern Creek and the Phillip Island circuit. Steve is one of the most genuine and caring human beings I have ever met – and one of the fastest riders

I have ever seen. What he does for a living is teach people how to ride better, and consequently, faster. This confluence of qualities and skills was unbeatable as far as I was concerned, and quite crucial to me in my current straits.

'Steve, you gotta help me,' I mewled into the phone.

'What's wrong, mate?' he asked, his voice filled with genuine concern.

'I've decided to go racing,' I said.

'That's ... great,' Steve replied. Like any serious racer, he was always keen to spread his gospel of speed, but wary of who might suddenly decide to take up the faith.

'No it's not,' I went on, babbling like a fool. 'I'm scared I'm gonna die. I'm even more scared of riding like a moron and being so slow I'll be laughed off the track right after qualifying. And I lost my licence for sixteen months and I haven't ridden a bike in almost three months, and I have to race in eleven weeks and I'm totally rooted.'

'What are you racing?' Steve asked.

'A Yoshimura-kitted GSX in a Harris frame.'

A meaningful silence followed that disclosure. 'What are you racing that in?'

'BEARS Formula Three.'

A more meaningful silence followed the second revelation. I broke it. 'I'm going to die, aren't I?'

'I hope not,' Steve said. 'Look, you need to come down to the school and we'll see what we can do.'

'I will buy you whores and make them do dirty things to you,' I declared with all sincerity.

'I'm good, Borrie,' Steve replied evenly. 'I'll manage without that.' Steve's a practising Mormon, so there isn't a lie in him. Had he been a Catholic, I would have been suspicious at his declaration.

The next week I presented myself at Eastern Creek California superbike school. I spent the next two days being intensively coached by Big Al (one of the instructors) and Steve himself, and I was also mentored on the track by the other instructors. I was riding one of the school's Suzuki GSX-R600s, a light, responsive and very enjoyable middleweight that was ideal for instilling confidence in me as I learned the fast way around the track.

Despite the fact that I had almost three decades of riding behind me, and literally more than two million kilometres of motorcycle experience, I was a nappy-messing newborn when it came to racing and racecraft. Of course, there was no hope of teaching me racecraft in the time allotted – like roadcraft, it can only be learned on the job, so to speak. What Steve and Big Al hoped was to teach me enough to avoid death or maiming and to at least finish the two five-lap races I had entered.

Ideally I would have learned all this on the Manbike, but even that was conspiring against me. Ian had taken the beast on a shakedown run at a track day a few weeks earlier and fired one of the pistons and the attached conrod out through the front of the motor. This had dumped four litres of oil on the race-line between Turn Ten and Turn Eleven (the fail-stain was still visible as I circled the track), and had caused two Ducatis to come crashing down in his *Exxon Valdez*-like wake. He was rebuilding the motor and swore it would be ready in time for the race; I wouldn't be able to try the bike out on the racetrack until a week before the race at the earliest. When I communicated this to Steve and Big Al they exchanged concerned looks.

'So you're not gonna get a chance to ride the bike you're racing until a week before you race it?' Steve asked.

'Yeah,' I nodded. 'Is that a problem?'

Instead of answering me, Steve redoubled his tutelage. As a result I managed to shave some thirty seconds off my pre-school lap-times around the Creek in the two days of coaching, which left me hovering right on the two-minute mark and culminated in three breathtaking and life-affirming laps following Steve's bike – which are probably the fastest laps I will ever do around Eastern Creek.

While the other students were learning the theoretical basics of corner entry and throttle control, Steve took me aside, told me to put on my helmet and follow him around the track. 'I'll show you the race-line that seems to work the best around here, then I'll follow you and see how you go,' he said.

So I jammed the helmet on my head, zipped up my leathers and followed him out of the pit lane, my stomach doing backflips and bouncing off my squealing kidneys. I'd already done lots of laps around the track, both during the superbike school as well as a few track days I'd been to, so it was not unfamiliar to me. But when a former 125GP racer offers to take you by the hand and lead you around the circuit, it is a special and most revelatory experience. As I did my best to keep Steve in sight, trying to mimic his lines and body, I realised how truly special these fast boys were. Every movement is smooth and calculated; every corner entry is measured, sure and precise; every exit is hard and true and a set-up for the next corner. They all make it all look so damnably easy. And maybe it is for the very best of them. But I am certainly not one of them and racing is not remotely easy for me. Pretty much everything on a racetrack takes place at horrifying speeds that challenge the swiftness of human thought – never mind the casual, sauntering rubbish my middle-aged brain is usually occupied with. Just as I was happily congratulating myself for not dying in my own bloody poo after not crashing on Turn Three, I had to deal with not dying at Turn Four, setting up for Turn Five so as not to perish there, and so on, and all the time trying to go faster and faster, so as not to look like a total cock-blanket when the race came.

Then, as I started my second lap in Steve's wake, things started to come together. I stopped trying to think and just started to ride. I tried to remember to breathe. I remember coming out of Turn Twelve and onto the straight about sixty metres behind Steve, tucking in with my head down, my eyes up, and snicking the screaming Suzuki up through the gears as Turn One, coincidentally one of the fastest totally blind left-hand corners in the world, began to loom ahead of me. You actually have to 'know' somehow just when to tip into that corner, because it *is* blind and because it *is* fast and because it very quickly sorts the stallions from the mares. You can't look through it, you just have to 'know' it. It's a Jedi mind-trick that happens at more than 200 kms per hour, and no matter how many times you do Turn One (and I have now done it hundreds of times) the approach to it still fills my belly with bitter acid and terror.

I banged down a gear as I saw Steve begin his entry and even though I wanted to close my eyes, I didn't. I just followed him.

And it was glorious and faster than I was able to think – so I didn't think, I just leaned.

Yowling down the short straight after Turn One, I took a fast, ragged breath, slammed down into second gear and set up for Turn Two – a horrid uphill hairpin that's claimed more scalps than an Apache war-party. There's a strange ridge in the bitumen just where it shouldn't have a ridge and there are apparently two lines you can take through it – the wider one manages to avoid the bump, while the tighter one forces you to deal with it. There is a third line, but that will spear you into the tyre wall and is therefore best avoided. Steve chose the tighter one, I followed, feeling the bike soak up the fault-line, and then it was hard on the gas for a nanosecond and up a gear as Turn Three displayed its right-hand arrogance for your delectation. Screw this one up and you'll leave the earth's gravitational pull and sail into the sky, whereupon you will return to earth and will briefly behold the distant pit garages as dirt and pain and tufts of shitty yellow grass are force-fed into your helmet and your body disassembles itself inside your leathers. If you make it, you're now hurtling downhill into another right-hander, Turn Four, which dips and must be held tightly in order for Turn Five's left-handed evil not to slaughter you and leave you smeared along the concrete wall that's meant to stop you tumbling into the adjoining drag-racing complex a kilometre away. Turn Six was a slight left with a strange slab of concrete bastardry on the apex (for which the whole turn was removed in the track's subsequent redesign) which you had to avoid so your pulverised organs would not be poured into a medical waste bucket when the ambos came to get you. Turn Seven followed, a sharp, spirited left that catapults you up a rise and into the blind, hateful crest of the left-arcing Turn Eight swerving around the strangely named Corporate Hill upon which no corporation has ever stood.

I saw Steve disappear as he crested the rise, and stopped breathing again. I was banked hard left as I apexed and could see Steve and the track again, now on a trailing throttle because it went sharply downhill into the rude, brutally carnivorous hairpin of Turn Nine. This is one of the best places to overtake slow-moving degenerates and pussies, because there is a massive weight transfer onto the front-end under all the fear-braking, causing the back-end to become light, and as you suddenly realise you're not actually able to steer the bike into the hairpin anymore because you're going too fast and you've locked all your shit up, the men who ride better than you will pass you as your front-end tucks and you face-plant into the bitumen. With any luck you'll slide off the track and avoid being run over, but you can never be sure. If you don't crash, and your knee-slider isn't on the ground anywhere else on the track, it is here where it will rub itself along the bitumen like a dog dragging its worm-filled arse along the carpet.

Steve was then hard on the gas out of Nine and heading for the outside of the track, and I followed. This set us up for the gentle right-hand kink that is Turn Ten and then the all-important double-apex, slightly uphill nonsense of turns Eleven and Twelve, which must be taken as one corner lest you are lapped like a chicken-flavoured bitch by men with bigger balls and get to sail down the main straight to the laughs of derision and contempt of the crowd. But because Steve's take on turns Eleven and Twelve was perfect, so was mine. As we hurtled down the straight, I saw him lift his left arm off the bars and signal a thumbs-up to me. This meant that I had done good. His approval warmed me like sunshine – I remember grinning like an idiot and then totally stuffing up the entry point into Turn One by turning in too early, which sent me wide and almost transformed me and the Suzuki into a screamy earth-moving combination. Had I come down, my soil-ploughing efforts would have thrown up a respectable dirt embankment about a hundred metres to the right of Turn One's exit. I did another lap with Steve watching me from behind, then returned to the pits, dry-mouthed and goggle-eyed.

'That was good, mate,' Steve said, clapping me on my armoured shoulder. 'Just do that for five laps and you'll be fine.'

I just nodded. We both knew there was no way I could do that for five laps and that what had just happened was one of those crazy, flukey things that happens from time to time and would probably never be repeated even if I spent the rest of my life cutting laps around the Creek. Because racing is not just cutting laps, it is racing. As Steve explained at the end of that wonderful, wonderful day, no track day, no coaching, and no amount of superbike school training laps is a substitute for actually racing. Until you've raced, you don't understand racing.

There is an apocryphal tale about Mick Doohan, five-time world MotoGP champion and one of the greatest racers of all time, which sums up racing pretty accurately. One day when Mick was at some racetrack, a young racer who bumped into him in the pits began to babble about the race he had just finished. 'Man, it was insane!' the young bloke screeched. 'I was coming into Turn Three and I was drifting out wide and I felt the front start to squirm and I just kept the power on and I felt it shake its head, then I was coming into Nine and I felt the back-end step out and the whole bike was outta line and I thought it was gonna high-side me! It was fucken intense! I was on the absolute edge!'

Mick listened to him and when the young bloke had finished huffing and puffing, he looked him in the eyes and said: 'When you're on the edge like that on every single corner on every single track and in every single race, that's when you're racing.' I don't actually know if that conversation ever happened, but I like to think it did because it defines racing perfectly. I went home that day exhausted, satisfied and packing shit, all in equal measure.

Over the next few weeks leading up to my race I was a regular visitor to Eastern Creek. I would do lap after lap after lap. I didn't get faster, I just got more consistent. As my race day approached, I felt I would be able to string together at least three or four non-shameful laps on the Manbike.

The week before the race, Ian brought the Manbike to the Creek so I could finally ride it. He did a great job prepping the animal: everything that needed to be race-wired was race-wired. If you look closely at a race-prepped bike, you'll notice small lengths of twisted wire adorning various nuts, bolts and other bits of bike. This is to prevent them flying off during a race and hitting the people behind you. Given that there would in all like-lihood be no one behind me during the race because I would be motherless, dead last, I thought it was a bit funny, but Ian said it was necessary for the bike to pass the scrutineering.

We poured petrol into it, warmed it up as I donned my helmet and for the first time in my life, I rolled out of the pits on a set of racing slicks on a bike my mate had built in his carport, and hit the track. Two laps later I was back in the pits, my right leg covered in hot engine oil, roiling clouds of greasy smoke surrounding me as Ian looked on, perturbed. 'I think it's coming out of the head,' he muttered, squatting on his haunches and peering at the engine. 'Probably seeping out past the studs.'

'Make it stop,' I said. 'It's making the rear tyre want to kill me.' I had felt the rear-end step out rather alarmingly on the last lap as I came out of Turn Nine and began to throttle on. But it was the first thing the big bike had done wrong. Sure, it was heavy compared with the Suzuki GSX-R600 I had been banging around on, but it held a nice line once you muscled it into the corner, and while the throttle and clutch were a bit heavy and clunky and medieval compared to the modern smoothness Suzuki served you, the Manbike repaid your efforts by offering you stupid amounts of power and a noise that made your spine crawl with pleasure. I liked it. It terrified me, but I liked it.

But now that it was leaking oil, I was reconsidering my feelings. Ian fiddled around for a few minutes and I went back out again. The leak had slowed down, but not stopped, and after another five laps I was back in the pits, smelling like an oil refinery and leaving oily right-foot prints where I walked.

'I'll have this sorted by next week,' Ian assured me.

'How?' I wanted to know.

'Ronnie Beck is coming down for the weekend. He'll go over it before the race and he and his son Steve will be our mechanics on the day.'

'What does that make you?'

'The crew chief – I'm like Alberto Puig,' he grinned, naming the mentor of the perennial bridesmaid of MotoGP, Dani Pedrosa.

So after less than ten oily laps, I went home and tried to explain to my wife that I intended to actually race a motorcycle the following weekend.

'You're a fucken idiot,' she said to me. 'You have no business racing motorcycles at your age.'

'Lots of blokes my age race,' I protested.

'How many of them started racing at your age?'

She had me there, but I was not going down without a fight. 'What's that got to do with it?'

She stared at me intently, her luminous brown eyes flashing with serious displeasure. 'Do not fall off and hurt yourself,' she said evenly. 'Just don't.'

I nodded sombrely. 'Don't worry. I have no intention of falling off. I'll take it easy.'

In retrospect, what I had just said to her was complete and utter nonsense, and she probably knew that as well as I did, but she also knew that once I had committed to doing something I would see it through to the end – no matter how bitter that end might be. And this, after all, was racing, which is based on one iron-clad rule: fish or cut bait.

And so came the race weekend. I was to race twice – two five-lap sprints, as they are known in the trade. Being only five-lappers, they are ferocious from the get-go because no one has time to settle down, work out a plan, watch what the bastard in front is doing, or plan passing manoeuvres on some future lap. Bring it all, bring it now and keep on bringing it until you see the chequered flag seemed to be the prevailing wisdom.

I had a light breakfast and only one cup of coffee, but as my friend The Door was driving me to Eastern Creek, my bladder felt like it was going to burst and I was certain I was going to vomit into his car's foot well.

'You okay?' The Door asked. 'You look a little strange.'

Clearly he had never seen me display primitive, naked terror before. 'I'm nervous as hell,' I muttered.

'You'll be fine. What could go wrong?'

I shot him a sideways look. 'Lots. I could die, or I could lose both my legs, or my arms, or my heart could burst, or my pancreas could explode. My kidneys could liquefy. My spine could be severed ...'

The Door laughed, then we were driving through the Creek's Gate Seven, making our way to the back of the pits and I ran out of things to say.

Ian was as good as his word: the Manbike was waiting for me in Pit Garage 25, along with Ron Beck and his son Steve. Seeing Ron, I felt a little bit better. Mechanically at least, the bike would be as good as it could be. Ron was almost seventy years old and about the size of Yoda but he raced a wonderful old Vincent motorcycle and was an aircraft engineer of rare genius, having won a coveted Rolls-Royce award for his skills. He grinned when he saw me, clapped me on the back and told me it was a good day to die. I forced a laugh, but really didn't feel amused.

I'd ridden a few kilometres with Ron's son Steve, who had also raced a bit, and when he came over to help me get into my leathers he also expressed the view that I would be okay. 'You'll be fine,' he said as I shrugged myself into my one-piece race-suit. 'Just have fun. That's what this is all about.'

Fun? Really? And here I was thinking that racing was all about winning and that fun was what happened after you'd won and were in a nudie bar snorting cocaine off some stripper's pierced belly.

The bike was up on its race stands, its tyre-warmers were on, and Ron and Ian were poking around it with tools. 'Get the fuck out of the light,' I heard Ron tell Ian, who instantly retreated a metre and left the master to deal with the sticky throttle and the oil leak that had plagued the bike all along. While the oil leak was worrying for its own reasons, when combined with a throttle that wouldn't respond to my input but went on eagerly delivering geysers of petrol into the carbies when I wanted it to stop doing that (like when a corner appeared), the Manbike became rather problematic.

I left Ron to his tinkering and went to the toilet for the fourth time since arriving at the track and forced a few nervous drops out of my shrunken penis. Ian had gone to get the transponder to be fitted to the bike which would allow the race callers and stewards to keep track of my times and where I was on the track.

When I returned, Ron had fixed the two outstanding problems and sorted out a heap of smaller mechanical issues I was too dumb and distracted to understand. But he did laugh tenderly at the stupid way I checked my tyre-warmers – basically by burning myself on them.

My race number was number 70 – a randomly allocated pair of digits which emanated no ill luck that I could discern, and having been painted a heroic blue and red, the bike looked every inch a proper race bike. This was good – because after catching a glimpse of myself in the toilet mirror, I did not look like a racer at all. I looked like a silly fat circus-freak who had been poured into tight all-black leathers and was about to be shot out of a cannon.

My nerves were manifestly obvious to all. I lost count of the number of fellow BEARS members, who were all racing that day, too, who went out of their way to come over, shake my hand and wish me well. When you've come to race for your first time, it is certainly overwhelming and confusing and nerve-wracking, and their generous good wishes went a long way to allay my overwhelmed and confused nerves.

But I was still packing a serious amount of shit. Then I had no more time to pack shit because I was required to get out onto the track and qualify, to determine where I would start on the grid. The quality of my courage would also play a large part in this. I rolled out of the pits and onto the track to try to go as fast as I could for at least one of the three laps allotted to my class for qualifying. I returned dry-mouthed and panting to a smiling pit crew a few minutes later.

'Good on you!' Ian trumpeted as Steve levered the rear, then the front of the bike up onto its race stands.

'Yes!' I honked. 'I didn't fall off!'

'You qualified fourth!' he grinned, clapping me on the shoulder.

I blinked in confusion.

'Look!' he said, waving a sheet of paper in my face.

The paper was a readout of everyone's times and where they would start the race as a result. There it was, my name and the corresponding time of 1:54.296. I had indeed qualified fourth in my class and eighteenth overall in a field of thirty-six. This put me on Row Five of the grid, but by the way my crew were smiling and backslapping me you'd think I'd just handed Rossi his arse at Jerez.

Fuck me, I thought, this is what 300 laps of Eastern Creek gets me. But there was no more time to analyse anything, there was no more time to be nervous, there was no more time to do anything but get out there and line up for the start.

Men have found God while perched on the starting grid of a racetrack. Others have vomited into their helmets or squirted fiery fright-piss into their leathers. I did none of that, but sitting on that grid, I did realise it was the perfect time to ponder the size and quality of my testicles. Mercifully, that time was brief, because I was downsizing them with every passing second. Had the man with the red flag at the head of the grid stood there any longer, they would have been the size of rice grains.

My mouth was sand and ashes. My breathing, when I remembered to do it, was harsh and shallow. All I could see was the man with the red flag and a tiny (but gigantic) dead bug on my visor. Then the flag man walked off the track, the bug disappeared and my universe was the red light on the gantry above the track. While it remained on, I was safe. When it blinked off, I would be racing.

'Shitfuckshitfuck,' I muttered to myself, my mind chattering in the nanoseconds in which my safety was now measured. 'I'm really doing this! Shitfuckshitfuckshitfuck!'

The red light blinked off and I began to pay for my sins as my world became sound, fury and speed while I prepared to hurtle into Turn One along with thirty-five like-minded maniacs. But since thirty-six riders cannot enter Turn One simultaneously, it follows that some of them will back off the throttle a bit.

I had been told time and again, by Ian, by Ron, by Steve and by everyone who had raced and who had bothered to give me advice: 'Just make it through Turn One.' So that was my immediate mission, and a feat I could normally perform with ease at a track day. But as I was rapidly discovering, a track day is, by an order of quite immense magnitude, not at all at all at all like a race meeting. The former is like a Boy Scout camp where you tie knots, sing 'Kumbaya' and jerk off onto a biscuit. The latter is like a Marine Recon unit assaulting a beach-head and killing everything it sees several times over.

I remember Turn One being crowded and tried, as instructed by wiser heads, to run as wide as I could in order to come tightly into Turn Two to prevent faster blokes from cutting under me into that hairpin. It didn't make a pinch of shit's bit of difference – three bikes went around on the outside of me anyway.

I remembered to breathe, which made me feel a little better because I was close to fainting with oxygen deprivation – I had not taken a breath since the red light went out. Thus revivified, I held my own through turns Three and Four, but was slain by a Supermotard in Turn Five, a Ducati in Turn Six. I somehow managed to block some traffic coming into Turn Seven, though not by design. I think I had just stuffed the entry into that corner in every way possible and the blokes following me were waiting for me to crash so they could race on past. My teeth were clenched to aching as I got on the gas up the hill into Turn Eight and I could sense but not actually see bikes all around me. Great, I thought. There will be lots of bastards running over me when I crash in Turn Nine. Everyone crashes in Turn Nine. I will be no different. But Ron and Ian had both insisted I run through Nine as tightly as possible, so I banged the bike down into second, levered my vagina off the seat and aimed for the inside of the corner as if my life depended on it – which it kinda did, because no one around me was slowing down much at all. Astonishingly, I came out the other side of Nine, jammed the throttle open and actually passed someone into the fast approach for Turn Ten. But then someone passed me and suddenly I was far too hot into Turn Eleven with bikes all around me and my spine melting out of my tightly clenched rectum.

The track hit me in the face with a savagery that took my breath away. In an eye-blink the front-end of the Manbike had tucked, slid out, and my hip, arm and head slammed into the ground and I slid off the track in a dazzling, flash-fast sequence. It sounded like a truck diff had fallen off a building and rolled down the street. Bikes were still whizzing past, but all I could hear was the roaring of blood in my head. If there is a rushing, whooshing, echoing silence more complete and profound than the one immediately following a bike crash, I could not tell you what it is.

I levered myself up, lurched to my feet and hauled the bike upright. My chest sang with pain each time I tried to draw a deep breath, my hip was numb and I could only see part of the colour spectrum. But I was standing. And when I managed to wheel the bike a few more metres away from the edge of the track without suffering a massive coronary, I figured I would probably live.

There was a race marshal directly opposite me, and I indicated to him that I was alright so that he wouldn't stop the race by red-flagging it. I did not want the burden of guilt that ruining the other riders' day would bring.

I knew why I'd face-planted. And the burden of that guilt was elegantly sufficient. I had touched the front brake while I had the bike heeled over into the entry of Turn Eleven at about 120 kms per hour. Just like a nappy-wearing dickhead. My inner-voice had even begun chanting 'Dickhead, dickhead, dickhead' as I tried to count how many ribs I had managed to crack.

The ride back to the rear of the pits in the Your Race Is Over ute was a sombre affair. I was devastated. Not particularly for myself, mainly for Ian, Ron and Steve, who had worked so hard on my behalf. There was certainly no question of a bruised ego at my end, but one needs to be good at something before one can develop an ego that can then be kicked to pieces. When one stupidly taps the front brake and lowsides off the track, ego is just an old Skyhooks song.

I lumbered painfully into my pit garage, panted apologies to the blokes then limped and swayed my way to the track's medical centre. I emerged twenty minutes later with a Band-Aid on my finger (I had somehow managed to cut myself through the glove) and a high blood-pressure reading. Gimping my way back to my pit garage I once again said sorry to everyone within earshot.

'Stop apologising or I will hit you,' Ian said. 'This is racing. Look around you. How many unmarked leathers do you see?' He had a point. My shiny new ensemble now resembled everyone else's well-worn and crashed-in outfits.

'The bike's good to go,' Ron chimed cheerily as Steve finished beating something under the Manbike's seat with a hammer, and offered me a cigarette with a sympathetic grin.

'I'm fucken not,' I whined. I was still unable to take a deep breath and stuff was starting to throb alarmingly from my hip down. Standing upright was fast becoming quite a challenge.

'You sure?' Ron asked. 'The bike's straight and ready to go.'

If there was ever a spirit-willing, flesh-weak moment in my life, that was it. I went home. It was the only thing I could do that would afford me any shred of dignity. Certainly, I could have fainted on the floor of the pit garage and soiled myself like a diseased animal, but I chose to depart the field of valour with my armour torn and my body spent. I had contended with other men for supremacy, as men have for millennia, and had been beaten by my own incompetence. It wasn't by any kind of fear. I had peered through the red mist of battle and had ridden faster and harder than I had ever ridden in my life. Had I died or had my face sheared off, then so be it. Jesus hates a pussy.

Should you ever decide to get drunk, lose your licence then go completely mad and decide to take up motorcycle racing to get your riding fix, let yourself be guided by the words of Kai Ka'us ibn Iskandar, a tenth-century Persian prince, who declared that: 'Once you engage in battle, it is inexcusable to display any sloth or hesitation; you must breakfast on your enemy before he dines on you.'

When my wife beheld my shattered form an hour later, I was happy she was not a great reader of tenth-century Persian warlords, or she would have probably stomped the crap out of whatever remained of me. As it was, she began nurturing me back to health by declaring me to be among the greatest fools who ever trod the earth. But she did do the hard yards when my needs were most desperate.

As my smashed ribs and bruised organs slowly calcified and healed, and I was able once again to wipe my own arse – thus sparing us both from what is one of the harshest tests of matrimonial love – she became more and more contemptuous and dismissive of my needs. The cold drinks she had brought me as I lay panting in agony on the couch I would now have to fetch for myself. The healthy snacks she had so lovingly prepared were now hastily thrown-together constructs of fats, salts, sulphites, emulsifiers, food colourings and shitty carbohydrates prepared by me when I limped into the kitchen during commercial breaks.

And so I did slowly heal.

I did the remainder of my no-riding-for-foolish-arseholes-like-you sentence in complete agreement with her.

SECRET MEN'S BUSINESS

Fear and love are the two great motivators of the human condition. Combining the two into a single situation is an unbeatable combination. Imagine a caveman fending off a mountain bear at the mouth of his cave. The caveman is terrified of the bear, but he is more terrified of what is going to happen if the bear gets past him and eats his beloved family. Thus he will fight that bear with a grimness and determination he never knew he possessed. That bear just shall not fucken pass.

As a motorcyclist and a former outlaw, I am no stranger to fear. As a father, son and husband I am no stranger to love. But I was not remotely prepared for the feelings I would have when I purposely put what I loved in harm's way. But yes, I did it anyway. And no, the bear did not pass.

'You don't raise heroes, you raise sons.
If you treat them like sons, they'll
turn out to be heroes, even if
it's just in your own eyes.'

WALTER SCHIRRA SR

'He is to be warm, he is to be dry and he is to be unmarked. If he is hurt in any way, do not come home, bastard. Just keep riding.' These were the words my beloved wife said to me when I told her I'd like to take our son, Andrew, to the Phillip Island MotoGP on the back of a motorcycle.

Andrew was fourteen and in some cultures there would have been dried heads hanging from the roof of his hut, writhing girls warming his bed which would be strewn with the tawny hides of freshly slain lions, and long blood-stained spears ranged before his kraal. But I didn't figure this line of reasoning would succeed in getting my wife to approve and ratify this latest Great Idea. So I adopted the Compliant, Obsequious and Reverential Husband persona.

'I understand,' I said to her, my hands clasped meekly before me, shielding my offensive and aggressive male genitals in the time-honoured display of male timidity.

My wife eyed me with a gimlet stare. Hunting falcons behold their prey in just such a fashion. 'You do understand there is no "try",' she said in her best Yoda voice. 'There is just "do".' She was right, obviously. There could be no compromises here. There could be nothing but a favourable outcome. Nothing at all *but* that.

While I'm keen to risk my life doing what I love doing, I'm not a parent who casually inflicts that kind of risk upon my off-spring. Of course, Andrew was no stranger to riding on the back of motorcycles. I first sat him on the back of my Triumph Speed Triple when he was about four and just old enough to hang on, and ferried him ever so gently around the cul-de-sac at the top of our street. As time went on, we ventured further and further afield and by the time he was ready to go to kindergarten, he could easily do so on a motorcycle. Which was handy, because we only had one car and my wife needed it to get to work. Then the government, in its relentless quest to create a society entirely averse to risk, made it illegal to carry children under the age of eight and Andrew enjoyed a brief hiatus from my pillion seat.

A quiet and thoughtful child, Andrew had never expressed any interest in actually riding himself, and I was not the type of father who was going to push him into riding motorcycles. No one is more aware of how dangerous motorcycles are than motorcyclists themselves – a fact that goes a long way towards explaining why we ride the bastards in the first place – and as such, we grapple with a most awful paradox when it comes to our nearest and dearest. One part of us wants them to understand and to share the atavistic glee and stomach-lurching rush that riding serves up so readily. Another part of us wants to shield them forever from the possibility of being turned into blood-speckled paste under the wheels of some truck.

In Andrew's case, I adopted a wait-and-see approach. Sons don't always take up their fathers' passions, and it seemed this was to be the case with my son. But if he suddenly, at some stage, decided he wanted to ride, I would facilitate this desire and ensure he received the best possible training, no matter how much my wife cut me with her cruelly edged meat knives.

In the meantime, and once Andrew was of legal age, we'd duck into the city occasionally, or go for brief spin somewhere not too far. It would be fair to say that while he enjoyed our short rides, he never really made any noises that made me think he wanted to go further and faster than our sedate cruises. Then one day, a month or so before my annual 2000-plus-kilometre blast down to the MotoGP at Phillip Island and back, he came to me and said: 'Dad, I'd like to go to the GP with you this year.'

That I would agree to take him was a given. I am a doting father, and an easy touch. The thought of sharing one of my greatest joys with one of my greatest joys was certainly causing my joy-glands to juice, but there were a few not-entirely-inconsequential hurdles to jump over. The biggest was, of course, my wife, Lynette, and her natural concern for the safety and well-being of her only son. When this concern was coupled with her vast and altogether encyclopaedic knowledge of me and all the manifold evil I have been known to get up to when I go away with my friends, I was going to have to jump pretty high to ensure I didn't leave my balls swinging redly from the razor wire at the top of this hurdle.

Like all long-term, survival-minded husbands, my instincts regarding my wife are honed like the blade of a samurai master. There are times when she can be approached with outlandish proposals and be remarkably amenable to them. And there are times when the most banal of propositions will be greeted with steel-hearted scorn and contempt. My success lies in being able to differentiate these times. Most of the time.

So I chose my time and I chose my place and put my case to her, making sure I ticked all the boxes before she even identified them as boxes, then I closed with the big trump card: 'We [note the use of the collective pronoun that allows a sharing of responsibility] need to look at this as a rite of passage. He's fourteen, he's on the cusp of manhood. He needs to do this.'

My wife stared at me protractedly. Her incredible and entirely bewitching gaze searched me, clearly seeking to discover if the shit I was shovelling so robustly was even remotely digestible. She then made her decision and the 'He is to be ...' speech followed.

The other hurdles were considerably easier to negotiate. I had more than enough motorcycle gear to accommodate Andrew, and as he tried on my stuff, I realised he was quite a substantially sized fourteen-year-old. My gear was a little large on him, but not glaringly so. Next came the big question. What bike?

When I asked Andrew what kind of bike he'd like to ride to the Island, he shrugged. 'I don't know much about bikes,' he said. 'What do you reckon?'

'I reckon it should be as comfortable as possible,' I replied, wondering if I should inflict a Yamaha R6 on the boy as a means of toughening him up some. Then I thought about my own ageing bones and decided he could be toughened up some other time.

'What about a Harley?' I offered.

Andrew grinned. 'They are so hell cool.'

I grinned right back at him. May the Road Gods grant us all the same clarity of reason they give to the young. For a teenager, the final word in motorcycle cool is, of course, a

Harley-Davidson. It's primeval and utterly irreconcilable in its cool. It exudes this cool effortlessly and constantly – and not all the sad pirates and dire wannabes running around on them will ever de-cool the marque. A Harley will be cool forever, world without end, Amen.

I called the good folks at Harley-Davidson and told them that I wanted to do a story for *Australian Motorcycle News* which involved me taking my teenage son to the MotoGP, and the right bike for this journey was surely one of their vast and marvellous Ultras. These are the über-Harleys, the ones specifically designed for two-up touring in supreme comfort. The ones with the top-box, panniers and fairing and a multi-speaker stereo. And cruise control and, most importantly, a pillion seat that resembles a deliciously padded lounge chair.

The good folks at Harley-Davidson agreed to supply the bike. Job done. Hurdles conquered. All that remained was to ride there and back.

As our departure date drew near, and the piles of gear we were planning to take began to occupy the dining room table, Andrew became more sparkle-eyed with excitement with each passing day. He'd experienced my pre-run packing ritual year after year and had assisted in it when he was old enough to fetch and carry the many bits and pieces I take with me on trips. This time it was different, he was an integral part of it, and I was loving it.

He asked the right questions and my heart sang with pride. 'How many pairs of undies, Dad?'

'One for each day we're away and one spare pair.'

'How many pairs of socks?'

'Same as undies.'

'Will I need a torch?'

'Always have a torch.'

'Will I need a knife?'

'Always have a knife.'

Steadily, the surface of the table disappeared beneath changes of clothing, a tyre-repair kit, rope, spare batteries, cameras, a first-aid kit, wet-weather gear and a vast plethora of items I would probably never need, but decided to take in case I suddenly did. Calling my wife and telling her that I had somehow neglected to bring some crucial-to-Andrew's-happiness-and-comfort item was not something I wanted to do. And it's not like the Harley Ultra Classic didn't have the room to carry it all. I could have taken two hay bales, a hundred-kilogram bag of potatoes and a tubby little pig as well as all our gear, and the Harley would have swallowed it all within its cavernous luggage compartments.

Two days before take-off, it suddenly dawned on Andrew that this was the real deal. Five days away with Dad and his mates on a man-weekend replete with all the indescribably beaut and hitherto-secret men's business he had been hearing only whispers about for years.

Of course, what I do on my own when I go away and what I do when I'm with my son are two vastly different things. So while it's perfectly acceptable for me to roam the Island's major town of Cowes at 18 o'clock in the morning stenched up on beer, hooliganism and cop-hate, it is not perfectly acceptable to do that with my teenage son. At least, not yet. So keeping in mind how my trip was going to be different this time, I was determined to ensure Andrew's was spot-on.

On the day of departure, I woke him at 3.30 am. By 5 am we were bearing down on the Pheasant's Nest servo to rendezvous with my companions. It was misty and cool and our fully laden Ultra Classic seemed to float along the dark road emanating Canned Heat tunes from its speakers. I always enjoy reconnecting with these gigantic tourers – they offer a unique take on the ride, especially if you're two-up and taking it easy.

We collected Crew, Rob, Biffa and The Door and made for Gundagai, where we were to pick up Whale and rid ourselves of the mindlessness of the Doom Highway. At Gundagai, the sun was shining, my son was smiling and Whale was waiting. We fuelled up and aimed for Tumbarumba and the natural wonders of the Snowy Mountains.

Andrew and I chatted happily as I pointed out various sights (the Ultra Classic is so well-faired you can have inside-voice conversations up to about 120 kms per hour; over that speed, your outside voice is needed) and he played Spotto the whole way – that's a game where each time he sees a yellow car, he yells 'Spotto!' and drives his fist into my spine. Of course, I am also allowed to belt him if I see a yellow car and yell 'Spotto!' but in practice I'm far too busy piloting more than one metric tonne of American awesomeness to pay attention to car colours.

New South Wales was radiantly green thanks to the recent plentiful rain – like Ireland without the sectarian violence – but the forecast was decidedly unpleasant. Worrying about the weather is altogether pointless. How bad could it get? I asked myself.

At Towong on the NSW–Victoria border, I stopped to show Andrew a swollen and muddy Murray River and told him he was now in Victoria. He said he'd always imagined the river would be bigger and asked when lunch was.

In short order we were in Corryong, where Andrew enjoyed his first-ever counter-meal – he was only fourteen but he was consuming man-size meals with ease and gusto. During the gluttony, we got a warning from one of the locals that the cop near Tallangatta was twenty kinds of motherless bastard and we should proceed with that in mind.

'What's going to happen at Tallangatta?' Andrew asked me as we zipped up our jackets and prepared to ride on.

'We'll be treated to a demonstration of quality policing,' I beamed, climbed aboard the bike, nodded Andrew onto the back and headed south. When the stormtrooper goose-stepped out onto the road to arrest my progress, I was blithely unconcerned. I hadn't been speeding, the bike was perfectly road-legal, my licence was current and valid, and if God existed, He would have been in His Heaven and all was pretty much right with the world.

It was the first time in a long time I was actually grinning as I coasted to a gentle halt in front of a policeman. Observing my smugness, the Highway Patrol officer, who was actually wearing jodhpurs and a leather cap despite the fact that we were not in a gay nightclub and he did not have a horse, clearly felt it was his duty to de-smug me, sharpish.

'I have stopped you for the purposes of a licence check,' he intoned. I had been subjected to this inane nonsense for most of my riding career, so I was still smiling as I handed my licence over. Andrew really was going to get a life-lesson here. That life-lesson goes like this: If the police want to pull you over and get up into your shit, record your identity and whereabouts, or just strut around you with their hands on their guns exuding author-ity and menace but they don't really have a reason to do so, they will always invent one. A 'licence check' is the usual nonsense – presumably because so many unlicensed idiots are hurtling about the countryside, especially during massively policed events like the MotoGP at Phillip Island.

So Andrew and I sat in the sun by the side of the road as the jodhpur-wearing officer laboriously scrawled my details on a bit of paper. There was no 'check' of my licence at all. He did not walk back to his car and call my details through to Cheap Thought, the police supercomputer that resides inside the secret police ultrabunker in the middle of Australia. He just copied them onto a shitty piece of paper. I was hoping he might have at least used his notebook, or a clipboard, but at least it wasn't as silly as the time one of them wrote my details down on his hand.

Andrew was confused. What was this all about? What had we done wrong? I told him this was how Victorian police gath-ered intelligence on interstate motorcyclists and the policeman was angry because I wasn't speeding and therefore couldn't be Tasered on the side of the road.

'Why isn't he checking your licence on the radio?' Andrew asked.

'Because he knows my licence is valid and there is nothing to check.'

'You're serious, aren't you, Dad?'

'Absolutely,' I grinned. I was still smiling when the police-man in the jodhpurs handed my licence back. He'd clearly heard Andrew and I talking, so he was not smiling. But neither was he ordering me off my bike at gunpoint, so things were not all that bad.

We rode on and paused briefly at the pretty little town of Kiewa only to be told the Kiewa Valley Highway was washed out, but a detour ran parallel to the unrideable road and was a bit of a hoot. It was, and as we climbed over Tawonga Gap and down the other side (which is a bit of a hoot, too) I told Andrew our day's riding was nearly done.

The town of Bright greeted us with cold drinks, hot pizzas and emptiness. We seemed to be the only game in town that night, but since our numbers had grown with Res, Jonesy and Jamie arriving in town, it was still a party. That evening Andrew got to taste a little of the enticing 'oneness' that binds riders on a big trip and laughed along with us at all the vile jokes and utterly merciless ribbing. My friends didn't exclude him, but they didn't overwhelm him either, and I was as proud of them as I was of my son. The weather was gentle, the evening was mild, and the beer was plentiful, which was all the encouragement a few of my mates needed to race to the top of the nearby Mount Hotham and back.

Andrew watched them hair off up the street, their exhausts yowling. 'You not going, Dad?' he asked, a half grin on his face.

'Nah. I'm too old for that nonsense,' I lied, and I'm pretty sure he forgave me for it, too.

I thought Andrew's daily report to his mother that evening as we settled down to sleep in a nearby motel was overwhelmingly positive: 'I'm really good. Yes, Dad's fed me. Pizza. No, he's not drinking out of a bottle. Yes, I can see him. Okay. I will. Bye.'

The next morning it was raining as if it had never rained

before. Andrew was still asleep as I stood in the doorway of our motel room in my underpants at 6 am and watched agog as literally oceans of water tumbled out of the heavens. My shit got a little more agog as I looked at the Harley and saw that I had left one of its panniers open all night, and it was now brimming with water. Anything that was capable of floating on top was doing so; the heavy stuff lay submerged on the bottom. Fortunately, it was my stuff, not Andrew's, which was in the other closed pannier.

So while Andrew woke up and endured his first motel breakfast, I shoved towels into the pannier to soak up the water and called myself names. Then began the most traumatic and nerve-wracking ride of my life. It was raining like the world was ending. I'm not at all perturbed by crap weather when I am on my own, but the combination of a fully laden and massive motorcycle with the road manners of a felled pine tree, my son as a passenger, serious wind gusts, insane amounts of rain and some of the twistiest roads in Victoria, had me a little dry-mouthed. The only consolation was that the cops would all be tucked up snug and warm in their little beds and not performing those crucial licence checks.

We made for Myrtleford, then Moyhu, Whitfield and the awesome road that runs from there to Mansfield. Except it's ever so much more awesome on an Ultra Classic in the teeming rain – primarily because I could not see the road through the rain-speckled plexiglass of the fairing and was reduced to half-guessing where it was while simultaneously giraffing my head up to try to see over the top of the screen – an action that caused cold water to cascade down the neck of my jacket and ice up on my chest. Waterproof jackets, in case you were wondering, mostly do a pretty fair job of keeping the water out. Nothing in their design parameters, however, requires them to deal with water that is poured down the neck of the jacket and into the lining and inner pockets. But being wet was about Number Seven on my list of Shitty Issues right about then. Not dying was Number One. With a bullet.

I was grateful Andrew had no terms of reference, so he had no idea how close we were to plunging off a cliff every hundred metres or so. At times I rode through puddles so appalling I felt both tyres lose all traction. At other times I felt the front-end abandon all hope as the bike floated free of the road and disaster was only averted by ABS and swearing. I wasn't breathing so much as I was sucking in gulps of wet air every five minutes or so.

I was trembling when I got off the bike at Mansfield, but Andrew was all smiles. 'That was a really twisty road, Dad!' he grinned and went to pee in the service station toilet. I rattled some petrol into the Harley's cavernous tanks and paid the smug dry prick behind the counter with wet money.

The road opened up after Mansfield and the rain got harder but the Ultra Classic was once again in its element, which is wide open highway, and it split groups of slower-moving motorcycles like a whale dispersing plankton. I was still as wet as if I was sitting at the bottom of a swimming pool, but I wasn't as cold as I had been earlier. The only grief I was having was with the bastard screen. I could no longer see through it at all, didn't dare touch it in case I scratched the Perspex forever, and was reduced to peering over it like a panting ostrich. The rain was just so overwhelming and relentless.

'You okay?' I asked Andrew as we hurtled through the spray.

'Yep,' he replied.

'You wet?'

'Nope.'

I did not know how this was possible, since my gear had long since failed, but figured the boy was bright enough to know wet from dry and that lying to me was counterproductive. Then I pushed that from my mind and concentrated on negotiating the narrow, slippery, winding and breathtakingly beautiful stretch of road known as the Black Spur. I was tired, I was cold again and I'm pretty sure I could have walked faster around some of the corners I waddled that Harley through. But I didn't sail off the road, and that's what was important to my screaming mind.

When we docked outside the Healesville pub about 1 pm, I was shakingly haggard, utterly soaked and truly grateful to be alive. How we made it down the Black Spur and the Whitfield–Mansfield road on that massive rhinoceros of a bike, I still have no idea. But fear of my wife's reaction to an unsatisfactory result was a great motivator: I have never ridden with more terror, care or caution than I did that day and I was weak with relief.

Andrew *was* dry. Sure, his gloves were finally letting the water through, but his pants, jacket and boots were still watertight and he was as warm as a fresh piece of toast. I, by contrast, was soaked through and shivering. It was still raining and the Island was still some hours away. Res only half-jokingly offered Andrew his Hayabusa to ride if he could take his place on the back of my Harley.

After a quick but warming meal, we made for Pakenham via Cockatoo and Woori Yallock, then as we hit the Bass Highway at

Koo Wee Rup, the infernal Bass Strait wind slammed us, the icy rain turned sideways and the last hour to the Island was a feat of teeth-gritting endurance.

We made it, whole and complete. We didn't lose a single bike or rider, and as we stood on the verandah of our locked rental house waiting for Crew to bring the key from the real estate agent, sipping Stone's Green Ginger wine to ward off ice-death, we were smiling through chattering teeth. Except Andrew, whose teeth were not chattering as he called his mum. 'Hi, Mum. We're here. Yep. I'm fine. My hands got a little wet. Dad's soaked. He can't talk to you, he's shivering too much. Yes, he is drinking out of a bottle. Okay. I'll tell him.'

The weekend proper commenced later that afternoon after we'd dried off and watched Res (who for reasons best known to himself only brought the clothes he was standing up in) slow-roast his jeans in the oven. The house we were in did not have a functioning heater, so we were reduced to turning on all the stove's burners and opening the oven so as to dry our gear. This made the whole house smell like a giant, wet and somewhat manky animal, but there was an Antarctic ice-gale blowing outside so we endured the stench.

The next day Andrew was treated to everything the MotoGP had to offer – the glorious sound and spectacle of the bikes, the Third-World facilities offered to the fans, the hectares of Russian Front-type mud, the garbage trackside food, the inane over-policing, and the unrestrained and indefatigable good humour of my friends.

We went to parties where old mateships were renewed, we attended the track where promo girls smiled through their goosebumps and cheerfully posed for photos ('What did you do on those days you had off from school, Andrew?' 'I hung out with hotties at a racetrack.'), and we danced and yelled at the Euphoria café on Saturday night, ate its restorative breakfasts every morning and went to sleep each night with goofy grins on our dials.

I will never forget my son's face when he beheld the start of the MotoGP as his eardrums quivered and all speech was impossible. If I had shown him the birth of a sun he wouldn't have been more amazed. 'It's not like this on TV,' he breathed when the pack had done its first lap. 'They are so … so *fast!*'

For my part, I felt better than I'd ever felt before at Phillip Island, primarily because I was not hungover, but also because I was enjoying again through my son's eyes all the stuff I had grown used to over the years.

I may have not done the things I sometimes do at the Island, but I had done more than I had ever done before, and I did it all with my son – which is a pleasure and gift I shall treasure forever. Did he become a man on the trip? No. He did not. It will take a few more years and a few more trips before he can make that claim. He was, however, no longer the child he was when we left Sydney. He collected some serious kilometres and tasted a little of his father's madness. I believe he quite liked it.

THROUGH THE EYES OF A FOURTEEN-YEAR-OLD

Andrew saw things he had never seen before on this trip and his questions and observations gave me so much pleasure, it was like I was seeing the same things for the first time, too …

Andrew on Service Station Toilets
'Dad, why are there always condom machines in those toilets? And what's Horny Goat weed?'

My Friends
'Dad, did you know Res is drying his jeans in the oven?'

Beer
'Dad, look at that truck! How cool is that! It's like a pub with dancing girls! What does XXXX stand for?'

Promo Girls
'They look cold. Hot, but cold, if you know what I mean.'

A Silly Hat He Bought
'Dad, isn't this the most awesome hat you've ever seen?'

The Hume Highway
'Dad, this is bullshit.'

The Police
'Dad, this is bullshit.'

ACKNOWLEDGEMENTS

So that's that, then. All that's left in this book is for me to thank the people who have helped and steadied me during the writing process.

Certainly, no amount of thanks is adequate for the sacrifices my wife, Lynette, and my son, Andrew, make for me during the procedure. I just wish to assure them once again that it is perfectly normal for me to damage unco-operative computer equipment after questioning it in a loud and angry voice for half an hour.

I must also thank Phil Canning and Nick Cruth, who saw some early drafts of three of the stories and made constructive noises at me about them, while doubtlessly wondering about my sanity. My gratitude also goes out to Nick Warne, the fellow who berated me endlessly to stop talking about writing books and actually start writing them. I suppose he is really to blame for all of this.

And once again, the wondrous team at Hachette – headed up by Vanessa Radnidge, who's the kind of publisher I had always hoped I'd get, and my brace of brilliant editors, Jacquie Brown and Karen Ward. Thank you all for giving me another crack at this book-writing business.

And finally, I will always remain in awe and wonder at the amazing collection of brothers, friends and sparring partners who inhabit the cyber-temple of the Road Gods at www.bikeme.tv

Hail motorcycles, bastards!

Three of the stories in *At the Altar of the Road Gods* were published in a very much abridged and vanilla-flavoured form before they could be injected with the correct amount of seasoning on these pages.

'Race Me Off' – This tale first appeared in *Australian Motorcycle News* in 2007, but without context, or any detailed explanation as to why I foolishly decided, and indeed was impelled, to imagine I could race high-powered motorcycles on a racetrack.

'Secret Men's Business' – Once again, *Australian Motorcycle News* was the place where this tale of paternal angst was told, albeit in a somewhat truncated form, back in 2009.

'Going Postal' – I wrote about my time with Australia Post in *Australian Postal Worker* magazine back in 2009, but as you can imagine, the straitlaced and stolid nature of that industry publication ensured that I was only ever going to tiptoe around my experiences.

ABOUT THE AUTHOR

Boris Mihailovic first began riding motorcycles more than thirty-five years ago and soon after became a telegram boy for Australia Post (the only other option at the time that would pay him to ride motorcycles was to become a police officer). It was a job that left him with plenty of time to write vitriolic letters to motorcycle magazines, one of which offered Boris a job as a 'cadet journalist'.

The magazine was *Ozbike* and in a few years Boris became the editor of that title, which went on to be the largest-selling motorcycle magazine in Australia. It was there Boris discovered that he had a knack for telling a good yarn. He then landed a job at *The Picture* magazine. Eventually Boris was offered an editor's position at *Picture Premium*. And apart from a stint as editor of *The Picture*, he has remained in the role of editor of *Picture Premium* and *Premium Babes*. Boris has contributed to a host of other magazines, including *Ralph*, *FHM*, *UFC*, *Zoo Weekly*, *Australasian Dirt Bike* and Britain's *Motor Cycle News* (*MCN*). He is also a regular columnist with *Heavy Duty*, *Australian Motorcyclist* and *Australian Motorcycle News*.

Boris continues to enjoy the entire rich smorgasbord that

motorcycling offers – racing, enduro trails, commuting, drag-racing, motorcycle lobbying, shows and trade expos. He was also the president of an outlaw motorcycle club for ten years. Boris has ridden all over Australia and Europe – and plans on doing just that until it is no longer physically possible.

Boris has a wife and son and two bull terriers who look like alien pig-foetuses and act like potatoes.

To find out more about motorbikes and Boris visit:

www.bikeme.tv